SP Pvt. Ltd.

Women Empowerment *for* Inclusive Growth

Pradeep M.D
Srinivas Institute of Management Studies
Mangaluru, Karnataka – 575 001

2017

Studium Press (India) Pvt. Ltd.

Women Empowerment *for* Inclusive Growth

ISBN: 978-93-80012-93-3

Published by:

Studium Press (India) Pvt. Ltd.
4735/22, 2nd Floor, Prakash Deep Building
(Near Delhi Medical Association),
Ansari Road, Darya Ganj, New Delhi-110 002
Tel.: + 91-11-43240200-15 (15 lines); Fax: 91-11-43240215
E-mail: studiumpress@gmail.com

Printed at:

Printed In India

Foreword-I

Women deserve to be in highest reverence in any civilized society because she performs the dual role of mother and bread winner for the family. The role of the mother imposes several biological, physiological and psychological limitations on her. To be a breadwinner she has to compete with men in a competitive world of the complex workforce. Paradoxically, they are the worst sufferers in war or peace despite those wars is created by men for their own sake. Some historians say that during the nomadic days men by virtue of his muscle power established superiority over women. Segregation of family functions like care of children, has widened this gender-based cleavage and limited women to home-based economic activities. Somewhere in the later time, religion has been brought to justify the inferior status of women. By and large, all major religions over the world have been discriminatory to women giving her a secondary role and ensured that she comply through harsh punishment for violations. In the present day, women have differential status with many countries in the west opening up endless opportunities to women tantamount to men and many politically and religiously rigorous regimes assigning relatively suppressive life for women. This book on *Women Empowerment for Inclusive Growth* is an apocalyptic disclosure of the journey of Indian women from past to present and provides valuable insights into their integration for inclusive growth. The book covers the historical development of women in Indian society from the Vedic period to present day, the legal protection given by the Indian constitution at home, workplace and the society in order to give confidence and security for her development, and equality in society. The book also contains an in-depth analysis on empowerment of women through education, political power, social, and economic power. The book discusses the need for women empowerment and the strategies to be followed in domestic empowerment through self-help groups. At best you will also agree if, I say that women deserves a fair deal and we have miles to go in empowering her for her rightful share of the national cake. This book is expected to be a reference guide for every woman in order to plan their growth and future endeavor in the society.

Dr. P. S. Aithal
M.Sc., Ph.D (Phy.), MIT, M.Tech., M.Sc, Ph.D (Mgt.)
Principal
Srinivas Institute of Management Studies
Mangaluru, Karnataka, India

Foreword-II

The study of *Women Empowerment for Inclusive Growth* is of great significance in the modern times. I am happy to write a foreword for this book written by a committed Professor covering several aspects of women empowerment like Historical, Social, Political, Economic and legal perspectives. The author has adopted a holistic approach, which is quiet interesting. After the commencement of the Indian Constitution, India has developed in several fronts but as far as male domination aspect is concerned, it still continues may be because, we cling to customs, traditions and conventions. In the era of Globalisation State has played a predominant role in passing suitable legislation to prevent discrimination of women and by giving effect to Article 15(3) of the Indian Constitution. Several customary practices have been struck down by the court as unconstitutional. To name a few practices like Sati, Narabali, Bethle Seve etc. Several new laws like Domestic Violence Act, Prevention of sexual harassment at workplace, Women Right to Property and treating women on par with men as coparceners are some of the legislations which has strengthened the hands of women. India after signing the UDHR has taken all precautions to protect the women and children from all dimensions particularly from Human Right perspective not only in safeguarding their rights but also in Empowering them to take the recourse of law whenever their right is violated. The author has not only traced the position of women in ancient and medieval days but also he has discussed the position of women in the present period and particularly chapter II and VI have carved out a niche for itself and it is worth reading because it is not only informative but also an enlightening one. I wish this book be an eye opener for all academicians and law makers.

Dr. B.K. Ravindra
M.A, LL.M, Ph.D
Vice Chancellor
Alliance University
Bengaluru, Karnataka, India

About the Author

Mr. Pradeep M.D Born on in Kollegal, Mysore District. Until XII Std perceived his education from Jawahar Navodaya Vidhyalaya, affiliated to CBSE Board, New Delhi. In Class XII with Commerce specialization honoured for being among 0.1 per cent meritorious students among the schools. Completed LL.B from Mangalore University in 2006. Perceived Master of Social Work in HR & IR Specialisation securing First Rank with Gold Medal from Mangalore University in 2008. From Directorate of Distance Education, Kuvempu University, Shimoga completed his Masters in Law (LL.M) in Business Law in 2011 securing First Rank, Post Graduate Diploma in Business Administration (PGDBA) in 2012 securing Sixth Rank and M.A (Sociology) in 2014 securing Second Rank respectively. Registered for Ph. D in 2015 at Alliance University, Bangalore to perceive research in the field of Law. Presently Working as Assistant Professor, in Srinivas Institute of Management Studies, Mangalore holding 8 years of teaching experience for PG Students and coordinates Distance Education Programme from Manasa Educational Foundation for Mental Health, Shimoga since 7 years. He has attended 11 Faculty Development Programmes, Organised

17 Social Outreach Programmes. With his keen interest in Research has guided nearly 70 research projects and Published many research articles in reputed National and International Journals. Has Introduced "Pradeep Consistent Learning Model" for slow learners and Technology Aided Social Work Profession (TASWP) Model for Higher Education.

Acknowledgement

It is my duty to render my gratitude to all who have helped me to realize this work. At the outset I am Thankful to Mr. J.N. Govil, Vice President (Publications) & Managing Editor, Studium Press (India) Pvt. Ltd, New Delhi for giving me an opportunity for writing this book and for his continuous guidance for making this work a reality.

My thankful acknowledgements are due to those authors of the source material indicated in the bibliography.

My sincere thanks are due to Ms. Sangeetha Rai, Chief Librarian, Mangalore Academy of Professional Studies, Mangalore for providing materials from different sources.

My sincere thanks to my mother Mrs. Meenakshi K. N whose dedicated service in the Health Department in the State of Karnataka, India, her sense of humour to serve the poor, caring for the family and confidence to face challenges has inspired me to be empathetic towards women folk and encouraged me to write this book. I am also due to my father Mr. Devadasan T.K, and my brother Mr. Prathap M.D. for their constant encouragement and support.

My thanks are due to Dr. P.S. Aithal, Principal, Srinivas Institute of Management Studies, Mangalore for his encouragement and support in this venture.

My gratitude is due to Mr. Sajith S Nair, System Admin, Srinivas College of Hotel Management, Mangalore for designing attractive cover page.

I am thankful to Studium Press (India) Pvt. Ltd, New Delhi for bringing out this book in an impressive manner.

I thank all those who have contributed directly or indirectly in its making.

Mangaluru **Pradeep M.D**

Preface

I am happy to place before you this book entitled "*Women Empowerment for Inclusive Growth*" covering the Historical, Legal, Political, Social and Economic perspectives of Women Welfare. This book is based upon my experience as a Researcher and Academician. The Development and Growth of India is not uniform across all sections of the society. Women constituting half of the total population but are kept outside the perview of nation building activities. Indian society traditionally considered that 'women' are generally weak compared to 'men' in all spheres of life. The prevalence of 'Son syndrome' among the orthodox elders resulted in marginalizing women in the society. The orthodox social structure projected men to be unjustifiably superior over women. This resulted for the creation of paternal bias, discrimination, powerlessness and dependency of women upon the men. The social thought of 'having a daughter was equalent to planting a tree in the neighbors land'. Women were only confined to the domestic works like collecting fuel, cooking, rearing children etc. Crimes like Child Marriage, Sati, Purdah, Jauhar, Devadasi, Discrimination, Harassment, Rape, Domestic violence, Sexual assault, Dowry started galoring in the society boosting opportunities for vulnerability. The gender discrimination in the society will definitely invade upon the dignity of life and right to privacy of women in contravension to the internationally ascribed human rights norms.

After Indian Independence, The Constitution of India made a deliberate radical departure from the inherited social system, by granting equal rights to women. The guarantee of dignified life of women lies at the threshold of social justice intervention for women. Hence, the Government began to direct its effort towards mainstreaming of women into the national development process to safegurad equality, social justice and fraternity in the country. The legal system should ensure gender equity through providing equal opportunities for Education, Health, Freedom, Safety, Dignity, and Justice to women. The post independence strategies of Revolution, Public Interest Litigation and Judicial Activism for ensuring positive dimensions of right to life and Justice has become rewarding for women welfare. Empowerment of women for bringing them into the mainstream of society to enable them to contribute equally to the national development is the need of the day. The process of women empowerment aim to increase their Political Participation (political empowerment), ensure Education and Health (social empowerment), enhance Opportunities for Employment (economic empowerment) granting right over Property and Legal Aid (legal empowerment) creating Freedom and Autonomy in the family (Domestic empowerment). India should always follow Inclusive Growth Strategy for the the prosperity and growth of the country at the global level.

This book is prepared to give an overall view about 'Women Life and Status' since Vedic period to the 21st century. To introduce the reader to the concept of women empowerment, I have tried to trace the historical development of women through the ages. The book is based upon the recent research outcomes and updated data and presented in a simple form without compromising the quality. The presentation style in this book I presume, will be pleasing and very useful. The book include 13 chapters covering topics like Historical Development of Women in Indian Society, Legal Framework for Women Welfare, Protection of women under Special Laws, Protection of Women at Workplace, Judical activism towards Women issues, Need for Women Empowerment, Revolution towards Women Education & Health, Political, Social, Economic & Domestic Empowerment through Self Help Groups (SHGs) and Gender Equity and inclusive Growth of Women in India.

Mangalore **Pradeep M.D**

Table of Contents

1

Historical Development of Women in Indian Society

Women are the embodiment of all divine virtue on earth by soma blessing all his purity on them, Gandharva has rendered sweetness of speech, fire has showered all his brilliance to make them most attractive. There were contradictory schools of thoughts among which one has described women as 'the equals of men' while the other tried to spread hatred and disrespect by projecting women as weak minded and unworthy to be trusted. The school which protected the interest of women always proposed that women should enjoy freedom in marriage, inheritance and demand equal participation in public affairs. But in society issues of inequality and discrimination towards women was prevailed because of social attitude and social practice[1]. Varahamihira during the Sixth Century A.D says that the pursuit of the ends of 'dharma' which is righteousness and 'artha' the wealth of the society depends on women. Manu under the smriti said that "if women live in grief and trouble, such family will perish and if they are happy such family intern will become prosperous'. Male and female are complementary to each other like 'Purusha' and 'Prakriti' even though they are bisexual in nature. The society had compartmentalized the occupation on the basis of gender.

The girl child was entrusted with the works like weaving, needlework, household responsibilities and oversee the cropping.

[1] Indira (1951). Status of Women in Ancient Times, Bombay, pp. 12-13.

Even then, the occupational education was considered to be important but which was provided based on the occupation of the family. Brahmin girls were taught in vedic wisdom, Kshatriya girls were taught in using bow and arrows. The involvement of women in the social activities during the early India can be known only through some of the famous writers works. The very old Barhut Sculptures represented about horsewomen, Patanjali mentions about 'Saktikis' who are supposed to be the spearbearers in the army, Megasthenes in his book 'Indica' specifies that the King Chandragupta had Amazonian women as his bodyguard, Kautilya mentions in his 'Arthashastra' about women archers in the houses and forest which gives the proof of involving women in all social aspects actively equally with men. Then Universities like 'Nalanda' and 'Thakshila' used to encourage women in fine arts like music, dancing and painting. Marriage has become a ritual for the people and till third century B.C. the marriageable age of women was sixteen. It is in 'Manusmriti' and 'The Dharmasastras' that the doctrine of the perpetual dependence of women on men is enunciated by telling that women was the fragile plant, to be cared and nourished by man. The contrary school of thought continued its dominance to create disrespect over the status and position of women by spreading "there is nothing more sinful than women and they are the burning fire and just a illusion that Daiya Maya has created hence she is like the sharp edge of razor". In Mahabharata also the 'Draupadi Vastra apaharana' depicts the disrespect towards the women. Further in Ramayana also, some of the related thoughts have been incorporated that "the faces of women are like flowers, their words are like the drops of honey, but their hearts are like sharp razor hence their real feeling cannot be understood by any one in the world"[2]. Though these statements were given in some context, the real status of women could be judged only through the discussion over the status in each age.

(1) LIFE DURING THE PERIOD OF VEDAS

The Indian Society was stratified upon the 'Chaturvarna System'.

[2] Altekar A.S. (1938). The position of Women in Hindu Civilisation from Prehistoric Times to the Present Day, Culture Publication House, Banaras Hindu University, p. 407.

According to this doctrine, the Hindu Society was divided into Four main varnas namely, The Brahmins who used to offer prayers and sacrifices to god, The Kshatriyas who used to defend the society from enemies, The Vaishyas who involve in various business and The Shudras meant for the service class. This system was prevalent during the Vedic period was mainly based on the division of labour and occupation. The position of women in Vedic India was not low. There was a belief among the people that women are graced with special qualities like grace, tenderness, peace, affection, surrender and sacrifice hence they used to believe that the duel role which a women plays as a wife and a mother is undoubtedly very important, highly skilled and difficult task. The 'Smritis' and 'Dharmashastras' mentions about basically eight forms of marriages that are practiced. The following three forms of marriages they are if any male marries a girl while she is asleep or unconscious or mad it becomes 'Paishacha' marriage, If women are regarded as prizes of war it amounts to 'Rakshasa' marriage it is mentioned in 'Rigveda' that Aryan masters purchased slave girl which depicts these types of marriage. If the husband buys the bride for a price it amounts to 'Asura' marriage. The Paishacha, Rakshasa and Asura marriages are distorted form of civilization as it deprives a women from equality by reducing her only as a sexual unit. The generally approved form of marriage was 'Gandharva Vivah' it was based on mutual consent where, the lover chooses the beloved. In Kalidasa's great drama 'Abhijnana Shakuntala' he quotes the interesting case of 'Gandharva Vivah' held between 'Dushyanta and Shakuntala'. normally 'Gandharva' unions will happen without the recitation of mantras hence to give the social approval it was laid that ceramonies should be performed after the union. Another form is 'Asura' marriage where the father of the bride is permitted to accept a cow and a bull from the son-in-law. In 'Daiva' form of marriage the sacrifice offers his daughter in marriage to the officiating priest. In 'Prajapatya' marriage the bride is offered to the bridegroom with due rites, and the couple are enjoined to be inseperable companions in the discharge of their religious duties. In 'Brahma' type, where the bride properly decorated, is offered to the bridegroom who is specially invited for the purpose and the husband takes the vow that he will always be closely associated with the wife in all spheres of activity hence, it is the approved and popular form of marriage among all classes. Normally, many practice 'Brahma' form to be the ideal, even then, here and there 'Gandharva' and 'Asura' forms were also seen.

The Hindu ideal of marriage was essentially a fellowship between a man and a woman who seek to live together to achieve Dharma, Artha, Kama and Moksha which are the four objects of life. Its purpose includes the generation of children, care and nurture, cooperation in a better social order but main aim is the enrichment of the personality of husband and wife, through the fulfillment of their needs for a permanent companionship in which each may supplement the life of the other and both may achieve completeness. The position of wife was honoured religiously because neither of them could reach heaven without being accompanied by the other. The highest expression of religion was the sacrifice. Prayers and sacrifices were offered jointly by husband and wife. Women who do not marry are known as 'Brahmavadini' who study Vedas and perform the prescribed rites. 'Sandyovadhu' are those who performed the ceremony of 'upanayana'. A single standard for both men and women was then laid down, "the wife who does not adhere to her husband will be sinful as she has committed a great and heinous sin as killing of an embryo. The men who will go to other women, neglecting a chaste and loving wife who has observed from her youth the vow of chastity, will commit the same sin". There was a practice of marriages between different castes also. 'Rigveda' expresses instances of intermarriages. Chanakya has said that "the bride can be choosen from any caste or community, even if it is low". As a proof to this, several inscriptions have even stated that 'Hindu princes married Foreign princesses'. Manu also says that "a man can marry a girl, even from a inferior and bad families, if the girl is a jewel among women". In 'Mahanirvana Tantra' says that in 'Daiva' form of marriage only conditions for marriage were women should not be within prohibited degree and she should not have husband at the time of marriage and the questions of age, caste are not hurdles for marriage hence, such social rule justified intercaste and widow marriages during this period. 'Monogamous' marriage was a cultural state, it being the ideal form as there is no double form of morality. The marriages between 'Shiva and Parvati', 'Rama and Sita', 'Nala and Damayanthi', 'Satyavan and Savitri' were ideal marriages for the traditional people. Even though the institution of marriage was well established rule but the concept of 'Sati' was not established during 'Rigveda' period[3]. 'Atharva veda' gives some clues about the practice of 'Sati' where about a practice of custom for a widow to lie by the side of her husbands corpse on the funeral pyre. 'Niyoga' is an ancient custom by which dead man's brother or next kin had to marry the widow as per the code of conduct according to 'Manusmriti' and widow remarriages were sanctioned at that time[4]. Women cannot hold any major rights in the society hence the economic capacity of women was only secondary by nature. Inspite of joint ownership of property by both husband and wife, the complete right over the property was vested only with the husband. Only women had right over the movable property specially upon 'ornaments' but later the same right was known as 'Stridhan'. A women as a daughter had no share in her fathers property and only sons used to get the entire property. Mothers property was equally divided among sons and unmarried daughters. However, a forsaken wife was entitled to one-third of her husband's property. Even though politically women were very weak, as they were not given the right to vote but religiously, wife enjoyed full rights[5]. The status of the women during Vedic period can be understood only through the freedom and restrictions they have faced during that time. They enjoyed freedom in selecting their mates, they were given high regards while taking religious decisions, widows were allowed to remarry, divorce was not permitted to both men and women which shows the value towards marital relationship during those period. Thus in the beginning, the social position of women was just and fair, economically they were given freedom to produce normally home based production was focused and all wives used to help the husband in agriculture. Women were respected and placed in the highest esteem during Vedic period[6].

---

[3] Krishna Chandra Pradhan (2008). Rural Women Issues and Options, Sonali Publications, New Delhi, pp. 01-04.

[4] Neera Desai and Maithreyi Krishnaraj (1987). Women & Society in India, Ajanta Publications, New Delhi, p. 35.

[5] Radha Kumud Mukherjee (1947, 1951). Ancient Indian Education (Brahmanical and Buddhist) 2nd Ed., Macmillan & Co. London.

[6] Gurudath (2006). Hindu Jurisprudence in Feminist Perspective-A Look, in the Collection of Essays titled women child law and society, Vidyavardhaka Law College, Mysore, 2006.

(2) LIFE DURING THE LATER VEDIC PERIOD

The chronology of Hindu Orders started from Vedas, Brahmana (1500 BC-500 BC), Upanishads, Grihashutras, Dharmashastras, Epics (500 BC-500AD), Smritis (500AD-1800AD) and Puranas. The position of women that was highly respected and treated as equal to men disappeared in the post Vedic period. The reason behind this may be that the number of subsidiary sciences, lengthy commentaries and written Vedic text appeared. With the change of society and culture the position of women was degraded. Their merit is not recognized by the male counterparts. In society pre-puberty marriage came to be practiced, widow remarriages become unpopular in the period between 300 B.C. and A.D. 200. Iberuni records that remarriage of widows was prohibited by custom, and this prohibition became extended to child widows. husband was given the status of god for women. The unfairness to women came in 'Manusmriti' Manu requires a good wife to adore even to a bad husband as her duty this seemed to be a sort of slavery to the husband. By such exaggerated teaching he attempts to submit the duty of devotion to the husband. 'Apastamba' has quoted that women should wear donkey skin and beg for food, the practice has however, been unkind to women. There is also a difference in the treatment of widowers and widows. Men obtain permission to marry after the wife dies, by the device that they cannot discharge their religious duties except by marrying a second time, though the presence of the wife is not indispensable for the performance of religious duties. The Aitareya Brahmana states that a widower can continue his Vedic sacrifices, even if he has no wife. 'Sraddha' or 'devotion' will function as his wife. Education was denied or made difficult. Age of marriage continued to be sixteen or seventeen. Most difficult laws were imposed on women. Polyandry prevailed in certain communities. The famous instance is that of Draupadi's marriage with five brothers. As in other early society Polygamy was the privilege of princes and noblemen. The 'Shastras' allow a husband to contract a second marriage with the consent of his wife. It is justified, where the first wife is found to be suffering from an incurable disease, or adulterous. Legal recognition of polygamy has resulted in great unhappiness. The concept "a wife and slave cannot own property" was practiced popularly. According to scholars and historians, women were totally denied the status of equality and tolerance. The reason behind may be Brahmanical religious domination on the entire society, rigid restrictions imposed by the caste system, the joint family stem, lack of educational opportunities to the women. Racial discrimination, among Aryans and non Aryans.

(3) LIFE DURING THE PERIOD OF JAINISM

Jainism has much in common with Buddhism has rejected the sanctity of the Vedas, the superiority of Brahmins, the sacramental notions of marriage, and considered all sex relations out of wedlock as inferior to celibacy. Jain teachers held extreme views on 'Asceticism' and 'Ahimsa'. The insistence of non-killing was so uncompromising that it closed many professions and occupations even to laymen. From the time of 'Parasvantha' down to the present, women have been admitted to the religious order of nuns. There is, however, some difference of opinion between the 'Digambaras' and 'Shwetambaras' about their title to Liberation. The Shwetambaras, in support of their contention, even assert that Malli, the Nineteenth Thirthankara, was a lady, which claim the Digambaras reject with contempt. The Digambaras further maintain that nudity is absolutely essential for perfection while the Shwetambaras hold that no harm can happen to the soul by wearing of white garments. Anyway, the Digambaras admit the difficulty of nuns appearing in public without clothes, and that is one of the reason for their belief in the incompetence of women for direct salvation. Marriage did not involve any indissoluble ties for the early jains and men were free to leave their wives and take to the monastic life if they so choose. In the earlier stages of Jainism, women too had the privilege of leaving their husbands and joining convents. All jains, maintain that in the monastic life the nun is inferior to the monk a view, by the way, shared by all great religions. Nuns are prohibited to study chapters of 'Mahaparijnana', 'Arunopapata' and 'Dristivada'. It is stated that the 'Dristivada' deals with magical formulate and as women are not strong enough but fickle, they are not allowed to study the above mentioned scripture. The climax is reached in the rule which lays down that a monk of three years standing can become a teacher of a nun of thirty years standing. Adultry was punished in Jain India with particular severity as we shall see presently but, a more tolerant attitude was adopted towards nuns who commits error. Jains had no regular convents and nuns lead a wondering life and wicked men often took advantage of their helplessness. Many cases of seduction, molestation and rape of nuns are recorded, but the children born to nuns in such unions were not condemned. The Jain text 'Brihat kalpa Bhashya' maintains that it is possible for women to become pregnant without actual sexual intercourse, and the mere fact of pregnancy should not be taken as proof of guilt in an unmarried women or nun. Four causes are mentioned as capable of producing pregnancy in women without coitus, namely (1) Sitting without cover at a place smeared with semen, (2) Introduction of semen into the genitals of a sleeping women by a desiring person. (3) Use of a garment stained with semen by a women in her rutu and (4) Drinking of water containing semen by a women. Due to the helplessness condition which often left them to the mercy of villainous men, a nun who got pregnant, it is specifically laid down in the Jain Canon, should not be turned out of the order. If possible, the culprit, if any, was to be punished, but the nun herself was to be protected from slander and calumny. If convenient, she was made to live in the house of a respectable householder, otherwise in an Upasraya or home for nuns from where she was not to be sent out for begging alms, which was a daily religious duty for regular nuns. "If any one made remarks, he must be told that she could not be abandoned in such a condition." Any way, the nun should be defended by citing the examples of 'Kesi' and 'Satyaki' who were born of nuns without being guilty, and should be looked after properly. This tolerance and humanitarian attitude of Jainism is marked contrast to the cruelty of later Hinduism which excommunicated and abandoned an unmarried women or widow found with child. Adultry by all people under all circumstances was not punished in the same manner. Jain monks too enjoyed certain privileges in this regard. Among many households there was a belief, it would appear, that learned monks were capable of producing geniuses in dull women. Intercourse with a strictly celibate monk was also considered a cure for sterility in women. The Jain text 'Acharanga' mentions that the wives, daughters, daughter-in-law, and slave girls of house holders among whom monks lives as guests, often approached the holy men for cure of sterility or for obtaining illustrious sons. Even prostitutes believed in the power of the pious to produce prodigies, and the efficacy of physical contact with monks in removing spiritual impurities. Child marriage become a fashion among the jains. The sati was confined to certain clans, and this would account for the fact that in ancient India some women survived their husbands while others immolated themselves on the funeral pyres of their husband. Kings considered women, as one of the fourteen jewels of royalty, and generally loved to display their splendor by the number and quality of the women they possessed. Some sort of Purdah was observed by ladies of the royal clans who did not wish to be seen by vulgar eyes. They held the mother in the greatest esteem[7].

(4) LIFE DURING THE PERIOD OF BUDDHISM

Buddhism and Jainism marked a revolt against the pretension of the Brahmins. The founders of both were 'Kshatriyas', Princes of ruling clans who lived in the sixth century before Christ. Both were contemporaries and hailed from East India. The conversion of the 'Mauryan' emperor Ashoka to Buddhism, made this religion the most important not only in India but in the whole Asia. From the time of Ashoka to the rise of Islam, Buddhism was reckoned in all countries east of Persia as the religion of civilized mankind.

(5) LIFE DURING THE PERIOD OF ISLAM

A man cannot marry more than four wives at a time, though he is allowed to keep concubines and slave girls, if he could afford them. Marriage being essentially a civil contract among Muslims, the essentials are that there must be a proposal by one party, and acceptance by the other. Such a proposal and acceptance must be made in clear terms in the presence and hearing of two male or one male and two female witnesses, who must be sane, adult Muslims. Both the offer and the acceptance must be at one meeting and no other writing or religious ceremony is essential for a valid marriage.

---

[7] Vijay Kaushik & Bela Rani Sharma (1998) Encyclopaedia of Human Rights and Womens Development. Indian Women Through Ages, Sarup & Sons, New Delhi, pp. 59-75.

There is optional registration for Muslim marriage, and divorce in some districts of Bengal and Assam, but it is expressely provided that the registrar, shall not be authorized to be present at the marriage ceremony unless invited. The contract generally involving economic obligations, a women is entitled to claim from her husband a sum of money as the dower. The duties of a wife, according to Muslim law, are residence in the house of her husband, obedience to him in his reasonable orders, and performing her marital functions whenever required by the husband at reasonable times and places with due regard to health and decency and observing strict conjugal fidelity and refraining from undue familiarity with strangers and all unnecessary appearance in public. Among Shia's mutah marriages is also prevalent where, a couple are married for a stipulated period after which the marriage becomes null and void without any divorce proceedings. Divorce is permitted under Muslim law. It can be given at the will of the husband without any legal proceedings. A man has to repeat the word 'Talak' three times and send his wife away. As a rule, unless it forms a specific stipulation of the marriage contract, a women cannot divorce herself. According to the Muslim Marriage Act, 1939 for instance, a Muslim women can claim divorce in case her husband takes another wife, on the ground that "there is unequality of treatment either psychologically or economically. A women is as much as heir as a man under muslim law, and the son does not exclude a daughter from a share in the fathers property. Marriage does not give the husband any rights over the property of his wife during her lifetime, which she can administer in her own right and even alienate without the permission of the husband.

'Purdah' system deteriorated the position of women further. In earlier days of Islam, women it would appear, were free to visit the mosque and prey. This practice was, later condemned as good men found it difficult to concentrate their mind on prayers in the presence of women, by the third century in the Muslim era, this system fell into disuse. As the 'purdah' became stricter, prostitution became more popular. Royal and Aristocratic households had extensive pleasure parks and sports grounds, they had the benefits of education, and lady teachers gave instruction to young ladies. The main disadvantage of the 'Purdah', among these upper classes was that they were denied knowledge of the outside world and the pleasures of a mixed society. The middle classes could afford none of these luxuries and seclusion made their women, anaemic, narrow minded and victims of many physical ailments. Within middle class households, 'purdah', however was less strict. Among middle classes, women could appear without the veil before visiting friends and relatives and converse freely with them. The Muslim conquest, as we have seen, led to large scale immolation of women, especially among the Rajputs who considered it lesser evil than capture by the invaders. The Muslims themselves, with their secular notions of marriage, were against the institution of Sati and did what they could to abolish or discourage it among the Hindus whom they ruled. Due to various reasons, they could not stop it by law in their dominions. By the time the Muslim rule was well established in India. Sati had become equally well established among the Hindus who came to look upon it as a religious institution with the sanction of tradition. The later Muslims, found it difficult to rule the country without the cooperation of the Hindus and were reluctant to interfere in the religious observances of the Hindus. Hence, even though many Muslim rulers tried to abolish Sati in their dominions, the institution for all practical purpose flourished without much hindrance[8].

(6) LIFE DURING MEDIEVAL PERIOD

From the beginning of the Medieval age upto the advent of British rule in India, the position of women witnessed many changes. During this period divergent philosophical ideas existed and affected not only in the society but also the position of women. Between A.D. 900 and A.D. 1200 the rights of a widow to inherit her husbands share came to be eventually recognized all over the country. But womens conditions in other fields deteriorated. Education was reduced to eight years and by A.D. 500 Sanction to widow marriage disappeared completely from the social scene. The later part known as the 'Mughal' age advanced Muslim customs and traditions in India and brought newer constraints on women. Among the unfortunate developments that took place in India was the growth of 'Purdah' or the seclusion of women. There is no record of 'Purdah' observed within the family

[8] Ibid, Note 6.

in the Hindu period. However, during the 15th century, the situation had undergone some change. Ramanujacharya organized the first 'Bhakti Movement' during this period, which introduced new trends in the social and religious life of women in India. The Bhaktas like Chaitanya, Nanak, Meera, Kabir, Ramdas stood for the right of women to religious worship. Though this did not drastically free women from the then prevailing attitude, it unlocked the gate of religious freedom to women by granting social rights, attending religious prayers freed them from the circumscribed domestic life. After 'Bhakti movement', the Christian Missionaries took interest in the education of girls. In 1824 the first girls school was started under Lord Dalhousie's Initiative. The Hunter Commission emphasized on the need for female education in 1882. Until 1875, girls were not allowed to take university education, the literacy percentage among females shows an increase then onwards. Education to women was given a boost since the 'Bhakti Movement' also encouraged women to read religious books. Moreover, the 'Grihasthashram' which was emphasized in the teaching of 'Bhakti Movement', did not permit saints to take the sanyas without the consent of the wife thus implying an important right to women during that period. But the economic structure did not undergo any change, so women continued to hold a low status in the society[9].

(7) LIFE BEFORE INDIAN INDEPENDENCE

The British ruled India form the Eighteenth century onwards till independence of India in 1947. While progress in improving the quality of life of women during the British rule of 200 years appeared to have invisibility. Yet some substantial progress was achieved in eliminating inequalities between men and women in education. Women again got an opportunity to come to the forefront only in the Nineteenth century with the 'Social Reform Movements' started by stalwarts like Raja Ram Mohan Roy, Ishwarchand Vidyasagar, Jyotirao Phule and at the time of the independence struggle led by Mahatma Gandhi, when women efforts were recognized and

[9] Kakolee Chakraborthy (2000) Women as Devadasis, Origin and Growth of the Devadasi Profession, Deep & Deep Publications Pvt. Ltd, New Delhi, pp. 6-7.

appreciated. Social reformers like Justice Ranade and Raja Ram Mohan Roy came forward to abolish some ill practices like Sati, Purdah and other sufferings. Ishwarchand Vidyasagar launched a movement for the right of widow remarriage and also pleaded for education of women. Maharishi Karve, considering the problems of widow remarriage, established SNDT Womens University in Maharashtra in 1916. Maharaja Sayajirao Gaekwad of Baroda State, worked for preventing child marriages, polygamy and giving the right to education to women and the right of remarriage to widows. This social movement awakened social consciousness for the liberation and equal rights for women[10]. Many reformative measures and laws were formulated. In 1829 Bengal Sati Regulation Act was passed which declared the practice of sati as illegal and punishable. Similarly, in 1859 Hindu Widow's Remarriage Act was passed. The Indian Penal Code of 1860 provides for the punishment of various offences against women like abduction, rape, bigamy, etc. also in 1874 Married Women's Property Act declares the property purchased by her, through employing her art and skills and all savings and investments shall be her separate property[11]. The use of English as a medium of instruction opened the doors to liberal thoughts. During this period two major developments took place which affected the movement and led to the betterment of position of women, The 'Social Reform Movement' and The 'Indian National Movement', of which the former has been considered to be a key to the intellectual processes which led to the 'National Movement'. The history of women large scale participation in the 'Nationalist Movement' is well known and in fact, one can go back to 1905 when women freedom fighters showed immense courage in fighting the British rulers. Mass participation of women was recognized during the 'Civil Disobedience Movement' in 1930 and 'Quit India Movement' of 1942, where thousands of women quoted as arrested. Some women participated in the 'Revolutionary Movement' as couriers distributing literature, risking police repression, imprisonment and even capital punishment. Similarly, in the 'Tebhaga Movement' for land reform,

---

[10] Report of the Committee on the status of women in India, New Delhi, Government of India (1974).

[11] Paras Diwan (1994). Women and Legal Protection, Deep and Deep Publications, New Delhi.

which took place during 1946-51 in Bengal, it has been reported that women participated at all levels. There was a 'Nari Bahini' a 'Womens Volunteer Force' which would help to guard villages at night. The issues which attracted the attention of the Nineteenth Century social reformers were Sati, ill-treatment of widows, ban on widow remarriage, polygamy, child marriage, denial of property rights and education to women.

Social reformers felt that these social evils should be eradicated by raising consciousness and making people aware to the injustice perpetrated on women. They thought that by giving women the access to education and by enacting progressive legislation, social change could be brought. Raja Ram Mohan Roy, Ishwarchand Vidyasagar, M.G. Ranade, Mahatma Phule, Lokhitwadi and others from all over the country raised their voices against some of the unjust practices, which revivalists like Dayanand Saraswati, Swami Vivekananda and Annie Beasant believed in reviving the old Vedic society presumed to be the ideal society for women. Another very powerful force which improved the position and attitude towards women was the 'Nationalist Movement', particularly during the Gandhian phase. Mahatma Gandhi was the first mass mobiliser who saw the potential of women for an organized movement. Khadi became the first common bond uniting the humble village spinners and urban families. By encouraging women to opt for Swadeshi and to discard jewellery Gandhiji encourage them to cultivate the habit of new activities and a new way of life. With the 'Swadeshi Movement' of the 1920s, Indian women from extremely traditional families began to come out without veils, raise their voice against oppressed and give up caste and clan prejudices[12]. Gandhiji criticized the custom of child marriage, prohibition of widow remarriage, temple prostitution and purdah. He had immense faith in women inner strength and her moral appeal. The 'Nationalist Movement' helped women to organize and to fight for their own cause, rather than depend on 'benovolent' men in society to promote their cause. The formation of All India Women's Conference in 1927, was a crucial event in Women's march towards

[12] Indu Prakash Singh (1991). Indian Women: The Power Trapped, Galaxy Publications, New Delhi, p. 4.

equality[13]. Thus, the pre-independence period created a favourable climate to improve the status of women through legal reforms. To mention a few, the Child Marriage Restraint Act 1929, popularly known as Sarda Act prohibited marriage below the age of 14 for a girl, Hindu Womens Right to Property Act recognized womens right in joint family property. In short, during the phase prior to Independence an awareness of the need to remove social disabilities of women was created, the doors of education was opened to them due to which the political participation of women increased. During the phase prior to Independence, an awareness of the need to remove social disabilities of women was created; the doors of education was opened to them, the following women organisation emerged to represent the needs and causes of women like Bharat Mahila Parishad founded in 1904 with the main aim being to struggle for the emancipation of women, Bharat Stri Mahamandal founded in 1910, Womens Indian Association started in 1917 by Annie Besant, National Council of Women in India founded by lady Aberden and Lady Tata, All India Women's Conference established in 1927. Thus in the Nineteenth Century, the rise in understanding of women problems continued on one hand whereas women in India also suffered from disabilities like child marriage, practice of polygamy, sale of girls and specially women exploitation under the cover of religion, like Devadasis. The Indian Succession Act, gave women the same right to the property of her husband as the husband has on the death of his wife.

(8) LIFE AFTER INDIAN INDEPENDENCE

Dr. Ambedkar, who is known as the father of the 'Indian Constitution' felt that injustice to women which is laid by the 'Manusmriti' should be cured only through the legal measures. As the first law minister he tried to introduce Hindu Code Bill which emphasized equal rights to women by diluting the obstructions of law for the social advancement of women[14]. The Constitution of free India came into

[13] Neera Desai and Maithreyi Krishnaraj (1987). Women & Society in India, Ajanta Publication, New Delhi, p. 35.

[14] Kuber W.N (1979). Dr. Ambedkar: A Critical Study, Peoples Publishing House, New Delhi.

force on 26th January, 1950 granting equality among all. The Preamble to the Constitution initially declares India to be a 'Sovereign, Democratic and Republic'. The words 'Secular and Socialist were added to it by 42nd Amendment. Besides the preamble, the directive Principles of State Policy embody the major policy goals of the welfare state. Indian Women are beneficiaries of these rights as much so as Indian men. The preamble to the constitution of India resolved to secure to all citizens Justice, social, economic and political, liberty of thought, expression, belief faith and worship, equality of status and opportunity to promote among them all fraternity assuring the dignity of the individual and the unity and integrity of the Nation. In 1948, an important step was taken by passing acts pertaining to employment they are The Factories Act, 1948, The Employee State Insurance Act, 1948 in which focus is given to health, welfare, safety and ensures sickness, maternity, disability and medical benefits. In addition to the reform of Hindu Personal Laws, parliament also enacted the Special Marriage Act, 1954 which permits members of two different religious to marry without either party renouncing his or her religion. The social evils of Sati and child marriage were out of the picture by this period. The enactment of Hindu Law guaranteed The right to divorce and re-marriage to Hindu women, The Inheritance Act provided equal share to women in the property, establishing the principle of monogamy are some of the important innovations introduced in the Indian social structure affecting women status and role. The Termination of Pregnancy Act, The Maternity Benefit Act, The Dowry Prohibition Act are some of the measures of relief for all women irrespective of caste, creed or religion. Indian emphasis on being a welfare state, had significant impact on women position and their role. The Government of India, in 1953 established a Central Social Welfare Board with a nation wide programme of grant in aid for promoting welfare and development services for women, children and under privileged groups. The Hindu Marriage Act which came into force in May 1955 ended the age old institution of marriage as a one sided sacrament and enforced monogamy on the male also. Secondly, the Hindu Marriage Act for the first time permitted divorce, provision for which was a necessary corollary of enforcing monogamy. Divorce could be sought on the grounds of adultery, desertion, cruelty, insanity or incurable disease. The Hindu Succession Act which became effective from June 1956 gives the daughter and other women relatives a share in the succession to the property of Hindu males. Widow Remarriage Act, Hindu Adoption and Maintenance Act was also enacted in 1956. In 1961, The Dowry Prohibition Act, was passed to curb the social evil of dowry. Abortion was legally treated as a criminal offence. In 1971, the Medical Termination of Pregnancy Act was passed which legally regulated both pregnant women and abortionist to cause miscarriage. Similarly right to property, inheritance, equal wages, working conditions, maternity benefits, job security, etc. were extended equally to daughter, wife and widows. In this narrative of women participation in mass movements, the illustration of the 'Chipko Movement' stands out prominently. There is a feeling that a genuine mass based women movement can grow out of the grassroot participatory organizations of women. The Chipko Movement initiated in 1972-74 is an example of the powerful impact about women initiative can have on the power brokers, contractors and family members. Where women shoulder major burdens of bringing fuel, fodder and water from long distances, any action which affects these sources of livelihood adversely will surely bring sharp resentment among them[15]. Equal Remuneration Act of 1976 was passed. After 1990s women were encouraged to work in the industrial establishments equally as like men for wages and other emoluments. Many international agreements were entered by the Government of India to empower women in all the spheres of life. The government adopted philosophy of 'Promotion of women's welfare' until 1970, during 1980's it aimed towards 'Development of Women' and after 1990's the focus was towards 'Empowerment of Women' by guiding all the major activities towards women's progress. With the emphasis towards Women empowerment to build potential community and ensure human welfare the world started recognizing 1975th year as 'International Year of Women' as per the call of the NGO's, every 8th March as 'International Women's Day', the Decade between 1991-2000 AD as 'SAARC Decade of the Girl child and Year 2001 as the 'Year of Women Empowerment'.

The cases of Gender equity is focused very much after 2010 one of the incidence where Hundreds of women thronged the Shani

---

[15] Noor Mohammad and others (2004). Rethinking of Women Participation, women's link, Volume 10, No. 03, July-September.

Shingnapur temple in Nevasa taluka of Ahmednagar district after the four century old ban restricting women entry into the sanctum sanctorum was lifted. The temple trust allowed women to step into the sanctum sanctorum following directives of the Bombay High Court. The Shani Shingapur village wore a festive atmosphere. The Trupti Desai led Bhumata Ranragini Brigade (BRB), spearheading a crusade against gender bias in temples in Maharasthra. The Shri Shaneshwar Devasthan Trusts decision has been hailed by the women activists across the country. "To progress in this 21st century then it is important that we remove this concept of discrimination of caste and gender from the minds of the people completely" said Maharashtra Chief Minister Devendra Fadnavis. This development is a culmination of a spirited campaign against gender bias in temples by the Bhumata Ranragini Brigade (BRB) activists, effective intervention by the Bombay High Court and the undertaking given by the Maharashtra Government that it will scrupulously implement the Maharashtra Hindu Place of Worship (Entry Authorisation) Act 1956 which prescribed six months imprisonment to those prohibiting anyone from entering the place of worship. "Ultimately it is the fundamental right of a women and others fundamental duty to protect this right chief justice D.H. Waghela had said[16]. The legal, economic, social, political, domestic empowerment strategies towards women are explained in the further chapters.

CONCLUSION

In every society, there are sections of deprived and disadvantaged people who need special facilities and concessions for their uplift. In India, scheduled castes, scheduled tribes and backward classes have been exploited since long and denied their rightful places in the society. Similarly, women and children constitute weaker sections deserving special care. Thus one can see that after independence and particularly after the making of the Indian Constitution, a lot of reformative measures were taken concerning women. These measures touched important aspects of a women life and the Hindu

[16] Deccan Herald, Mangaluru, Volume 19, No. 199, Sunday, April, 10 (2016).

Personal Law especially is considered to be a landmark in the history of legal provisions for women. Various phases in the changes in the position of women. The women of the Vedic age held an esteemed position in society with fewer of the discriminations which plagued women in the later period. Women have started regaining their position in the society only since the latter part of the Nineteenth century. One of the striking achievements has been the acceptance of the need to spread women education. Today women are stepping out of their homes and taking up careers. One more development is the emergence of women's movement wherein women have started raising their voice against inequality and a society bound by patriarchal values and traditions. Along with this, political and consciousness rights were also given to women. The Indian Constitution gives two important political rights to females like franchise right and eligibility for the legislature. In this regard Government of India Act, 1935 is important for women's right since it grants enfranchisement on the basis of educational qualifications. Accordingly, the state, the community and voluntary associations undertake various welfare measures. The government grants them reservations in services, facilities for free education upto the highest level, reservation of seats in medical and technical educational institutions. Investigations into the role of women in Telangana and Naxalite movements subsequently have revealed that women not only gave shelter to the revolutionaries and served as liaison among various groups but also took leading part in direct political action. Recently, The Supreme Court comprising a bench of Justice Dipak Misra and Shiva Kirthi Singh however, agreed with additional solicitor General Pinky Anand on 25th April, 2016 said while directing the Maharashtra Government not to put hurdles in the way of dance bar owners to restart their business and held that Dignity of the women has to be protected but not by banning dance as it is a profession unless it is obscene. But regulation cannot enter into the realm of prohibition. It is better for women to perform in dance bars than beg on the streets or indulge in some objectionable activities to make their both ends meet, the State Government can make rules to regulate dance bar performances to protect the dignity of women and prevent obscene performances. Attitude must be towards regulation and not to prohibit performances. We are talking about art and women have the fundamental right to perform. We have to protect the dignity of women and mindset must change towards dance bars[17]. In this 21st century India should focus towards gender equity and equal right to women in all spheres which intern contributes to the national development.

[17] Amit Anand Choudhary, Times of India, 26th April (2016).

2

Legal Framework for Women Welfare

History of women in India has been eventful. Social evils like Child marriage, Sati, Purdah, Jauhar, Devadasi in the social system during the medieval period diluted the status of women in India. After independence, the Constitution of India made a deliberate radical departure from the inherited social system, by granting to women equal social and political status. The government began to direct its effort towards mainstreaming of women into the national development process by various acts to ensure equality, social justice and fraternity. Women constitute half of total population should be included in the task of nation building but instead are treated as the 'weaker sex'. Women suffer from many disadvantages as compared to men in terms of literacy rates, labour and autonomy. Women should be encouraged to participate in education, occupations, awareness programmes relating to health, family-life, nutrition, child care, home-management, women's rights, civil responsibilities, etc. The Planning Commission observes that the term 'Social Welfare Services' denotes services offered for the special needs of people who suffer handicapness and traditionally denied with the services of the community. Thus, the welfare services are designed to enable the underprivileged sections of the community to develop to the maximum extent. In India, social welfare services focus upon the under privileged groups like scheduled castes, scheduled tribes, denotified communities, orphans, widows, unmarried mothers, women in moral danger, aged, children, socially maladjusted, beggers, prostitutes, delinquent, physically and mentally disabled, diseased, mentally retarded, economically underprivileged, destitutes and unemployed sections of the society. Gender equality implies a society in which women and men enjoy the same opportunities, outcomes, rights and obligations in all spheres of life. Equality between men and women exists when both sexes enjoy equal access to education, opportunity to develop personal ambitions through sharing power and influence with equal opportunities and financial independence. Women have less access to medical care, property ownership, credit, training, employment and education.

Moreover, women are still widely under-represented in decision-making at household and public spheres. They are vulnerable to health problems, victims of domestic violence, unintended pregnancies, maternal deaths, disability, sexually transmitted infections like HIV, and gender based violence, etc. The roles that men and women play in society are not biologically determined but socially justified as being required by culture or religion. Economic disparities persist partly because much of the unpaid work within families and communities falls on the shoulders of women. Normally, women work longer hours than men, but are usually paid less thereby likely to live in poverty. Women spend much of the day performing tasks to maintain the household and agriculture. A critical aspect of promoting gender equality is through empowerment of women with a focus on identifying, redressing power imbalances, autonomy to manage their own lives, realization of human rights and sustainable development through empowerment is the strategy. The principle of gender equality is enshrined in the Indian Constitution in its Preamble, Fundamental Rights, Fundamental Duties and Directive Principles. Within the framework of a democratic polity, our laws, development policies, plans and programmes have aimed at women's advancement in different spheres. India has also ratified various international conventions and human rights instruments committing to secure equal rights of women.

A. THE INDIAN CONSTITUTION- GENDER EQUITY AND WELFARE[1]

India, a Union of States, is a Sovereign, Socialist, Secular,

[1] Kapoor N.D. and Rajni Abbi (2009). General & Commercial Laws, Sultan Chand & Sons Publishers, New Delhi, Seventh Edition, pp. 2.1-2.32.

Democratic, Republic. The Republic is governed in terms of the Constitution, which was adopted by the Constituent Assembly on 26th November, 1949 and came into force on 26th January, 1950. The Constitution which the people of India gave to themselves is a unique document considered to be the law of the land. The Parliamentary system of Government in India is based on adult suffrage, in which all citizens above the age of 18 years of age are vested with the right to vote for any election to the Lok Sabha and Legislative Assemblies of the States. The Constitution is federal in structure with unitary features. The areas of jurisdiction of the Union and States are demarcated. Even though The President is the executive head in India, Article 74(1) empowers the council of ministers headed by the Prime Minister to retain the real executive power who are responsible collectively to the house of the people Lok Sabha. Similarly, Governor is the executive head of the state, but virtually the Council of Ministers headed by the Chief Minister collectively responsible to the Legislative Assembly of the State. The Constitution guarantees to the citizens of India Fundamental Rights which are justifiable like, Right to Equality (Article 14-18), Right to Freedom (Article 19-22), Right to Education (Article 21 A), Right against Exploitation (Article 23-24), Right to Freedom of Religion (Articles 25-28), Cultural and Educational Rights (Article 29-30) and Right to Constitutional Remedies (Article 32). Constitution lays down a set of guiding principles known as Directive Principles of State Policy (Article 38-51) contained in the part IV which the state ought to follow both in framing laws and enforcing them. Even though these principles are not enforceable in the courts yet they are fundamental in the governance of the country. In a federal state, it is essential to have independent judiciary for preserving the sanctity of the Constitution hence, Constitution granted Independence to judiciary. The citizens of our country are free to follow any religion and they enjoy equal rights without any discrimination upon caste, creed, religion or sex. The Constitution of India not only grants equality to women but also empowers the State to adopt measures of positive discrimination in favour of women for neutralizing the cumulative socio-economic, education and political disadvantages faced by them[2].

---

[2] Justice Vishwanath Shetty P (2004). Hon'ble Judge, High Court of Karnataka Bangalore, Inaugural address delivered in the seminar Women-Legal Problems & Perspectives, 25th March, at Vidyaardhaka Law College, Mysore, Karnataka State, India.

(1) Fundamental Rights (Article 14-32)

(a) Right to equality (Article 14 to 18)

Article 14 guarantees equality to all before law, the state shall not deny to any person equality before the law or equal protection of laws within the territory of India. Article 15 prohibits discrimination on grounds of religion, race, caste, sex or place of birth or any of them. Article 15(1) guarantees the right of a citizen against the state from imposing any disability, liability, restriction or condition with regard to access to shops, public restaurants, hotels and places of public entertainment or the use of wells, tanks, bathing ghats, roads and places of public resort, maintained wholly or partly out of state funds or dedicated to the use of the general public. Article 15(3) The State to make any special provision in favour of women and children like reservation of seats in buses and rails, restrictions upon working hours for women and children. Union of India *Vs.* K.P. Prabhakaran[3]. The Supreme Court held that article 15(3) legislative or executive orders favouring women is not arbitrary. Article 15(4) the state can make any special provision for the advancement of any socially and educationally backward classes of citizens or for the scheduled castes and scheduled tribes like scholarships or fee concessions in public educational institutions.

(b) Equality of opportunity in matters of public employment (Article 16)

Article 16(1) guarantees equality of opportunity for all citizens in matters of employment or appointment to any post under the state. Article 16(2) prohibits discrimination against a citizen on the ground of religion, race, caste, sex, decent, place of birth or residence this was upheld in M.R. Balaji *Vs.* State of Mysore.[4]

(c) Abolition of untouchability (Article 17)

It is defined in Devarajiah *Vs.* Padmanna[5] High Court held that

[3] (1997)11 SCC 638
[4] AIR 1963 SC 649
[5] AIR 1961 Mad 35, 39

the principal object of Article 17 is to ban the practice of untouchability in any form. It also declares that the enforcement of any disability arising out of the practice will be an offence punishable in accordance with law. Consequently, Parliament passed Untouchability (Offences) Act, 1955 declaring punishment for the offence of Untouchability. In 1976, the act was amended and renamed as Protection of Civil Rights Act, 1955 which, actually enhanced the punishment of many offences and preaching of untouchability has been made an offence.

(d) Right to freedom (Article 19)

Constitution guarantees every citizen six fundamental freedoms. Article 19(1)(a) Grants right to express her convictions and opinions freely by word of mouth, writing, printing, pictures or any other mode but state may impose reasonable restriction in the interest of sovereignty, integrity of the state, the security, friendly relation with foreign states, public sector, decency or morality, on the ground of contempt of court, defamation, and incitement to commit an offence. Article 19(1)(b) to assemble peacefully without arms which includes the right to hold meetings and take out processions subjected to the reasonable restriction for the sovereignty of India or on public order. Article 19(1)(c) The right to form associations implies that several individuals get together and form voluntarily an association with a common aim, for legitimate purpose for common utility but it should not affect the sovereignty and integrity, public order or morality. Article 19(1)(d)&(e) Right to move freely throughout the territory of India, to reside and settle in any part of the territory of India is to remove internal barriers within the territory of India so as to enable every citizen to travel freely and settle down in any part of a State or union territory. These rights are subjected to the general public interest and protection of the interests of the Scheduled Tribes. Article 19(1)(g) to practice any profession, carry any occupation, trade or business which includes the right to close down, relinquish or sell the business subjected to the interest of general public. The test of reasonableness of restrictions imposed by the state is that they should not be arbitrary, excessive or beyond what is required in the interest of General Public.

(e) Protection in respect of conviction for offences (Article 20)

Article 20(1) No women be convicted illegally of any offence except for the violation of law in force. It means if an act is not an offence at the date of its commission it cannot be an offence subsequently. Article 20(2) if a person has been prosecuted and punished for an offence, she cannot be prosecuted and punished for the same offence again in a subsequent proceeding. Article 20(3) provides protection to every person accused of any offence from being the witness against himself.

(f) Protection of life and personal liberty (Article 21)

No person shall be deprived of his life or personal liberty except according to procedure established by law. Women have the right to life and personal liberty. In case of any violation, women can take legal remedy (Please refer to the chapter Judicial Activism on women issues for further details)

(g) Right against exploitation (Article 23)

Traffic in human beings, beggar and other forms of forced labour are prohibited and any contravention shall be punishable accordance with the law. Traffic in human beings and beggar where a person is compelled to render involuntary and free service without wage and other similar forms of forced labour are prohibited and punishable in accordance with law. In Raj Bahadur *Vs.* Legal Remembrancer[6]. It was held that Traffic in human beings means "to deal in men and women like goods" to sell or dispose of them including slavery according to Section 370 of Indian Penal Code, 1860 whoever imports, exports, removes, buys, sells or disposes of any person as a slave against his will shall be punished

(h) Right to religion (Article 25)

It guarantees freedom of conscience and free profession, practice and propagation of religion to every man or women of any caste or creed subject to public order, morality and health of the people.

---

[6] AIR 1953 Cal, 522

(i) Right to constitutional remedies (Article 32)

Guarantees remedies for the enforcement of Fundamental Rights has been described as the 'Soul of the Constitution'. Rights without remedies would be just abstract declarations without any real content in them and will be of no use. This remedial right itself made a fundamental right, being included in Part III. The Supreme Court has been empowered to grant relief to those who move to the court for the enforcement of Fundamental Rights. The Supreme Court has the power to issue directions, orders or writs for the enforcement of these rights. The writs may be in the nature of Habeas Corpus which is an order requiring a person to be brought before a judge or into the court, especially to investigate the right of the law against keeping him in custody. Writ Mandamus is issued by a Superior Court commanding the performance of a specified official act or duty by the person to whom it is addressed. Writ Prohibition, is issued by a superior court to an inferior court forbidding the latter to continue proceedings therein in excess of its jurisdiction. Writ Certiorari in which, superior court calls for the records and entire proceedings of an inferior court and Writ Quo Warranto requires a person to prove the authority on which he hold a public office.

(2) Directive Principles of State Policy (Article 39 to 51)

Indian constitution lays down a set of guiding Principles, which the State ought to follow both in framing laws and enforcing them. These are contained in the part IV of the Constitution. They confer no rights and create no legal remedies, but still they provide a good guide in charting the path of the state in the governance of the country. Article 39 directs the state to secure the right to an adequate livelihood, and ensure equal pay for equal work for both men and women. Not to abuse the health and strength of workers and not to force men and women to enter into profession which is unsuited to their age and strength due to their economic necessity. Article 39-A directs equal justice and free legal aid under suitable legislation or scheme by ensuring that justice is not denied to any citizen by reason of economic or other disabilities. Article 42 directs that state shall make provision for securing just and humane conditions of work and for maternity relief. In article 44 state shall endeavour to secure to the citizens a Uniform Civil Code throughout the territory of India. Article 46 directs the State to promote educational and economic interests of the weaker sections to protect them from social injustice and all forms of exploitation. Article 47 guides the State to raise the lovel of nutrition and the standard of living of the people. Article 51(A)(e) ensures to promote harmony and the spirit of common brotherhood among all the people of India and to renounce practices derogatory to the dignity of women. Article 243 D (3) Not less than one-third (including the number of seats reserved for women belonging to the Scheduled Castes and the Scheduled Tribes) among the total number of seats to be filled by direct election in Panchayat shall be reserved for women. Such seats to be allotted by rotation to different constituencies in a Panchayat. Article 243 D (4) not less than one- third offices of Chairpersons to be reserved for women. Article 243 T(3) not less than one-third (including the number of seats reserved for women belonging to the Scheduled Castes and the Scheduled Tribes) of the total number of seats to be filled by direct election in every Municipality to be reserved for women. Article 243T(3) such seats to be allotted by rotation to different constituencies in a Municipality. Article 243T(4) not less than one-third offices of Chairpersons in Municipalities shall be reserved for the women.

(3) Fundamental Duty (Article 51-A)

Rights always travel with corresponding duties as a balancing force in any civilized society. Fundamental Duty is introduced by the Constitution (Forty-second) Amendment Act, 1976 enumerates the fundamental duties of the citizens of India. These duties like the Directives mentioned above are also not enforceable in the courts. Article 51-A(e) impose a duty upon the people to promote harmony and the spirit of common brotherhood amongst all the people of India transcending religious, linguistic and religion or sectional diversities, to renounce practices derogatory to the dignity of women.

B. PROTECTION OF WOMEN UNDER PENAL AND PROCEDURAL LAWS

To uphold the Constitutional mandate, the State has enacted various legislative measures intended to ensure equal rights to women by countering social discrimination, violence and atrocities. Although women are the victims of numerous crimes including Rape, Kidnapping, Murder, etc., which are characterized as 'Crime against Women' The following are the legal protections for protecting the life and provide welfare to women.

(1) Protection under Indian Penal Code (IPC) 1860[7]

(a) Protection against Rape

Section 375 defines Rape as "a man is said to commit 'rape' if he penetrates his penis, any part of the body or mouth to any extent, into the vegina, mouth, urethra or anus of a women or makes her to do so with him or any other person or manipulates any part of the body of women so as to cause penetration against her will and without her consent." It amounts to rape even with her consent if her consent is obtained by putting her or any person in whom she is interested in fear of death or hurt or when the man knows that he is not her husband and she had consented believing that he is a man to whom she believes to be lawfully married, consent due to unsoundness of mind, intoxication or the administration of unwholesome substance to her so that she cannot understand the nature and consequences of the act to which she has consented. Finally, with or without consent if she is under 18 years of age or situation where she is unable to communicate consent. Sec. 376 prescribes punishment for the offence Rape as whoever commits rape, shall be punished with rigorous imprisonment of either description for a term which shall not be less than 07 years, but which may extend to imprisonment for life, and shall also liable to fine. Rape committed by persons with authority, any relative, guardian or teacher who hold a position of trust, offence committed during communal violence, after knowing her to be pregnant, upon anyone who is less than sixteen years of age, who is incapable of giving consent, by misusing the position of dominance, upon a mentally or physically disabled, and caused grievous bodily harm, disfigure or endangered her life or repeated rape on the same

[7] Misra S.N. (2013). "Indian Penal Code" As amended by Criminal Law (Amendment) Act, 2013, Central Law Publications, Allahabad, Nineteenth Edition.

women shall be punishable with rigorous imprisonment for a term which shall not be less than 10 years, but which may extend to imprisonment for the remaining life and fine. Sec. 376 A Punishment for causing death or resulting in persistent vegetative state of victim shall be punished with rigorous imprisonment for not be less than 20 years, may extend to life. Sec. 376 B whoever has sexual intercourse with his own wife, who is living separately, whether under a decree of separation or without her consent, shall be punished with imprisonment of either description for a term which shall not be less than 02 years it may extend to 07 years and fine. Sec. 376 C Sexual intercourse by a Police Officer, Public Servant, Member of Armed Forces deployed in an area, being in Management or staff of a Jail, Remand Home, Place of Custody, Institution and Hospital commits Rape under custody shall be punished with rigorous imprisonment of either description for a term which shall not be less than 05 years, but may extend to 10 years and fine. Sec. 376 D where a women is raped by one or more persons constituting a group shall be punished with rigorous imprisonment for not less than 20 years, but may extend to the remainder of that persons natural life and with fine. Sec. 377 whoever voluntarily has carnal intercourse against the order of nature with any women shall be punished with imprisonment for life, or with imprisonment for 10 years and fine.

(b) Protection against kidnapping and abduction

Sec. 360 defines Kidnapping as whoever conveys any person beyond the limits of India without the consent of that person or some person legally authorized to consent on behalf of that person. Sec. 361 defines kidnapping from lawful Guardianship as whoever takes any minor girl who is under the age of 18 years or any unsound person out of the keeping of the lawful guardian without the consent of such guardian. Sec. 362 defines Abduction as whoever by force compels, or by any deceitful means induces, any person to go from any place. Sec. 363 prescribes imprisonment of either description for a term of 07 years and fine for the kidnap. Sec. 363-A says whoever kidnaps any minor for the purpose of begging shall be punishable with imprisonment for life and fine. Sec. 364 Whoever kidnaps or abducts any person in order to murder shall be punished with imprisonment for life or rigorous imprisonment for a term of 10 years and fine. Sec.

366 Kidnapping, Abduction or inducing women to compel her marriage against her will, or to force to illicit intercourse, shall be punished with imprisonment for 10 years and fine. Sec. 366-A whoever, induces any minor girl under the age of 18 years to go from any place and induced to have illicit intercourse with another person shall be punishable with imprisonment for 10 years and fine. Sec. 366-B whoever imports into India from any outside country any girl under the age of 21 years to seduce her to have illicit intercourse with another person shall be punishable with imprisonment of 10 years and liable for fine.

(c) Protection against trafficking

Under Sec. 370 whoever for the physical exploitation or any form of sexual exploitation, slavery or practices similar to slavery, servitude or forced removal of organs recruits, transports, harbours, transfers or receives any person by using threat, force, abduction, fraud, abuse of power and inducement commits the offence of trafficking shall be punished with rigorous imprisonment for a term not less than 07 years, but which may extend to 10 years and fine. Trafficking of more person or minors shall be punished with rigorous imprisonment of 10 years or imprisonment for life and fine. More minors with imprisonment for not less than 14 years or life imprisonment and fine. If the person is convicted more than once shall be imprisoned for the remainder of his natural life and fine and finally if any public servant or police officer is involved in the trafficking then they will be punished with imprisoned for the remainder of that persons natural life. Sec. 370 A whoever engages a trafficked person for sexual exploitation shall be punished with rigorous imprisonment for a term not less than 05 years and fine. Sec. 372 whoever sells minor for the purpose of prostitution shall be punished with imprisonment 10 years and fine. Sec. 373 whoever buys minor for the purpose of prostitution shall be punished with imprisonment for 10 years and fine.

(d) Protection of marriage

(i) Sec. 493 cohabitation caused by a man deceitfully inducing a belief of lawful marriage

Every man who by deceit causes any women who is not lawfully married to him to believe that she is lawfully married to him and to cohabit or have sexual intercourse with him in that belief, shall be punished with imprisonment of either description for a term which may extend to 10 years and shall also be liable to fine.

(ii) Sec. 494 marrying again during lifetime of wife

Whoever having a wife living, marries in any case in which such marriage is void by reason of its taking place during the life of such wife shall be punished with imprisonment of either description for a term which may extend to 07 years, and liable to fine. Except when any persons marriage has been declared void by a court of competent jurisdiction or if wife at the time of subsequent marriage, shall have been continually absent from such person for 07 years, and has not heard by such person as being alive within that time, were the person contracting such subsequent marriage shall before such marriage takes place, inform the person with whom such marriage is contracted of the real state of facts so far as the same are within his knowledge. This section make punishable that marriage which under English law is known as 'bigamy'. This section applies to all Hindus, Christians and Parsis whether male or female. But in case of Muslim it applies only to females but not to males as Muslim personal law permits the male to have four wives at a time but a female is not permitted to have more than one husband at one time.

(iii) Sec. 495 concealment of former marriage from person with whom subsequent marriage is contracted

Whoever conceal from the person with whom the subsequent marriage is contracted, the fact of former marriage, shall be punished with imprisonment of either description for a term which may extend to ten years, and shall be liable to fine.

(iv) Sec. 496 marriage ceremony fraudulently gone through without lawful marriage

Whoever dishonestly with a fraudulent intention, goes through the ceremony of being married, knowing that he is not thereby lawfully married, shall be punished with imprisonment of either description for a term which may extend to 07 years and liable to fine.

(v) Sec. 497 adultry

Whoever has sexual intercourse with a person whom he knows to be the wife of another man, without the consent of that man, such sexual intercourse not amounting to the offence of rape, is guilty of adultery and shall be punished with imprisonment of either description for a term which may extend to 05 years, or with fine or with both. In such case the wife shall not be punishable as an abettor.

(vi) Sec. 498 enticing or taking away or detaining with criminal intent a married women

Whoever takes or entices away any women who is the wife of any other man, from that man, or from any person having the care of her on behalf of that man, with intent to have illicit intercourse with any person, or conceals or detains with that intent any such women, shall be punished with imprisonment of either description for a term which may extend to 02 years, or with fine or with both.

(vii) Sec. 498-A husband or relatives of husband of a women subjecting her to cruelty

Whoever, being the husband or the relative of the husband of a women, subjects her to any willful conduct which is of such a nature as is likely to drive the women to commit suicide or to cause grave injury or danger to life, limb or health of the women or harassment of the women where such harassment is with a view to cohercing her or any person relating to her to meet any unlawful demand for any property or valuable security or is on account of failure by her to meet such demand shall be punishable with imprisonment for a term which may extend to 03 years and shall also be liable to fine. This was introduced by Criminal Law (Amendment)Act, 1983 was seen as an expression of the social recognition against harassment of married women[8].

[8] Ammu Abraham (1992). A Legal Remedy for Harassed Wives, The Hindu, Nov. 22.

(e) Protection against offences affecting the human body and life

(i) Sec. 304-B dowry death

Where the death of a women is caused by any burns or bodily injury or occurs otherwise than under normal circumstances within seven years of her marriage and it is shown that soon before her death she was subjected to cruelty or harassment by her husband or any relative of her husband in connection with, any demand for dowry, such death shall be called as dowry death and such husband or relative shall be deemed to have caused her death and shall be punished with imprisonment for a term which shall not be less than 07 years but which may extend to imprisonment for life.

(ii) Sec. 312 causing miscarriage

Whoever voluntarily causes a women with child to miscarry shall if such miscarriage be not caused in good faith for the purpose of saving the life of the women, be punished with imprisonment of either description for a term which may extend to 03 years, or with fine or with both. A women who causes herself to miscarry shall be punished with imprisonment of either description for a term which may extend to 07 years and with fine.

(iii) Sec. 313 causing miscarriage without women's consent

Whoever causes miscarriage without the consent of the women shall be punished with imprisonment for life, or with imprisonment of either description for a term of 10 years and with fine.

(iv) Sec. 314 death caused by act done with intent to cause miscarriage

Whoever, with the intent to cause the miscarriage of a women with child, does any act which causes the death of such women, shall be punishable with imprisonment of either description for a term which may extend to 10 years and with fine.

(v) Sec. 326A voluntarily causing grievous hurt by use of acid

Whoever cause permanent or partial damage, deformity, burns, maim, disfigures or disables any parts of body of a women or causes grievous hurt by throwing acid includes any substance which has acidic or corrosive character or burning nature, that is capable of causing bodily injury leading to scars or disfigurement or temporary or permanent disability, with the knowledge that he is likely to cause such injury or hurt, shall be punishable with imprisonment of either description for a term which shall not be less than 10 years but may extend for life and with fine which shall be just and reasonable to meet the medical expenses of the treatment of the victim. Any fine imposed under this section shall be paid to the victim.

(vi) Sec. 354 assault or criminal force to women with intent to outrage her modesty

Whoever assaults or uses criminal force to any women intending to outrage or knowing it to be likely that he will thereby outrage her modesty, shall be punishable with imprisonment for a term not less than 01 year but which may extend to 05 years and liable for fine.

(vii) Sec. 354-A sexual harassment

A man commits physical contact and advances involving unwelcome and explicit sexual overtures, demand or request for sexual favours, showing pornography against the will of a women shall be punishable with rigorous imprisonment for a term which may extend to 03 years, or with fine or with both and for making sexually coloured remarks shall be punished with imprisonment for a term which may extend to 01 year or with fine or with both.

(viii) Sec. 354-B assault or use of criminal force to women with intent to disrobe

Any man who assaults or uses criminal force to any women or abets such act with the intention of disrobing or compelling her to be naked shall be punished with imprisonment of either description for a term which shall not be less than 03 years but which may extend to 07 years and with fine.

(ix) Sec. 354-C voyeurism

Any man who watches or captures the image of a women engaging in a private act in circumstances where she would usually have the expectation of not being observed or disseminates such image shall be punished on first conviction with imprisonment of either description for a term which shall not be less than 01 year but which may extend to 03 years, and shall also be liable to fine, and be punished on a second or subsequent conviction, with imprisonment of either description for a term which shall not be less than 03 years, but which may extend to 07 years and with fine.

(x) Sec. 352-D stalking

Any man who follows a women and contacts to foster personal interaction repeatedly despite a clear indication of disinterest by such women or monitors the use by a women of the internet, email or any other form of electronic communication, commit the offence of stalking except for the purpose of preventing or detecting crime upon the condition imposed by any person under any law shall be punished on first conviction with imprisonment of either description for a term which may extend to 03 years, and shall also be liable to fine and be punished subsequently with imprisonment of either description for a term of 05 years and with fine.

(xi) Sec. 406 criminal breach of trust

It is usually applied in investigation of stridhan recovery from the husband and his family shall be punished with imprisonment of either description for a term which may extend to 03 years or with fine or with both.

(2) Protection under the Code of Criminal Procedure (Cr.PC) 1973[9]

(a) Protection of women during search by a police officer (Sec 97)

Where the women is confined in such circumstances as appear to amount to an offence, any District magistrate , Sub divisional

[9] Kapoor N.D. and Rajni Abbi (2009), General and Commercial Laws. Sultan Chand and Sons Publishers, New Delhi, Seventh Edition, pp. 5.1–5.29.

Magistrate or a Magistrate of the First class my issue a search warrant and the person to whom such search warrant is directed may search for the person so confined and the person, if found, shall be immediately taken before a Magistrate who shall make such order as in the circumstances of the case seems proper.

(b) Restoration of abducted females (Sec. 98)

Upon complaint made on oath of the abduction or unlawful detention of a women, or a female child under the age of eighteen years for any unlawful purpose, a District Magistrate, Sub-divisional Magistrate of First Class may make an order for the immediate restoration of such women to her liberty or such female child to her husband, parent, or other person having the lawful charge of such child, and may compel compliance with such order, using such force as may be necessary.

(c) Precautions for taking search of a women (Sec. 100)

Where any person in such place which is being searched, is reasonably suspected of concealing about his person or any article for which search should be made, such person is a women, the search shall be made by another women with strict regard to decency. Before making a search, the officer shall call two or more independent and respectable inhabitants of that locality and may issue an order in writing to them to be a witness of search. The search shall be made in their presence, and a list of all things seized shall be prepared and signed by such witnesses, but no person witnessing a search shall be required to attend the court as a witness of the search unless specially summoned by it. The occupant of the place searched, or some person in his behalf, shall in every instance, be permitted to attend during the search, and a copy of the list so prepared, signed by the said witnesses, shall be delivered to such occupant or person. When a person is so searched, a list of all things taken in possession, shall be prepared, and a copy thereof shall be delivered to such person. Any person who without reasonable cause, refuses or neglects to attend and witness such a search, when called upon to do so by an order in writing delivered to him shall be deemed to have committed an offence under section 187 offence of omission to assist public servant when bound by law to give assistance of Indian Penal Code 1860.

(d) Order for maintenance of wives, children and parents (Sec. 125)

If any person having sufficient means neglects or refuses to maintain his wife, who are unable to maintain themselves or his legitimate or illegitimate minor child whether married or not if unable to maintain itself or his legitimate or illegitimate child not being a married daughter who has attained majority, where such child is by reason of physical or mental abnormalities or injury, unable to maintain itself or his father or mother, unable to maintain himself or herself a Magistrate of the First Class may, upon proof of such neglect or refusal, order such person to make a monthly allowance for the maintenance of his wife or such child, father or mother, at such monthly rate not exceeding five hundred rupees on the whole, and to pay the same to such person as directed by the Magistrate. Provided that the Magistrate may order the father of a minor female child to make such allowance, until she attains her majority. If any person so ordered fails without sufficient cause to comply with the order, issue a warrant for levying the amount due and may sentence such person for the whole or any part of each months allowance remaining unpaid after the execution of the warrant to imprisonment for a term which may extend to 1 month or until payment. No warrant shall be issued unless application be made to the court to levy such amount within a period of one year from the date on which it became due. If such person offers to maintain his wife on condition of her living with him, and she refuses to live with him, such Magistrate may consider grounds for refusal and make order if he is satisfied upon the grounds for refusal like if husband contracted marriage with another women or keeps a mistress, it shall become a valid ground for refusal to live with him. No wife is allowed to maintenance if she is living in Adultry or refuse to live together without sufficient reasons or live separately by mutual consent and Magistrate can even cancel the order for Maintenance. In dealing with the quantum of maintenance to be allowed, net salary of the husband is to be calculated after deducting from the gross salary after the statutory deductions and not on the voluntary ones. Daughter unmarried or married having sufficient means liable to pay maintenance allowance to her father or mother who is unable to maintain himself or herself. This provision only gives wives, helpless and deserted children and destitute parents to secure the much needed relief. The Divorce by mutual consent under Sec 13-B of Hindu Marriage Act, does not relinquish the right of claiming maintenance under Sec. 125 Cr. PC. Conversion of a Hindu husband to Islam does not relieve the liability of the husband to maintain his divorced Hindu Wife and Children. The provision in the Code is intended to save deserted wives, children and parents form starvation as starvation may force them to be undesirable wives. In case where there is no other income of a neglected wife and the husband is a satisfied employee unless he has other unavoidable encumbrances it may not be unreasonable to direct the husband to pay even 1/3rd of his salary to his neglected wife depending upon the status of the parties, their acceptable habits and general mode of living provided such 1/3rd does not amount to luxurious allowance. The quantum of maintenance payable to a wife or child or parent has to be fixed in the light of the facts and circumstances of each case with due regard to the capacity of the husband and the needs of the claimant as also the cost of living bearing however in mind that the proceedings are merely 'maintenance proceedings' intended to provide not a lavish grant, but the necessary subsistence amount covering food, clothing and shelter. This provision are applicable to all persons belonging to all religions and has no relationship with the personal law of the parties. This will only gives effect to the natural duty of a man to maintain his wife and is essentially a speedier remedy available against starvation to be disposed off. If the provisions of Sec. 125 (1) are read with 127(3)(b) it becomes clear that the wife would continue to be treated as wife, although she has been divorced by the husband, so long as she is not in receipt of the whole of the sum payable under the customery or personal law applicable to the parties on such divorce. If the women has, after the date of such divorce, remarries then such order as from the date of her remarriage can be cancelled by the Magistrate. At the time of making any decree for the recovery of any maintenance the civil court shall take into account the sum which has been paid to, or recovered by such person as monthly allowance in pursuance of the said order.

(e) Requiring attendance of a women as witness by a police officer (Sec. 160)

Any police officer making an investigation may by order in writing, require the attendance before himself of any person being within the limits of his own or any adjoining station who, from the information given or otherwise appears to be acquainted with the facts and circumstances of the case, and such person shall attend as so required, but no male person under the age of 15 years or women of any age shall be required to attend at any place other than the place in which such male person or women resides.

(3) Protection under the Indian Evidence Act 1872

There are some facts of which evidence cannot be given before the court of law, though they are relevant facts. They are classified as priviledged communications. In relation to evidence, privilege means a right to refuse to disclose a fact. A privilege may permit or enquire a witness to decline to answer a question or to produce a document at the hearing or may permit or require a party to decline to answer an interrogatory or to disclose a document before trial. The principle of privilege from disclosure is based on public policy.

(a) Communications during marriage (Sec. 122)

No person who is or has been married shall be compelled to disclose any communication made to him during marriage by any person to whom he is or has been married. Likewise no person shall be permitted to disclose any such communication, unless the person who made it, or his representative in interest, consents, disclosure may however be made in suits between married persons, or in proceeding in which any married person is prosecuted for any crime committed against the other. This section rests on the obvious ground that the admission of testimony would have a powerful tendency to disturb the peace of families, to promote domestic broils, and to weaken, if not to destroy, that feeling of mutual confidence which is the most endearing solace of married life. The protection is not only a strictly confidential character, but the seal of law is also placed upon all communications of whatever nature, which pass between husband and wife.

(b) Presumption as to abetment of suicide by a married women (Sec. 113-A)

When the question is whether the commission of suicide by a women had been abetted by her husband or any relative of her husband and it is shown that she had committed suicide within a period of seven years from the date of her marriage and that her husband or such relative of her husband had subjected her to cruelty, the court may presume, having regard to the other circumstances of the case that such suicide had been abetted by her husband or by such relative of her husband.

C. INTERNATIONAL EFFORTS TOWARDS WOMEN WELFARE

The international community has applied the principle of gender equality since the United Nations was founded in 1945. It is enshrined in the UN Charter, the 'Constitution' of the United Nations. The United Nations Universal Declaration of Human Rights of 1948 also contains the principle that no distinction shall be made 'on account of sex'. The two human rights covenants that were adopted in 1966, which incorporated a ban on discrimination, made gender equality a legally binding principle for signatory states.

(1) The International Labour Organisation 1919

It worked in collaboration with the League of Nations after 1946, the economic and social council of the United Nations Organisation retained this organisation. The head quarters is situated at Geneva in Switzerland. This organisation regulates the hours of work, eliminates unemployment, to maintain just and fair conditions of labour, irrespective of caste, colour, race or sex, to provide for an adequate living wage, to promote moral, social, political and cultural welfare of the world peasants, to protect the worker against sickness, disease and injury, to protect children and yound persons and to bring the female labour upto the level of male labour, to provide old age pensions, to protect and guide the workers aginst exploitation of the capitalists and to organize professional and technical education and to recognize the principle of freedom of association.

(2) The International Labour Conference held at Philadelphia 1944

It decided that labour is not a commodity, poverty anywhere constitutes a danger to prosperity hence, freedom of expression and association are essential to sustain progress and war against want requires to be carried on with unrelenting vigour within each nation.

(3) Commission of the Economic and Social Council of the United Nations Organisation 1946

The commission on the status of women was constituted. It recommends for the promotion of women rights in the fields of social, political, economic and education by focusing the problems of women which requires immediate attention.

(4) Universal Declaration of Human Rights 1948

Article 2 declares that everyone is entitled to all the rights and freedoms set forth in this declaration, without distinction of any race, colour, sex, language, religion, political, national or social origin, property, birth and status but this declaration however, will not vest any binding force on the member states. It warns that the role of women in procreation should not be a basis for discrimination and exhorts for sharing of responsibility of upbringing of children. It warns that the role of women in procreation should not be a basis for discrimination and exhorts for sharing of responsibility of upbringing between men and women and society as a whole. It also obligates state parties to embody the principle of equity of men and women in their national constitution and legislations[10].

(5) Convention for the Suppression of Traffic in Persons and the Exploitation of the Prostitution of others July 25, 1951

United Nation consolidated International Convention for The

[10] Article 2 of UDHR (1948). International Covenant on Economic, Social and Cultural Rights, 1966 and International Covenant on Civil and Political Rights, 1966.

Suppression of the Traffic in Women and Children entered in 1921 and International Convention for the Suppression of the Traffic in women of full age of 1933 which were adopted by the League of Nations and agreed to punish any person who procures any person for prostitution or who keeps, manages, knowingly finances any brothel, or rents a building for the purpose of prostitution of others. The states also agreed to repeal or abolish any existing law, regulations or administrative provisions which allowed persons to engage in such activities.

(6) International Covenant on Civil and Political Rights 1966

It binds the states who have confirmed to the covenant through its Parliament or Sovereign Power to ensure the equal rights of men and women to the enjoyment of all civil and political rights of men and women to the enjoyment of all civil and political rights set forth in the covenant. Article 23 states that the family being the natural and fundamental unit of society, it is entitled to protect the society and the state. The right of men and women of marriageable age to marry and constitute a family shall be recognized. All the marriage shall be entered with free and full consent of the intending spouses. Appropriate steps shall be taken to ensure the equality of rights and responsibility of spouses towards marriage and even in its dissolution and provision to protect the children arising out of such marriage.

(7) International Covenant on Economic, Social and Cultural Rights 1968

State parties should render protection to family as it is responsible for the care and education of dependent children. Special protection shall be offered to mothers during a reasonable period before and after child birth by availing the facility of paid leave or leave with adequate social security benefits.

(8) Declaration of Mexico Plans of Action. World Conference of the International Women's Year, 19 June-2 July, 1975. United Nations December, 1975

In order to eliminate all obstacles that stand in the way of enjoyment by women of equal status with men, the Mexico Plans of Action decided to promulgate 30 principles on the equality of women and their contribution to national development and international peace. For implementation purposes, the objectives of the Mexico Plans of Action were divided into two categories-The World Plan of Action and The Regional Plan of Action. The main purpose was to stimulate National, International and Regional action to solve the problems of underdevelopment and of the socio-economic structure which place women in an inferior position[11].

(9) International Conference on Primary Health Care Alma-Ata, USSR, 6th to 12th September 1978

As decided by the Health Assembly of the World Health Organization (WHO)[12] and the Executive Board of the United Nations Children's Fund (UNICEF), and at the invitation of the Government of the Union of Soviet Socialist Republic, the International Conference on Primary Health Care was held from 6 to 12 September 1978 in Alma-Ata, capital of the Kazakh Soviet Socialist Republic. The Conference strongly reaffirms that health being a fundamental human right, the social target for Governments, International organizations and the whole world community in the coming decade is to attain a level of health to the people to lead a socially and economically productive life. It also emphasizes on Health Education, control the Health Problems, promotion of food supply, increase the level of Nutrition, adequate supply of Safe Water, Basic Sanitation, Maternal and Child Health care, Family Planning, Immunization against Infectious Diseases, Prevention of Epidemic Diseases, Treatment for Common Diseases and Injuries and Provision of Essential Drugs. The Conference calls for urgent and effective national and international action to develop and implement primary health care throughout the world and particularly in developing countries in a spirit of technical cooperation and in keeping with a New International

---

[11] Annexure to the "National Perspective Plan for Women" (1988-2000 A.D). Report of the Core Group set up by the Department of Women & Child Development, Ministry of Human Resource Development, Government of India.

[12] WHO (1977). Handbook of Resolutions and Decisions, Vol. I, 1973, pp. 29,30,31 and Vol. II (2nd Ed.) pp. 19, 20, 21, 148.

Economic Order. It urges governments, WHO, UNICEF, international multilateral and bilateral agencies, non-government organizations, funding agencies, all health workers and the whole world community should collaborate in introducing, developing and maintaining Primary Health through increased technical and financial support and cooperation.

(10) The Convention on the Elimination of all forms of Discrimination against Women 1981

The General Assembly of the United Nations has adopted a declaration on November, 1967 and a convention was adopted on December 18, 1979 which came into force in 1981. The Convention defines discrimination as any distinction, exclusion or restriction made on the basis of sex which impair the recognition, enjoyment or exercise of the human rights and fundamental freedom in the political, economic, social, cultural, civil or any fields by the women. The state parties condemned all forms of discrimination against women and agreed to eliminate it by embodying the principle of equality of men and women in their National constitution, other appropriate legislations by establishing legal protection of the rights of women. The convention also established a Committee on the Elimination of Discrimination against Women (CEDAW) to implement the convention in 1993. Article 10 of this Declaration declares that all appropriate measures shall be taken to ensure to women, married or unmarried, equal rights with men in the field of economic and social life. The women should not be discriminated on the grounds of marital status or any other grounds to receive vocational training to work, to free choice of profession and employment advancement, equal remuneration with men and to equality of treatment in respect of work of equal value, the right to leave with pay, retirement, privileges and provision for security in respect of unemployment, sickness, old-age or other incapacity to work, the right to receive family allowance on equal terms with men. In order to prevent discrimination against women on account of marriage or maternity and to ensure that effective right to work, measures shall be taken to prevent their dismissal in the event of marriage or maternity and to provide paid maternity to have with guarantee of returning to former employment, and to provide the necessary social service, including child care facilities. However, measures taken to potect women in certain types of work, for reasons inherent in their physical nature, shall not be regarded as discrimination. Article 11 requires the state parties to take appropriate measures to eliminate discrimination against women in the field of employment in order to ensure, on the basis of equality of men and women. To provide right to work as an inalienable right of all the human beings, the right to the same employment opportunities, including the application of the same criteria for selection in matters of employment, the right of free choice of profession and employment, the right to promotion, job security and all benefits and conditions of service and the right to receive vocational training including apprenticeship advanced vocational training and recurrent training. The right to equal remuneration, including benefit and to equal treatment in respect of work of equal value, as well as equality of treatment in the evaluation of equality of work, the right to social security, particularly in cases of retirement, unemployment, sickness, invalidity and old age and other incapacity to work, as well as the right to paid leave and the right to protection of health and safety in working conditions including the safe guarding of the function of reproduction. At present 179 countries has ratified to the convention.

(11) 41st World Assembly Adopted Resolution 41.24 in Geneva on 13th May, 1988

Avoidance of discrimination in relation to HIV infected people and people with AIDS. It urged member states to formulate national programmes for the prevention and control of HIV/AIDS, which should besides fostering compassion for infected people through IEC programmes, protect their human righs and dignity and also prevent any discrimination against them in the provision of services, employment and travel. They should also ensure the confidentiality of testing, counseling and other support services. The resolution also called upon the government, NGOs, International Organisations and Voluntary bodies involved in AIDS control programmes to take care of the health needs of all the people who are infected with HIV/AIDS.

(12) UN World Conference on Human Rights Held in Vienna 1993

The issue of 'Violence against Women' was discussed at the second UN World Conference on Human Rights held in Vienna in 1993. The concluding statement contains the specific condemnation of violence against women. It also specifies that 'Human rights of women and the girl child are an inalienable, integral and indivisible part of universal human rights'. Following the World Conference on Human Rights, the United Nations adopted a Declaration on the Elimination of Violence against Women in December 1993. The following forms of violence against women in the public and private domain were defined as human rights violations like Physical, sexual and psychological violence occurring in the family, including physical and sexual abuse of female children, Dowry-related violence, Marital rape, Genital mutilation and other traditional practices harmful to women, Non-spousal violence and violence related to exploitation, physical, sexual and psychological violence occurring within the general community, including rape, sexual abuse, sexual harassment and intimidation at work, in educational institutions and elsewhere, Trafficking in women and forced prostitution, all forms of physical, sexual and psychological violence perpetrated or condoned by the state. In 1994, the UN Human Rights Commission established the office of a Permanent Special Rapporteur whose area of work covers the forms of violence against women listed in the Declaration.

(13) International Conference on Population and Development, Cairo, 1994

Total 179 countries agreed that population and development are inextricably linked, and that empowering women and meeting people's needs for education and health, including reproductive health, are necessary for both individual advancement and balanced development. The conference adopted a 20-year Programme of Action, Advancing gender equality, eliminating violence against women and ensuring women's ability to control their own fertility were acknowledged as cornerstones of population and development policies. Concrete goals of the ICPD centred on providing universal education; reducing infant, child and maternal mortality; and ensuring universal access by 2015 to reproductive health care, including family planning, assisted childbirth and prevention of sexually transmitted infections including HIV/AIDS.

(14) The Beijing Declaration and Platform for Action was Adopted at the September 1995

Fourth World Conference on Women (FWCW) by representatives from 189 countries. The Platform reflects a new international commitment to the goals of equality, development and peace for all women everywhere. It builds on commitments made during the United Nations Decade for Women, 1976-1985 and on related commitments made in the cycle of United Nations global conferences held in the 1990s. The United Nations Millennium Declaration was unanimously adopted at the conclusion of the Millennium Summit. It focused to promote gender equality and empower women essential to achieving the other seven Millennium Development Goals as well.

(15) UN Security Council Resolution 1325 and Subsequent Resolutions 2000

The UN Security Council calls for women's 'equal participation and full involvement in all efforts for the maintenance and promotion of peace and security'. Several German federal ministries are tasked with implementing this resolution. Under the auspices of the Ministry of Foreign Affairs, these include the Federal Ministry for Economic Cooperation and Development (BMZ) and the Federal Ministries of Defence (BMVg), of the Interior (BMI) and of Justice and Consumer Protection (BMJ), along with the Federal Ministry of Family Affairs, Senior Citizens, Women and Youth (BMFSFJ). An interministerial working group has been established on the BMZ's initiative to involve women more effectively in conflict prevention and peace processes that has been the case in the past, and to promote equality in relevant missions. The working group meets regularly and in December 2012 adopted the National Action Plan to implement Resolution 1325, which sets out the framework for coherent and efficient implementation of this resolution by the Federal Government. UN Security Council Resolution 1820 of 2008 states that rape and other forms of sexual violence 'can be a war crime, a crime against humanity and/ or an act of genocide'. The resolution calls on UN member states to meet their obligations to prosecute those who commit such crimes. It also permits sanctions to be imposed on countries in which sexual violence occurs during armed conflicts. In follow-up Resolutions 1888 (30 September 2009) and 1960 (16 December 2010) the UN Security Council reiterated the importance of protecting women and girls in conflict situations. It called on states to put an end to impunity, to prosecute the perpetrators of sexual violence and to adapt justice systems accordingly. Resolutions 1889 (05 October 2009), 2106 (24 June 2013) and 2122 (18 October 2013) emphasis the importance of involving women in all areas of conflict prevention and peacebuilding, particularly during peace negotiations at the highest political level (Resolution 2122). Resolution 2106 highlights the significance of the International Criminal Court (ICC) for the prosecution of sexual and gender-based violence during conflict situations. A functioning criminal justice system is an important element of legal certainty and thus of violence prevention. To monitor the implementation of these resolutions and coordinate the commitment of the member states, the UN Security Council and the European Union in 2010 adopted indicators for the implementation of Resolution 1325. EU Indicator Reports outline the progress achieved at regular intervals. Apart from Germany's National Action Plan 1325, the EU indicators set the framework against which the German government's efforts to implement Resolution 1325 are aligned.

(16) MoU on Cooperation Between the Ministry of Youth Affairs and Sports of India and French Ministry of Sports, Youth Affairs, Public Education and Community Life 2015

Central Government under the leadership of Prime Minister Narendra Modi entered MoU to envisage cooperation and exchange of experiences in the fields of sports medicine, institutional cooperation, development of practice of sports in the context of proximity sports, support of participation of women and the disabled in sports, management and coordination of sports federations, training of executives and establishment of National Institute of Sports in India based on French model of INSEP.

3

Protection for Women under Special Laws

Women from half of the Indian Population. Women have always been discriminated against men and have suffered denial and discrimination in silence, self sacrifice and self denial are their nobility and fortitude and yet have been subjected to all kinds of inequalities, indignities, incongruities and discrimination[1].

(1) PROTECTION AGAINST TRAFFICKING OF WOMEN

According to the definition of human trafficking given by the Government of India in the annual report of crimes in India, it is a group of crimes involving the exploitation of men, women and children for financial gains, which is in violation of fundamental human rights. Victims are abducted from their homes and subsequently forced to work against their will by various means in houses or other establishments to involve in prostitution subjecting to various evils like killing or incapacitating for the purpose of begging and trade in human organs. The subject has received considerable attention in the world but very few detailed scientific studies have been done on it. Most of the trafficked women are between 14 and 18 years of age who are jobless in their own countries when they are

[1] Tripathi S.C., (2004). Law relating to Women and Children-Central Law Publication, p. 1.

helpless and are at the mercy of the traffickers who abuse and exploit them fully and do not even pay them properly. It is not surprising that they suffer from STDs, HIV/AIDS and many other diseases without any relief. Trafficking is a complex issue and addressing its causes and consequences requires action at many levels. As per the Platform of Action of Beijing in 1995 Government were exhorted to strengthen the implementation of all relevant human right interventions through international cooperation against organized and other forms of trafficking women for sexual exploitation, pornography, prostitution and sex tourism. The Governments will provide legal and social services through the international cooperation to prosecute and punish those responsible for organized exploitation of women. It allocate resources to provide Comprehensive Programmes for the rehabilitation of the victims of trafficking into the society by giving them job training, legal assistance and health care.[2] The Immoral Traffic Prevention Act, 1956 protects women against trafficking by the following provisions[3].

(a) Punishment for Keeping a Brothel or Allowing Premises to be used as Brothel (Sec. 03)

Sec. 3(1) It shall be punishable on first conviction with rigorous imprisonment for a term of not less than 01 year and not more than 03 years and also with fine which may extend to Rs. 2000/- and in the event of a second or subsequent conviction, with rigorous imprisonment for not less than 02 years and not more than 05 years and also with fine which may extend to Rs. 2000/-. Sec. 3(2) Any person who is a tenant, lessee, occupier, incharge, owner, lessor or landlord of any premises knowingly allows any other person to use such premises as brothel such person shall be punishable on first conviction with imprisonment for a term which may extend to 02 years and with fine upto Rs. 2000/- rupees and in the subsequent conviction, with rigorous imprisonment upto 05 years and with fine.

---

[2] Sudhir Varma, (2010). Gender, HIV and Social Work, Rawat Publications, Jaipur, pp. 48-51.

[3] Bare Act, (1999). The Immoral Traffic (Prevention) Act, 1956, Universal Law Publishing Co. Pvt. Ltd.

(b) Punishment for Living on the Earning of Prostitution (Sec. 04)

Prostitution means any female offering her body for promiscuous sexual intercourse for hire whether in money or in kind" including sexual exploitation or abuse of persons for commercial purpose. Any person over the age of 18 years who knowingly living with the company of a prostitute, have control or influence over the movements of a prostitute in such a manner as to show that such person is aiding, abetting or compelling her prostitution or acting as a tout or pimp on behalf of a prostitute, it shall be presumed that such person is living on the earnings of the prostitution of any other person shall be punishable with imprisonment for a term which may extend to 02 years, or with fine of Rs. 1000/-, or with both and where such earnings relate to the prostitution of a child or a minor, shall be punishable with imprisonment for a term of not less than 07 years and not more than 10 years.

(c) Procuring, Inducing or Taking Person for the Sake of Prostitution (Sec. 05)

Any person who procure, induce, takes a person from one place to another with a view to prostitution shall be punishable on conviction with rigorous imprisonment for a term of not less than 03 years and not more than 07 years and also with fine which may extend to Rs. 200/-, and if any offence under this sub-section is committed against the will of any person, the punishment of imprisonment for a term of 07 years shall extend to imprisonment for a term of 14 years. Violation by a child the punishment provided shall extend to rigorous imprisonment for a term of not less than 07 years but may extend to life and if he is a minor, the punishment of rigorous imprisonment for a term of not less than 07 years and not more than 14 years.

(d) Detaining a Person in Premises where Prostitution is Carried (Sec. 06)

Any person who detains anyone whether with or without his consent in any brothel any premises with intention that such person may have sexual intercourse with the person who is not the spouse of such person, shall be punishable on conviction, with imprisonment for a term which shall not be less than 07 years but which may be for life or the term may extend to 10 years and shall also be liable to fine. Court for any special reasons can impose a sentence of 07 years. Where a child or a minor found in a brothel is on medical examination, detected to have been sexually abused, it shall be deemed to be detained for the purpose of prostitution. If any women in a brothel is detained for the purpose of sexual intercourse with a man other than her husband. If anyone with intent to compel her to remain there withholds from her any jewellery, wearing apparel, money or other property belonging to her, or threatens her with legal proceedings if she takes away with her any jewellery wearing apparel, money or other property lent or supplied to her. Notwithstanding any law to the contrary no suit, prosecution or other proceeding shall lie against such women or girl by the person by whom she has been detained for the recovery of any money alleged to be payable by such women or girl.

(e) Prostitution in the Vicinity of Public Places (Sec. 07)

Any person, who carries on prostitution in any premises which is within a distance of 200 metres of any place of public, religious worship, educational institution, hostel, hospital, nursing home or such other public place notified by the Commissioner of Police or Magistrate shall be punishable with imprisonment for a term which may extend to 03 months. If the offence is committed against a child or minor it shall be punished with imprisonment of either description for life or upto 10 years and with fine. But court may on special reasons impose sentence of imprisonment for a term of less than 07 years. If any keeper, tenant, lessee, occupier, incharge, owner, lessor or landlord of any public premise knowingly permits prostitution shall be punishable on first conviction with imprisonment upto 03 months or with fine of Rs. 200/-, or with both and subsequent conviction with imprisonment for a term upto 06 months and fine of Rs. 200/-. If such place is found to be an hotel the license of carrying the business of such hotel shall also be suspended for 03 months to 01 year. And if offence is against child or minor the license shall be liable to be cancelled.

(f) Seducing or Soliciting for the Purpose of Prostitution (Sec. 08)

Whoever in any public place in such manner as to be seen or heard by words, guestures, willful exposure of her person (whether by sitting by a window or on a balcony of a building or house or in any other way) or otherwise tempts, or attracts the attention of, any person for the purpose of prostitution or solicits or molests any person, or loiters or acts in such manner as to cause obstruction or annoyance to persons residing nearby or passing by such public place or to offend against public decency, for the purpose of prostitution, shall be punished for first conviction, with imprisonment for a term which may extend to six month, or with fine of Rs. 500/-, or with both, and for subsequent conviction, with imprisonment for a term which may extent to 01 year, and also with fine of Rs. 500/-.

(g) Seduction of a Person in Custody (Sec. 09)

Any person who is having the custody, charge or care of over any person, causes or aids or abets the seduction for prosecution of that person shall be punishable on conviction with imprisonment of either description for a term not less than 07 years but may be for life or for a term which may extend to 10 years and with fine. But court may on special reasons impose a sentence of imprisonment for a term of less than 10 years.

(h) Reference of a Female Offender in a Corrective Institution (Sec. 10A)

Where a female offender is found guilty under this act and if the character, state of health and mental condition of the offender and other circumstances are expedient that she should be subjected to detention for such term for her correction, it shall be lawful for the court to pass, an order for detention in a corrective institution for not less than 02 years and not for more than 05 years, as the court feels after giving an opportunity to be heard and considering the report of the Probation officer appointed under the Probation of Offenders Act, 1958. Under Sec 10A(2) the provisions of Code of

Criminal Procedure, 1973 relating to appeal, reference and revision and of the Limitation Act, 1963 shall apply this regard also. In Sec 10A(3) the Government may at any time after expiration of 06 months, if it is satisfied that there is a reasonable probability that the offender will lead a useful and industrious life, discharge her from such institution, without or with conditions.

(i) Search without Warrant (Sec. 15)

If anybody finds that a female of his or her family has been abducted or kidnapped, after finding the place where that female is misused for prostitution, should directly approach the Special Police Officer and request him orally or through an application to make an immediate search of the place. If special police officer has reasonable grounds to believe that an offence punishable under this act has been committed in respect of person, after recording the grounds of his belief, enter and search such premises without a warrant. In Sec. 15(2) Such officer before making the search shall identify two or more respectable inhabitants at least one of whom shall be a women of the locality to attend and witness the search, and may issue an order in writing to them. Sec. 15(3) if any person who, without reasonable cause, refuses or neglects to attend and witness search shall be deemed to have committed an offence under section 187 of Indian Penal Code, 1860 (Omission to assist public servant when by law to give such assistance willfully neglects to aid a public servant). In Sec. 15(4) The officer, entering any premises for search shall be entitled to remove there from all the persons found therein and in Sec. 15(5) such person shall produce them before the appropriate magistrate. Such persons shall be referred to medical examination by a registered medical practitioner for determining the age or for detection of any injuries as a result of sexual abuse or for the detection of any sexually transmitted diseases under Sec. 15(5-A). In Sec. 15(6-A) Police officer making such search, shall be accompanied by at least two women police officers, and where any women or girl is removed, is required to be interrogated, it shall be done by a women police officer and if no women police officer is available, the interrogation shall be done only in the presence of a lady member of a recognized welfare institution or organisation.

(j) Rescue of Person from a Brothel (Sec. 16)

Magistrate on information supplied by police or any other person authorized by the state government that any person is carrying prostitution in a brothel, he may direct a police officer not below the rank of a sub-inspector to enter such brothel, and to remove such person from such place and produce before him.

(k) Intermediate Custody of Persons Removed or Rescued (Sec. 17)

When a special officer removing a person on search or rescuing on direction of Magistrate, for any reason unable to produce him before the appropriate Magistrate as required under law, he shall produce them before the nearest Magistrate of any place, who shall pass order for safe custody until he is produced before the appropriate Magistrate. The appropriate Magistrate can hand over rescued person to the parents, guardian or husband after proper enquiry or if feels that such person need care and protection, may summon a panel of five respectable persons three of whom shall be women after keeping the list of experienced social welfare workers, particularly women social welfare workers, in the field of suppression of immoral traffic in persons. Can order to detain not less than 01 year and not more than 03 years in a protective home, or in such other custody as he shall, for reasons to be recorded in writing, consider suitable after entering into a bond containing undertaking based on directions relating to proper care, guardianship, education, training, medical and psychiatric treatment of the person as well with supervision by a person appointed by the court in force for a period of not exceeding 03 years.

(l) Conditions before Placing Persons Rescued to Parents or Guardians (Sec. 17-A)

The Magistrate making an enquiry under section 17, may before passing an order for handing over the rescued person to the parents, guardian or husband, satisfy himself about the genuineness of such persons to keep such person by causing an investigation to be made by a recognized welfare institution.

(m) After Care Programmes

Social and Moral Hygiene Programme and After Care Programme is undertaken for rehabilitation of rescued women, adults and children discharged from Correctional and Care Institutions. The programme is implemented by the State Government with Central Assistance with the Central Social Welfare Board and the State Social Welfare Boards being associated with it in an advisory capacity. According to UNICEF, India contain half of the one million children worldwide who enter the sex trade each year. In recent years, prostitutes began to demand legal rights, licenses, and reemployment training, especially in Mumbai, New Delhi, and Calcutta. In 2002, the Government signed the South Asian Association for Regional Cooperation (SAARC) Convention on Prevention and Combating Trafficking in Women and Children for Prostitution. Girls as young as seven years of age were trafficked from economically depressed neighborhoods in Nepal, Bangladesh, and rural areas to the major prostitution centers of Mumbai, Calcutta, and New Delhi. NGOs estimate that there were approximately 1,00,000 to 2,00,000 women and girls working in brothels in Mumbai and 40,000 to 1,00,000 in Calcutta. In Bombay 269, in West Bengal 100, in Motihari 14 and Champaran 12 and in Orissa nearly 200 brothels are working. State Governments also enacted some legislations to prohibit the prostitution like Prevention of Prostitution Act 1923, UP Naik Girls Protection Act 1929, The Bombay Devadasi Protection Act 1934, Prevention of Dedication Act 1934, Madras Devadasi Act 1947. The implementation of these acts has become a challenge due to uncertain number about the trafficked people for bonded labours, servitude or for commercial sex. The ways of trafficking differs across the states hence difficult to track the traffickers. The reforms need to be taken to review the definition of trafficking by covering all the acts related with the offence, age of the victim, claim and compensation against the trafficker on the basis of tort law, the process of legal aid, procedure for legal representation and legal protection to the witness. Careful protection shall be extended to the Victim considering the degree of trauma. Provision for Gender sensitive Rescue and Rehabilitation Mechanism. State must allocate funds for better schemes and policies in the budget to implement this act. Pro-active Role shall be entrusted to the Panchayath's and awareness is required to be spread in the Community to be empathetic towards the victims and survivors.

(2) PROTECTION AGAINST INDECENT REPRESENTATION OF WOMEN

The Indecent Representation of Women (Prohibition) Act, 1986 prohibits certain acts made against indecent representation of women's body or style of living by way of advertisement. Sec. 02 defines indecent representation of women as depiction in any manner of the figure of a woman, her form, body, being indecent or derogatory or denigrating women, is likely to deprave, corrupt, injure the public morality or morals. An offence punishable under this act is cognizable but it is bailable. However, no suit, prosecution or other proceeding shall lie against the Central Government or any State Government for anything which is good faith done or under this act.

(a) Prohibition of Advertisements (Sec. 3)

No person shall publish any advertisement which contains indecent representation of women in any form including in the public medias.

(b) Prohibition of Publication or Sending by Post any Books, Pamphlets, etc. (Sec. 4)

No person shall produce, let to hire, distribute, circulate or send by post any book, pamphlet, paper, slide, film, writing, drawing, painting, photography, representation or figure which contains indecent representation of women in any form except such publication of any above mentioned items is proved to be justified as being for the public good on the grounds that such materials is in the interest of science, literature, art, for learning, for general concern or which is kept or used with good belief for religious purposes or any representation sculptured, engraved, painted or otherwise represented on or in any monument within the meaning of Ancient Monument and Archaeological Sites and Remains Act, 1958, any temple, or on any car used for conveyance of idols or used for any religious purposes and any firm in respect of which the provisions of Part II of the Cinematograph Act, 1952 is applicable.

(c) Power to Search (Sec. 5)

Any Gazetted officer authorized by the State Government having proper jurisdiction, enter and search at all reasonable times, with such assistance, any place where any offence is presumed to be committed and can seize any advertisement of any book, pamphlet, paper, slide, film, writing, drawing, painting, photograph, representation or figure contravening the provisions of this act. But no such entry shall be made into a private dwelling house without a warrant and the power to seize may be exercised in respect of any material without affecting the integrity, utility or saleable value thereof. Any seize shall be informed to the Magistrate as per the Code of Criminal Procedure Code, 1973.

(d) Penalty (Sec. 6)

Any person contravenes Sec. 3 and Sec. 4 shall be punishable on first conviction with imprisonment for upto 2 years with Rs. 2,000/- fine and subsequent conviction from 6 months upto 5 years imprisonment with fine from Rs. 10,000/- upto 1 lakh rupees.

(e) Offence by Company (Sec. 7)

If offence is committed by a company, every person, who at the time of committing the offence was incharge and responsible for the conduct of the business of the company, shall be deemed to be guilty of the offence and shall be proceeded against and punished accordingly. But no such person shall be rendered liable to any punishment, if he proves that the offence was committed without his knowledge or that he had excercised all due diligence to prevent the commission of such offence. And if the offence is due to the negligence of director, manager, secretary or other officer then, such persons will be punished accordingly.

(3) PROTECTION AGAINST COMMITTING SATI

The Commission of Sati (Prevention) Act, 1987 extends to whole of India except the state of Jammu and Kashmir. The act defines the practice of Sati means burning or burying alive of any widow along with the body of her deceased husband or any other relative or with any article. This Act seeks to prevent Sati practice and prohibits glorification of this action through the observance of any ceremony, participating in any procession, creating a financial trust, and the construction of a temple or doing anything to commemorate or honor the memory of a widow who committed sati. This practice was prevalent in historical India and considered as a social evil.

(a) Penalty (Sec. 3)

Attempt to commit sati is punishable under the act. Whoever any person attempts to commit sati and does any act towards commission of sati shall be punishable with imprisonment for a term which may extend to 01 year or with fine or with both. But the special court trying this offence shall, before convicting a person, take into consideration the circumstances leading to the commission of the offence, the act and the state of mind of the person charged with the offence at the time of the commission of the act.

(b) Abetting the Commission of Sati

Whoever abets the commission of such sati, either directly or indirectly shall be punishable with death or imprisonment for life and liable for fine. The following acts are deemed to be an abetment.

- Inducement to a widow to get her burnt or buried alive along with the body of her deceased husband, relative or any article irrespective whether she is in a fit state of mind or is under the state of intoxication, stupefaction, or other cause where she cannot give her free will.
- Making a widow believe that the commission of sati would result in some spiritual benefit to her or her deceased husband or relative or the family.
- Encouraging a widow to remain fixed in her resolve to commit sati and thus instigating her to commit sati.
- Participating in any procession in connection with the commission of sati or aiding the widow in her decision to

commit sati by her along with the body of her deceased husband or relative to the cremation or burial ground.

- Being at the place where sati committed as an active participant to such commission or to any ceremony connected with it.
- Preventing or obstructing the widow from saving herself from being burnt or buried alive.
- Obstructing or interfering with the police in the discharge of its duties of taking any steps to prevent the commission of sati.

(c) Glorification of Sati is a Punishable Offence (Sec. 5)

Whoever does any act for the glorification of sati shall be punishable with imprisonment for a term which shall not be less than 01 year but which may extend to 07 years and with fine which shall not be less than Rs. 5000/-, but which may extend to Rs. 30,000/-.

(d) Collector or District Magistrate Empowered to Prevent the Offence (Sec. 6)

Where the collector or the District Magistrate is of the opinion that someone is committing or is about to be committed either sati, any abetment or any glorification he may by order prohibit such act. whoever contravenes any such order shall if such contravention is not punishable under any other provision of this act, be punishable with imprisonment for a term which shall not be less than 01 year but which may extend to 07 years and with fine which shall not be less than Rs. 5,000/- but which may extend to Rs. 30,000/-

(e) Temples or any Structures in Memory or Glorification of a Sati may be Removed (Sec. 7)

The State Government, The Collector or The District Magistrate if satisfied that any temple or other structure where any worship or performance of any ceremony is carried on with a view to perpetuate the honour or to preserve the memory of any person committed sati, by order direct the removal of such temple or structure through a

Police officer not below the rank of Sub-inspector at the cost of the defaulter.

(f) Seizing the Property (Sec. 8)

Where The Collector or The Magistrate has reason to believe that any funds or property have been collected or acquired for the purpose of glorification of the commission of sati, may seize such funds or property. He shall report the seizure to the special court, and await the orders of such special court as to the disposal of the same.

(g) Obligation of Certain Persons to Report about Commission of Offences (Sec. 17)

All officers of Government are required and empowered to assist the Police in the execution of the provisions of this act. All village officers and other officers authorized by The Collector or District Magistrate, if they have reason to believe that sati is about to or has been committed in the area shall, report such fact to the nearest police station. If such people contravenes they shall be punishable with imprisonment of either description for a term which may extend to 02 Years and liable to fine.

(4) PROTECTION AGAINST ILLEGAL TERMINATION OF PREGNANCY

The Medical Termination of Pregnancy Act, 1971 protects women by the following provisions. It laid down liberal grounds through which women obtained the right to safe, scientific and legal abortions. It emerged as a landmark social legislation, which conferred on women the right of privacy and freedom of choice. It stops illegal and unsafe abortions performed by non-qualified, untrained and ill equipped medical practitioners under unhealthy conditions. Hence it is termed to be the milestone in the modernization of Indian Society through instrumentality of law[4].

[4] Gaur K.D., (1995). Abortion and the Law in Countries of Indian Subcontinent, Asian Region, United Kingdom, Ireland and the U.S.A, Journal of the Indian Law Institute, Vol. 37, No 3, July-September.

(a) Right of Women to Terminate Pregnancy Medically (Sec. 3)

Pregnancy may be terminated by registered medical practitioner who possess any recognized medical qualification and enrolled under the Indian Medical Council Act, 1956 who has such experience or training in gynaecology and obstetrics where the length of the pregnancy does not exceed twelve weeks if such medical practitioner of opinion in good faith that the continuance of the pregnancy would involve risk to the life of the pregnant women or of grave injury to her physical health or mental health or there is a substantial risk that after the birth of the child, it would suffer from such physical or mental abnormalities as to be seriously handicapped or where the length of the pregnancy exceeds twelve weeks but does not exceed twenty weeks, if not less than two registered medical practitioners are of the above mentioned opinion in good faith. The medical practitioner shall not be guilty of any offence under the Indian Penal Code, 1860 or any other law for the time being in force if the pregnancy is caused by rape and the anguish caused by such pregnancy shall be presumed to constitute grave injury to the mental health of the pregnant women, pregnancy occurs as a result of failure of any method used by any married women or her husband for the purpose of limiting the number of children and the anguish caused by such unwanted pregnancy may be presumed to constitute a grave injury to the mental health of the pregnant women.

(b) Place authorize for Termination (Sec. 4)

Pregnancy may be terminate only in a hospital established or maintained and approved by Government.

(c) Rule making Power of the Central Government (Sec. 6)

The Central Government may, by notification in the official gazette, make rules to carry out the provisions of this act regarding the experience or training, which a registered medical practitioner shall need under this act. By regulations require any opinion to be certified by a registered medical practitioner, to give intimation about the termination to the Chief Medical Officer of the State, and to prohibit the disclosure except to such persons and for such persons as may be specified. Any person who willfully contravenes or willfully fails to comply with the requirements of any regulation so made shall be liable to be punished with fine which may extend to rupees 1,000/-.

(d) Protection against Suit (Sec. 8)

The registered medical practitioners are protected against suit or legal proceedings for any damage caused by anything which is in good faith done under this act. A civil right to abortion does not amount to a social right but women can be protected from abortion only through the inculcation of safe abortion services as a social service in the health care, pre-natal care, child care, safe and reliable contraception, sex education, etc.[5].

(5) PROTECTION AGAINST DOWRY HARASSMENT

The ancient custom is rooted in the patriarchal family structure based on the objectification and subordination of women. Marriage in India is a sacrament, which create a bond between two families. The concept of 'kanyadaan' reduces the status of a daughter to a piece of object to be donated at the fathers or guardians will. The custom of dowry is embedded in social system that a liability to be disposed of at a discount in the inter family transaction that is marriage[6]. The Dowry Prohibition Act 1961 applies to the whole of India except the state of Jammu and Kashmir. It came into force on 1st July 1961. This Act prohibits the request, payment or acceptance of a dowry, "as consideration for the marriage"[7]. According to Butalia, Subhadra (1983) Modern dowry is different from the ancient custom of varadakshina or gift as prevalent among the upper castes and the

---

[5] Jesani, Amar and Iyer, Aditi, "Women and Abortion", EPW, Vol. XXVIII, No. 48, November 27.

[6] Krishna Gupta, (2001). Women, Law and Public Opinion, Rawat Publication, Jaipur, p 69.

[7] Achar M.R. and Vekannas T., Dowry Prohibition Act and Rules, The Law Book Co, Allahabad.

'Shulka' or bride price as existing amongst the lower castes. Somewhere, in the process of civilization, the two different practices adopted by the rich and the poor seem to have got incorporated and what emerged finally is dowry today[8]. Diwan, Paras (1997) Dowry conceptually and essentially, that property which is obtained under duress, coercion or pressure, is extorted, extracted or even snatched away from the parents or guardians of the girl by the bridegroom or his parents or other near relations[9]. Sec. 2 defines Dowry as any property or valuable security given or agreed to be given either directly or indirectly by one party to a marriage to the other party, by the parents of either party to a marriage or by any other person, to either party to the marriage or to any other person during or before or any time after the marriage in connection with the marriage of the said parties but does not include 'Dower' or 'Mahr' in the case of persons to whom muslim Personal Law (Shariat) applies. According to Sarkar L. (1987) Judiciary has shown sensitization to the problems faced by women especially in cases dealing with dowry related offences and dowry deaths. The Dowry Prohibition (Amendment) Act 1986 inserted section 304 B in the IPC provides "where the death of a women is caused by any burn or bodily injury if occurs within seven years of her marriage and before her death she was subjected to cruelty or harassment by her husband or his family in connection with any demand for dowry amounts to 'dowry death' punished with seven years imprisonment to life imprisonment. Under section 498 A Cruelty to married women includes willful conduct which may drive the wife to endanger her life, limb or health includes dowry harassments is punishable with imprisonment upto three years. Section 174 of Criminal Procedure Code says that investigation of death of women in suspicious circumstances within seven years of her marriage. The initial burden of proof is shifted upon the accused person and presumption against the husband or relative about abetment may be constituted under Section 13A of the Indian Evidence Act. On the whole, the entire procedure established by law brings with a pro-victim approach as a means of empowerment and justice.

[8] Butalia, Subhadra, (1983). Dowry and Attitudes, Womens link, Newsletter, No-18, March.

[9] Diwan, Paras, (1997). Law relating to Dowry, Dowry Deaths, Bride Burning, Rape and Related Offence, New Delhi, Universal Law pub. Co.

(a) Penalties for Demanding, Giving or Taking Dowry

Under Sec. 3 if any person, gives or takes or abets dowry shall be punishable with imprisonment for a term which shall not be less than 05 years, and with fine which shall not be less than Rs. 15,000/- or the amount of the value of such dowry, whichever is more. But the court may for adequate and special reasons to be recorded in the judgement, impose a sentence of imprisonment for a term of less than 06 months. Sec. 4 prescribes penalty if any person demands, directly or indirectly from the parents or other relatives or guardian of a bride or bridegroom, as the case may be, any dowry, he shall be punishable with imprisonment for a term which shall not be less than six months, but which may extend to 02 years and with fine which may extend to Rs.10,000/-. But the court may, for adequate and special reasons to be mentioned in the judgement impose a sentence of imprisonment for a term of less than 06 months. However, the aforesaid provision shall not apply to:

- Presents which are given at the time of a marriage to the bride without any demand having been made in that behalf if such presents are entered in a list maintained in accordance with the rules made under this act.
- Presents which are given at the time of marriage to the bridegroom without any demand having been made in that behalf if such presents are entered in a list maintained in accordance with the rules made under this act and further where such presents are made by or on behalf of the bride or any person related to the bride, such presents are of a customary nature and the value thereof is not excessive having regard to the financial status of the person by whom, or on whose behalf such presents are given. Any agreement for the giving or taking of dowry shall be void.

(6) PROTECTION AGAINST FEMALE INFANTICIDE

The Pre-Natal Diagnostic Techniques (Regulation and Prevention of Misuse) Act, 1994 prohibits misuse of pre-natal diagnostic techniques for determination of sex of foetus, leading to female infanticide, advertisement of pre-natal diagnostic techniques for detention or determination of sex, permission and regulation of the use of pre-natal diagnostic techniques for the purpose of detection of specific genetic abnormalities or disorders and prescribes punishment for violation of the provisions of this act. Foeticide of a female by getting it known through pre-natal diagnostic techniques is a crime and punishable under this act.

Regulation by Law

According to Sec. 3 any Genetic Counselling, Genetic Laboratory or Genetic Clinics are regulated and controlled by the law. It prohibits employment of any person who does not possess the prescribed qualifications. It prohibits medical genetist, gynaecologist, paediatrician registered medical practitioner or any other person from conducting or aiding in pre-natal diagnostic technique except for the purpose of detecting abnormalities like chromosomal abnormalities, genetic metabolic diseases, haemoglobinopathies, sex-linked genetic diseases, congenital anomalies and any other abnormalities or diseases as may be specified by the Central Supervisory Board. It puts condition to be fulfilled by the qualified person that, before pre-natal diagnostic techniques, the age of the pregnant women is above 35 years or she has undergone two or more spontaneous abortions or foetal loss or exposed to drugs, radiation, infection or chemicals or she is mentally retarded, physically deformed or facing any genetic diseases. Sec. 4 prohibits that no person, being a relative or the husband of the pregnant women shall seek or encourage the conduct of any pre-natal diagnostic techniques on her except for the purpose specified by law. In Sec. 5 the authorized person should explain the side and after effects of such procedure to the pregnant women and take her written consent for the test. No person conducting pre-natal diagnostic procedure shall communicate to the pregnant women concerned or her relative about the sex of the foetus by words, signs or in any other manner. Sec. 6 Prohibits Genetic Counselling center or Genetic Laboratory or Genetic Clinics from conducting the tests including ultrasonography for the purpose of determining the sex of the foetus. Sec. 22 prohibits Advertisements relating to pre-natal determination of sex. Sec. 23 prescribes the penalty of imprisonment upto 03 years and fine upto Rs. 10,000/- and on subsequent conviction imprisonment may extend upto 05 years and fine upto Rs. 50,000/-. Name of the registered Medical Practitioner may be got removed from the roll of State Medical Council. Sec. 25 Prescribes a penalty for contravention of this act with imprisonment for a term upto 03 months or with fine upto one thousand rupees or with both and for continuing contravention with an additional fine upto to five hundred rupees for every day of continuing contravention after conviction for first time. Even if the offence is committed by the company then any person who is responsible for the affairs and fails to prove his due care in this regard will be liable for penalty. Under Sec. 24 the court may presume unless contrary is proved that the pregnant women was compelled by her husband or a relative to undergo pre-natal diagnostic technique and such person shall be liable for the offence of abetment and shall be punishable.

(7) PROTECTION OF RIGHTS UNDER THE PERSONAL LAWS[10]

(a) Right to Conjugal Rights

(i) In case of a Hindu wife

In The Hindu Marriage Act 1955 Conjugal rights are the basic rights of matrimonial life. Under Sec. 9 the wife may apply to the family court when the husband without reasonable cause withdraws from or keeps back the society of wife, the wife has a right to get her conjugal rights with the husband restored. She may apply by a petition to the district court for a decree for restitution of conjugal rights.

(ii) In case of a Muslim wife

Under the Mohammedan Law, restitution of conjugal rights to a muslim wife would be meaningless, because the husband has infinite

[10] Om Prakash Tewari, (2002). Womens Rights in India, Sri Sai Law Publications, Faridabad, Haryana, 1st Edition, pp. 36-85.

and immediately effective rights to declare divorce of the wife at any time. It is impossible to enjoy restitution of conjugal rights to a wife against the sweet will of the husband. Under the Muslim law the restitution of conjugal rights appears to be available only to a husband and not to the wife. However the remedy is available for both the parties.

(b) Right to Judicial Separation

(i) Right of a Christian women

Under Sec. 22 of Indian Divorce Act, 1869 A Christian wife may obtain a decree of judicial separation, on the ground of adultery or cruelty, desertion without reasonable excuse for two years or upwards. In every case of judicial separation under this act, the wife shall from the date of the sentence be considered as unmarried with respect to property of every description which she may acquire or which may come to her. Such property may be disposed of by her in all respects as an unmarried women, and on her death intestate go as the same would have gone if her husband had been then dead.

(ii) Right of a Hindu women

A Hindu wife may separate herself from her husband in certain circumstances, under a decree of the court under Section 10 of the Hindu Marriage Act, 1955 on any of the below mentioned grounds for which petition for divorce is presented and includes the husband after the solemnization of the marriage, had voluntary sexual intercourse with any person other than his spouse or he has deserted the petitioner for continuous period not less than two years, treated her with cruelty, he has ceased to be a Hindu by conversion to another religion, he has been incurably of unsound mind or has been suffering continuously from mental disorder that the petitioner cannot reasonably be expected to live with the respondent, he has been suffering from virulent and incurable leprosy, he has renounced the world by entering any religious order, that he has been suffering from veneral disease in a communicable form, that he has not been heard of as being alive for a period of seven years or more by those persons who would naturally have heard of it, had that party been alive.

(iii) Right of judicial separation of a Muslim wife

A Muslim wife has no right of judicial separation under the Muslim Personal Law. Most of the grounds of judicial separation or divorce are the same. Muslim law does not recognize judicial separation as it is under the Hindu Law.

(c) Right to Divorce or Dissolution of Marriage

(i) Right of divorce of a Hindu wife

A Hindu wife may seek divorce on any of the grounds like continuous adultery, conversion of husband to another religion, incurable unsoundness of mind for continuous period of three years, virulent and incurable form of leprosy for three years, veneral disease in a communicable form, renunciation of the world by entering any religious order, the husband not having been heard for seven years, non resumption of co-habitation between the husband and wife after judicial separation for one year, or upwards, failure to comply decree for restitution of conjugal rights for one year, or upwards, husaband having more than one wife at the time of solemnization of marriage with her, husband being guilty of rape, sodomy or bestiality under section 13 of Hindu Marriage Act, 1955. Under Section 13-B a Hindu wife may present a petition for dissolution of her marriage with the other party on the ground that she has been living separately for a period of one year or more. They have not been able to live together and they have mutually agreed that marriage should be dissolved. On the request of both the parties made not earlier than six months after the date of the presentation of the petition by the wife and not later than eighteen months after the said date, if the petition is not withdrawn in the meantime, the court shall, after hearing to parties pass a decree of divorce declaring the marriage to be dissolved with effect from the date of the decree.

(ii) Right of a Christian wife

Where a marriage has been solemnized under the provisions of the Special Marriage Act, 1954, a wife may present a petition to divorce her husband under section 27 of the act on the ground of having sexual intercourse with any other women after solemnization of marriage, for deserting the petitioner for a continuous period of not less than two years, respondent is undergoing a sentence of imprisonment for seven years or more for an offences declared by the Indian Penal Code, 1860, the respondent has treated the petitioner with cruelty, has been suffering from unsound mind due to which the petitioner cannot reasonably be expected to live with the respondent, her husband is guilty of rape, sodamy or bestiality or in a suit under section 18 of Hindu Adoptions and Maintenance Act, 1956, or in a proceeding under section 125 of the Code of Criminal Procedure, 1973. There has been no resumption of cohabitation as between the parties to the marriage for a period of one year after the passing of a decree for judicial separation in a proceeding to which they were parties or no restitution of conjugal rights for a period of one year upwards after the passing of a decree for restitution of conjugal rights. Under section 27-A divorce by mutual consent of persons married under the provisions of this act, is allowed.

(iii) Right of divorce of a Muslim wife

A women married under Muslim Law is entitled to obtain a decree for the dissolution of her marriage on any one or more of the following grounds, namely where the husband have not been known for a period of four years, the husband has neglected or has failed to provide for her maintenance for a period of two years, the husband has been sentenced to imprisonment for a period of seven years or upwards, husband has failed to perform without reasonable cause, has marital obligations for a period of three years, husband was impotent at the time of marriage and continues to be so, husband has been insane for a period of two years or is suffering from leprosy or a virulent veneral disease, that she having been given in marriage by her father or other guardian before she attained the age of fifteen years, repudiated the marriage before obtaining the age of the eighteen years and finally the husband treats her with cruelty by habitually assaults, associates with women of evil repute, attempts her to lead a immoral life, disposes of her property, obstructs her in the observance of her religious profession, do not treat her equitably with other wives or on any other ground which is recognized for the dissolution of marriage under Muslim Law[11].

[11] Law of Divorce in Islam, ILR, (2005). Karnataka Series.

(d) Right to Maintenance

(i) Right of maintenance to a Hindu wife

(a) Hindu marriage Act, 1955

Under Sec. 24 provides if it appears to the court that either the wife or the husband has no independent income sufficient for them to meet the expenses of the proceeding, it may on application by the wife or the husband order the respondent to pay to the petitioner the expenses of the proceeding, and monthly during the proceeding such sum as, having regard to the petitioners own income and the income of the respondent, it may seem to the court to be reasonable. While granting maintenance to a wife, the court must have regard to the wife's own income and the income of the husband before it can fix the amount of maintenance that should be awarded to the petitioning wife. In Sec. 25 provides that on application by the either wife or the husband, the court can order that the respondent shall pay to the applicant for her or his maintenance such gross sum or such monthly, periodical sum for a term not exceeding the life of the applicant after considering the respondents own income and other property. The income and other property of the applicant, the conduct of the parties and other circumstances of the case may seem to the court to be just, and any such payment may be secured, if necessary, by a charge on the immovable property of the respondent. If the court is satisfied that there is change in the circumstances of either party at any time after it has made an order it may modify or rescind any such order.

(b) Hindu adoption & maintenance Act, 1956

Sec 18 provides that a Hindu wife, shall be entitled to be maintained by her husband during her life time even living separately without forfeiting her claim for maintenance. If he is guilty of desertion without reasonable cause either without her consent and against her will or willfully neglects her, treated her with such cruelty as to cause a reasonable apprehension that it will be harmful or injurious to live with him, if he is suffering from leprosy, if has other wife living, if he keeps a concubine in the same house in which his wife is living or habitually resides with a concubine elsewhere, if he has ceased to be a Hindu by conversion to another religion or any other cause which justifies the living separately. A Hindu wife shall not be entitled to separate residence and maintenance from her husband if she is unchaste or ceases to be a Hindu by conversion to any other religion. Sec 19 provides that a Hindu wife shall be entitled to be maintained after the death of her husband by her father-in-law if she is unable to maintain herself out of her own earnings or other property or where she has no property of her own, is unable to obtain maintenance from the estate of her husband or her father or mother or from her son or daughter, if any, or his or her estate. Provided that if father in law has no means to do so from any coparcenary property in his possession out of which the daughter in law has not obtained any share and any such obligation shall cease on the remarriage of the daughter in law. Sec. 20 specifies about maintenance of Children and aged parents that a Hindu is bound, during his or her lifetime to maintain his or her legitimate children and his or her aged parents including a childless step mother. Sec. 21 specifies listed women dependents of a person and includes his or her mother, his widow so long as she does not remarry, his or her unmarried daughter, or the unmarried daughter of a predeceased son of his predeceased so long as she remains unmarried if she is unable to obtain maintenance, in the case of grand daughter from her father or mothers estate and in the case of a great grand daughter from the estate of her father or mother or father's father or father's mother. His widowed daughter if she is unable to obtain maintenance from the estate of her husband or from her son or daughter if any, or his or her estate or from her father in law or his father or the estate of either of them, any widow of his son or of a son of his predeceased son, as long as she does not re marry. His or her illegitimate daughter so long as she remains unmarried. Sec. 22 provides that the heirs of a deceased Hindu are bound to maintain the dependents of the deceased out of the estate inherited by them from the deceased. Where a dependent has not obtained, by testamentary or interstate succession, any share in the estate of a Hindu dying, the dependent shall be entitled to maintenance from those who take the estate. Sec. 23 It shall be in the discretion of the court to determine what maintenance shall be awarded. In determining the amount of maintenance, if any to be awarded to a wife, children or aged or infirm parents under this act, regarding to the position and status of the parties, the reasonable wants of the claimant, justification of any separation, the value of the claimants property and any income derived from such property and number of persons entitled to maintenance under this act.

(ii) Right of Muslim divorced women to maintenance

A five Judges Bench of the Supreme Court, in Mohd. Ahmed Khan *Vs*. Shahbano[12] delivered a historical judgement declaring the right of a Muslim divorced women to maintenance, that a muslim husband having sufficient means must provide maintenance to his divorced wife who is unable to maintain herself. It was held in this case that such a wife is entitled to the maintenance even if she refuses to live with the Muslim husband because he has contracted another marriage within the limit of four wives allowed to him by the Quran. It laid down that the religion professed by a spouse or the spouses has no place in the scheme of section 125 of the code which is a measure of social justice founded on an individuals obligation to the society to prevent vagrancy and destitution. If there is any conflict between personal law and section 125 of the Code, then it is clear from the language of the section that it overrule the personal law. Under The Muslim Women (Protection of Rights on Divorce) Act, 1986 section 3 provides that a divorced women shall be entitled to a reasonable and fair provision and maintenance within the iddat period by her former husband where she herself maintains the children born to her before or after her divorce, a reasonable and fair provision and maintenance to be made and paid by him for a period of two years from the respective date of birth of such children, an amount equal to the sum of 'Mahr' or 'Dower' agreed to be paid to her at the time of her marriage or at any time thereafter according to Muslim Law and all the properties given to her before or at the time of marriage or after her marriage by her relatives or friends or the husband or any relatives of the husband or his friends. She can also make an application to a Magistrate for an order for payment of such provision of Mahr or Dower for her and her children if it is not decided. If any person against whom an order has been made fails without sufficient cause to comply with the order, the Magistrate may issue a warrant and may sentence such person for the whole or

[12] Cr. L. J. 875 (SC), (1985).

any part of any amount remaining unpaid after the execution of the warrant to imprisonment for a term which may extend to one year or until payment whichever is sooner[13].

(iii) Right of alimony of a Christian wife

Under Indian Divorce Act, 1869 wife may present a petition for alimony pending the suit. Such petition shall be served to the husband, and the court, on being satisfied of the truth of the statements therein contained, may make such order on the husband for payment to the wife of alimony pending the suit as it may deem just. But alimony pending the suit shall in no case exceed one-fifth of the husbands average net income for the three years next preceding the date of the order, and shall continue in case of a decree for dissolution of marriage or of nullity of marriage, until the decree is made absolute or is confirmed, as the case may be.

(8) PROTECTION AGAINST CHILD MARRIAGE

The Child Marriage Restraint Act, 1929 extends to whole of India except the state of Jammu and Kashmir. This act will restrain the solemnization of child marriages.

(a) Punishment for Male Adult below 21 Years of Age Marrying a Child (Sec. 3)

Whoever, being a male above eighteen years of age and below twenty one, contracts a child marriage shall be punishable with simple imprisonment which may extend to 15 days, or with fine which may extend to Rs. 1000/- or with both.

(b) Punishment for Male Adult above Twenty One Years of Age Marrying a Child (Sec. 4)

Whoever, being a male above twenty one years of age, contracts a child marriage shall be punishable with simple imprisonment which may extend to 03 months and shall also be liable to fine.

---

[13] Maintenance under Muslim Law from Shahbano to Danial Latifi: Criminal Law Journal (2003).

(c) Punishment for Solemnising a Child Marriage (Sec. 5)

Whoever conducts or directs any child marriage shall be punished with simple imprisonment which may extend to 03 months and shall also be liable to fine.

(d) Punishment for Parent or Guardian Concerned in Child Marriage (Sec. 6)

Where a minor contracts a child marriage, any person having charge of the minor, whether as parent or guardian or in any other capacity lawful or unlawful who does any act, to promote the marriage permits it to be solemnized, or negligently fails to prevent it from being solemnized, shall be punished with simple imprisonment which may extent to 03 months and shall be liable for fine. Provided that no women shall be punishable with imprisonment and unless and until the contrary is proved, where a minor has contracted a child marriage, the person having charge of such minor has negligently failed to prevent the marriage from being solemnized.

(e) Offences to be Cognizable for Certain Purposes (Sec. 7)

The Code of Criminal Procedure, 1973 shall apply to offences under this act as if they were cognizable offences, for the purpose of investigation of such offence and for the matters other than matters referred to in section 42 of the code and the arrest of a person without a warrant or without an order of a Magistrate.

(f) Power to Issue Injunction Prohibiting Marriage in Contravention of this Act (Sec. 12)

The court may issue an injunction against any of the persons prohibiting such marriage. Whoever knowing that an injunction has been issued against him under this section disobeys such injunction shall be punished with imprisonment of either description for a term which may extend to 3 months, or with fine which may extend to Rs. 1000/- or with both. Provided that no women shall be punishable with imprisonment.

(g) The Prohibition of Child Marriage Act 2006

In India traditional, cultural and religious protection was offered to this evil so that girl child used to face loosing opportunities for education, segregation from family, exploitation, early pregnancy, health risks, domestic violence, higher infant mortality rate, low weight babies, pre-mature birth, etc. This Act is armed with enabling provisions to prohibit child marriage, protect and provide relief to victim and enhance punishment for those who abet, promote or solemnize such marriage. Child Marriage Prohibition Officer implements the act. The District Court make order directing contracting party, to pay maintenance to the female up to her remarriage. The District court may also issue suitable order as to the residence, custody of the children of such marriage. Child conceived of such child marriage shall be deemed to be legitimate children. Child marriage shall be punishable with rigorous imprisonment for 2 years or with Rs 1 lakh fine or both.

(9) PROTECTION AGAINST DOMESTIC VIOLENCE

Domestic violence needs to be recognized as a public health issue under the Protection of Women from Domestic Violence Act 2005. Family Counselling Centres (FCCs) was constituted in 1983 by the Central Social Welfare Board to provide counselling, referral and rehabilitative services to women and children who are victims of atrocities, family maladjustment, social ostracism, natural disasters, etc. FCCs have been recognised as service providers under the Protection of Women against Domestic Violence Act in several States. Moreover, in some States, Counsellors have been designated as Protection Officers. In view of its continuing relevance, the scheme is proposed to be continued in the XII Plan. The scheme, which has 787 counselling centres at present, is yet to cover all districts. The honorarium of the Counsellors is also proposed to be reviewed. The state Government should constitute Independent Protection Officers and Dowry Prohibition Officers with supporting staff at district for implementing the act and constitute competent authorities to register direct information reports and counselors at block level to resolve issues. Collateral responsibility of funding has to be vested with Centre and State Governments. The Medical Curriculum can inculcate training the professionals in Medical Services on the issues of domestic violence. The Protection of Women from Domestic Violence Act, 2005 a civil remedy was brought into the picture in 2005 (amended in 2006). Domestic Violence includes the demand for dowry, harms, injures, endangers the health, safety, life, limb or well-being, whether mental or physical, causing physical abuse, sexual abuse, verbal and emotional abuse and economic abuse or coerce her or any other person related to her to meet any unlawful demand for any dowry or valuable security. The lower courts can issue "protection orders" like restraining order on husband and others, monetary compensation and residence order on the complaint of a woman. Though, it is a civil remedy violation of orders result in criminal penalties including imprisonment[14].

(10) PROTECTION OF RIGHT OVER PROPERTY

A women comes in contact with many types of property, such as joint family property, coparcenary property, self acquired property, women's property of Stridhan under the Hindu Law, limited estate, etc. There are different mode of succession of property to females in various systems or faiths. A married women earns independently from her husband or joint family. Her wages or salary even were supposed to be her husbands or joint family property. She could not use her self acquired property even independently at her sweet will and discretion.

(a) Property Rights of a Married Women Under The Married Women's Property Act, 1874

(i) Married women's right to her self-earnings and properties (Sec. 4)

The wages and earnings of any unmarried women acquired or gained by her from any employment, occupation or trade carried on by her, any money or other property so acquired by her through the exercise

[14] Veeraraghavan and Vimla, (1995). Violence in Families: A Bio Psychological and Naturalistic Perspective, Trends in Social Science Research, Special Issue on Family Studies, Vol. 2, No.1, pp. 83-90.

of any literacy, artistic or scientific skills and all savings from and investments of such wages, earnings and property shall be deemed to be her separate property and their husbands do not by their marriage acquire any interest in such property.

(ii) Married women may effect policy of insurance (Sec. 5)

States that any married women may effect a policy of insurance on her own behalf and independently of her husband, all the benefits shall ensure as her separate property and the contract evidenced by such policy shall be valid as if made with an unmarried women.

(iii) Married women's right to take legal proceedings (Sec. 7)

Married women may maintain a suit in her own name for the protection or security of such separate property described under this act or Indian Succession Act, 1865 and she shall be liable to such suits, processes and orders in respect of such property as she would be liable if she was unmarried.

(b) Property Rights Under Hindu Succession Act, 1956

(i) Womens absolute right in property (Sec. 14)

This act abolished the concept of limited estate of women and established womens absolute right in property. Any property movable or immovable property acquired by a female Hindu, at or after the marriage, or by her own skill or exertion, or by purchase or by prescription, or any such property held by her as 'Stridhan'. Nothing shall apply to any property acquired by way of gift, will, under any instrument or under a decree of Civil Court where the terms of the gift, will or other instrument prescribes a restricted estate in such property. Modern Hindu Law describes 'Stridhan' by including gifts which are made to women during maidenhood, coverture or widow hood by her parents and their relations or by the husband and his relations, property given by gifts by strangers other than relations to a women, Properties purchased by a women with her 'Stridhan' including any savings, accumulations and any savings, property acquired by women under a compromise, property acquired by prescription or adverse possession by a women, property obtained as maintenance or in lien of maintenance by a women, property obtained or to be obtained under a decree or order of a court by a women, property obtained by inheritance from her husband, in-laws or parents or any other relatives, property obtained on partition as share of a women in the joint property.

(ii) Devolution of interest in coparcenary property (Sec. 6)

If a Hindu male dies having an interest in Mitakshara coparcenary property, his interest in the property shall devolve by survivorship upon the surviving members of the coparcenary and not in accordance with the Hindu Succession Act, 1956. But if the deceased had left surviving female relative specified in Class I of the Schedule or a male relative specified in that class who claims, through such female relative, the interest of the deceased in the Mitakshara coparcenary property shall devolve by testamentary or intestate succession, as the case may be, under this act and not by survivorship. Hindu Succession (Amendment) Act 2005, Hindu Women's Property Rights under the Hindu Succession Act 1956, Women are entitled to an absolute estate like men when they inherit any property. Women Heirs of Class I were are daughter, widow, mother, daughter of a pre-deceased son, widow of pre-deceased son,widow of a pre-deceased son of a predeceased son and daughter of a predeceased daughter. Again the daughter of a predeceased son and the daughter of a predeceased daughter are raised to a higher rank. They became Class – I heirs and get a share along with the son and other Class – I heirs. The daughters are included in the Class – I in order to remove the discrimination on the basis of sex. the distinction between male and female heirs in the case of succession has been taken away and they are treated on equal basis if they belong to the same degree of relationship. Women will no longer be disinherited on the ground of unchastity. Under Section 14 of The Hindu Succession Act 1956, the limited interest of Hindu female is converted into absolute rights. If she gets property from her husband she can sell it and the purchaser gets absolute right in the property.

CONCLUSION

The empowerment of women and improvement of their status are important ends in themselves and are essential for the achievement of sustainable development. Men play a key role in bringing about gender equality since, in most societies, they exercise preponderant power in every sphere of life. Governments should promote equal participation of women and men in all areas of family and household responsibilities, inculcate responsible parenthood, healthy sexual and reproductive behavior by preventing sexually transmitted diseases, encourage mutual contribution to family income and children's welfare. Strict enforcement of laws to ensure marriage on free and full consent of the spouses. Eliminate all forms of exploitation, control discrimination, harassment and violence, eliminate the root causes of son preference from the society through awareness, prevent abuse, infanticide, prenatal sex selection, trafficking, prostitution and pornography. Enable women to access social, political and economic excellence through an integrated approach towards the special health and education which builds their self-esteem. Collective efforts of the people should evolve from each family and spread throughout which depicts the path towards success.

4

Protection for Women at Workplace

A distressing fact is that the prevalence of partriarchy prevents women from accepting crucial roles in the Society. In a recent conference on the problems of working women and their participation in trade unions a scholar noted "Today after more than a decade of our struggle we find to our satisfaction that the question and problems of working women and women in general are being discussed widely in our country by various organizations, individuals, press and also by the government. The question is also highlighted in international forums". Despite these efforts, many Trade Unions in the country are yet to pay adequate attention to women issues. Joint efforts have to be made to make a common cause to fight for the demands of working women. The issues which affect women such as rejection of maternity benefits and child care facilities, retrenchment of women workers and non payment of equal wage in spite of Equal Remuneration Act, have not been taken up seriously by Trade Unions. It is well known that women constitute majority among the unorganized labour force where the working conditions are miserable and no security for their job, no fair wages, no welfare facilities and no rights to demand anything, etc. It goes to the credit of gross root level organizations such as the Women Welfare Foundation and SEWA where, the researchers have highlighted the problems of these women, that attempts are now taken to create some kind of structure to ventilate their problems. Issues such as low wages, inhuman working conditions, health hazards, harassement and victimization for rape need to be checked properly.

Employers preferably use 'putting out', 'piece rate' strategies to enroll women on their pay rolls. The recently published report of the National Comission on Self Employed Women and Women in the Unorganised sector, has made several recommendations to ensure the inclusion of women in the unorganized sector in the entire gamut of Trade Union activities.

(1) INDIAN CONSTITUTION AND LABOUR WELFARE

Indian Constitution acts as a guideline to various labour laws for their effective implementation and functioning. The Articles 14, 19, 21, 23, 24, 38, 39, 39-A, 41, 42, 43, 43-A and 47 depicts the responsibility over the Government both Central and State, to secure social order and living wages, keeping with the economic and political conditions of the women in the country. Articles 21, 23 and 24 form part of the Fundamental Rights guaranteed under Part III of the Constitution. Articles 38, 39, 39-A, 41, 42, 43, 43-A and 47 form part of the Directive Principles of State Policy under Part IV of the Constitution[1].

(a) Right to Equality Before Law (Art. 14)

The concept of equality does not mean absolute equality among human beings which is physically not possible to achieve. It is a concept implying absence of any special privilege by reason of birth, creed, etc. It only means that all similar circumstance shall be treated alike both in the privileges conferred and liabilities imposed by the laws.

(b) Right to Form Association (Art. 19(1)(c)

This right is granted with restrictions mentioned under Art. 19 (4) where, the State may by law impose reasonable restrictions on this right in the interest of public order, morality or the sovereignty and integrity of India. It thus gives the right to form companies, societies,

[1] Kasibhatta Subrahmanyam, (1991). Women and Law, Asia Law House, Hyderabad, 3rd Edition, pp 1-3.

partnership, trade union, and political parties. The freedom to form association implies even to join or not to join, an association.

(c) Right to Life (Art. 21)

Right to life conferred under this article includes right to means of livelihood. 'Life' means something more than mere animal existence. No person can live without the means of living. If the right to livelihood is not treated as a part of the constitutional right to life, the easiest way of depriving a person of his right to life would be to deprive him of his means of livelihood to the point of abrogation. Such deprivation would not only deny the life of its effective content and meaningfulness but it would make life impossible to live. There is thus a close nexus between life and the means of livelihood. In Maneka Gandhi's case the Court held that the right to 'live' is not merely confined to physical existence but it includes within its ambit the right to live with human dignity.

(d) Prohibition of Traffic in Human Being and Beggar and Other Similar Forms of Forced Labour (Art. 23)

'Traffic in human beings' means selling and buying men and women like goods and includes immoral traffic in women and children for immoral" or other purposes. Though slavery is not expressly mentioned in Article 23, it is included in the expression 'traffic in human being'. Article 35 Parliament is authorized to make laws for punishing acts prohibited under this act. In pursuance of this Article Parliament has passed the Suppression of Immoral Traffic in Women and Girls Act, 1956, for punishing acts which result in traffic in human beings. Article 23 protects the individual not only against the State but also against private citizens. It imposes a positive obligation on the State to take steps to abolish evils of "traffic in human beings" and "beggar and other similar forms of forced labour" wherever they are found. Article 23 prohibits the system of 'bonded labour' because it is a form of force labour within the meaning of this Article. "Beggar" means involuntary work without payment. What is prohibited by this clause is the making of a person to render service where he was lawfully entitled not to work or to receive remuneration of the services rendered by him. The protection is not confined to beggar only but also to "other forms of forced labour". It means to compel a person to work against his will.

(e) Prohibits Employment of Children Below 14 Years of Age in Factories and Hazardous Employment (Art. 24)

Constitution imposes upon the State an obligation to ensure that the health and strength of workers, men and women, and the tender age of the children are not abused by forcing them to enter a vocation unsuited to their age or strength. In M.C. Mehta *Vs.* State of Tamil Nadu The Supreme Court has held that children below the age of 14 years cannot be employed in any hazardous industry. Exhaustive guidelines was laid down as to how State authorities should protect economic, social and humanitarian rights of millions of children , working illegally in public and private sections.

(f) Right to Constitutional Remedy (Art. 32)

It is true that a declaration of fundamental rights is meaningless unless there is an effective machinery for the enforcement of the rights. This article provides that in case of violation of fundamental right any person can approach Supreme Court by "appropriate proceedings" for the enforcement of the fundamental rights. It confers power on the Supreme Court to issue appropriate directions or writs like habeas corpus, mandamus, prohibition, quo-warranto and certiorari for the enforcement of any of the rights conferred by Part III of the Constitution. Under article 226 High court of the state is empowered to enforce the fundamental rights. Traditional rule of locus standi that a petition under these articles can only be filed by a person whose fundamental right is infringed has now been considerably relaxed by the Supreme Court in its recent rulings by introducing Public Interest Litigations or Social Interest Litigations

(g) Directive Principles of State Policy

The constitution embody the Directive Principles of State Policy which though cannot be enforced through a court of law are nevertheless fundamental in the governance of the country, but it casts a duty on the State to apply those principles in making laws. This seems to be the 'conscience of the Constitution' and without faithfully implementing the Directive Principles by the state, it is impossible to achieve the goal of welfare State. Directives pertaining to workers are like below. The State should ensure Equal right of men and women towards adequate means of livelihood, Equal pay for equal work, to protect health and strength of workers and tender age of children to ensure that they are not forced by economic necessity to enter a vocation unsuited to their age or strength (Art. 39), State shall ensure operation of the legal system to promote justice, on a basis of equal opportunities and free legal Aid (Art. 39A). In pursuant to this Parliament has enacted the Equal Remuneration Act, 1976. State to ensure the people within the limit of its economic capacity and development to assist in employment, education, and public assistance during unemployment, old age, sickness and disablement and any other undeserved want (Art. 41), State to make provision for securing just humane conditions for work and maternity relief (Art. 42), take steps, by suitable legislation to secure the participation of workers in the management (Art. 43). Free and compulsory education for all children until the age of 14 years (Art. 45) for abolishing illiteracy from the country. In a landmark judgment in Unni Krishnan *Vs*. State of A.P. The Supreme Court has held that the "Right to education" upto the age of 14 years is a fundamental right within the meaning of article 21 of the constitution. Raising the level of nutrition, standard of living, and the improvement of public health (Art. 47), Promotion of education and economic interest of the weaker sections of the people belonging to the Scheduled Castes and Scheduled Tribes (Art. 46)

(2) THE FACTORIES ACT 1948

In every factory the following mandatory measures shall be provided to the women workers. Sufficient Latrines and Urinal accommodation separately maintained for men and women, adequately lighted and ventilation shall be provided at convenient places to be maintained in a cleaned at lease once in a seven days with disinfectants (Sec. 19), Prohibition of Employment of Women and Children near Cotton-

Openers (Sec. 27) No woman or child shall be employed in any part of a factory for pressing cotton in which a cotton-opener is at work. Provided that if the feed-end of a cotton-opener is in a room separated from the delivery end by a partition extending to the roof to such height as the Inspector specify in writing. Women and children may be employed on the side of the partition where the feed-end is situated. In every factory wherein more than thirty women workers are ordinarily employed there shall be provided and maintained a Creche for the use of children under the age of six years of such women. Such rooms shall provide adequate accommodation, lighted and ventilated, and maintained in sanitary condition to be kept under the charge of women trained in the care of children and infants. The State Government may make rules requiring the provision in any factory for free milk or refreshment both for such children and mothers to feed children at the necessary intervals (Sec. 48). In every factory wherein five hundred or more workers are ordinarily employed the occupier shall employ such number of Welfare Officers as may be prescribed (Sec 49). No women and child shall be employed or permitted to work during the night. No female child shall be required or allowed to work except between 8 a.m. and 7 p.m. (Sec. 71). Where the State Government is of opinion that any manufacturing process or operation carried on in a factory exposes any persons employed in it to a serious risk of bodily injury, poisoning or diseases, it may prohibit or restrict the employment of women, adolescents or children in the manufacturing process (Sec. 87).

(3) THE CONTRACT LABOUR (REGULATION AND ABOLITION) ACT 1970

All Women contract labours should get separate enclosed accommodation for toilet and washing. Contractor employing more than 30 women shall provide a crèche, they are allowed to work only between 6 a.m. to 7 p.m. She is not allowed to work more than 9 hours on any day. Employment of women is restricted in dangerous manufacturing process. The employer under Sec. 21 is ultimately liable to provide the welfare and wage to the contract employees in case the contractor fails.

(4) THE KARNATAKA SHOPS AND COMMERCIAL ESTABLISHMENTS ACT 1961

The Act prohibits the employment of Women and Young Persons during Night shift provided that the State Govt can exempt the IT industries if it provides transportation and security.

(5) THE MINES ACT 1952

Sufficient number of latrines and urinals adequately lighted and ventilated separately for males and females at convenient and accessible places shall be provided to the employees. The Central Government may specify the number of latrines and urinals to be provided in any mine. (Sec. 20). No women shall be employed in any part of the mine which is below the ground and in any mining activity above the ground except between 6 a. m to 7 p.m. (Sec. 46).

(6) THE PLANTATION LABOUR ACT 1951

Sufficient number of latrines and urinals are to be provided separately to men and women in the plantation. It shall be maintained in a clean and in sanitary conditions (Sec. 9). In every plantation wherein fifty or more women workers (including women workers employed by any contractor) are employed or number of children of women workers is twenty or more, suitable rooms shall be maintained in clean and sanitary conditions kept under the incharge of a women trained in the care of children and infants (Sec. 12). Except with the permission of the State Government, no woman or child worker shall be employed between the hours of 6 a.m and 7 p.m. provided that nothing in this section shall be deemed to apply to midwives and nurses employed as such in any plantation (Sec. 25). Every worker shall be entitled to obtain from his employer in the case of sickness certified by a qualified medical practitioner, sickness allowance, as may be prescribed. The State Government may make rules regulating the payment of sickness allowance (Sec. 32).

(7) THE MINIMUM WAGES ACT 1948

Defines wage as all remuneration , capable of expressing in terms of money, which is paid to the employee when the terms and conditions of labour are expressed or implied, were fulfilled, be payable to a employment. It includes House Rent Allowance but does not include Light, Water and Medical charges, Contribution to Provident Fund and Traveling Allowance. In any scheduled employment minimum wages have been fixed by the appropriate Government, the employer shall pay to every employee wages at a rates not less than the minimum rate of wages fixed for that class of employees.

(8) THE MATERNITY BENEFIT ACT 1961

This facility enables women to meet the challenge of motherhood. This Act extends to whole of India except the state of Jammu and Kashmir. No employer shall knowingly employ a woman during the six weeks immediately following the day of her delivery or her miscarriage in any work which is of arduous nature or involves long hours of standing, or is likely to interfere with her pregnancy or the normal development of the foetus, or is likely to cause her miscarriage or adversely affect her health (Sec. 5). Every woman who has worked for not less than one hundred and sixty days shall be entitled for the maternity benefit at the rate of average daily wage for six weeks prior and after the delivery including the day of the delivery. In Sec 6 any woman employed may give notice in writing stating the date of her absence to her employer, seeking maternity benefit. The amount of Maternity Benefit for the period preceding the date of her expected delivery shall be paid in advance by the employer on production of such proof of pregnancy. The amount due for the subsequent period shall be paid within forty-eight hours of production of proof of delivery. The failure to give notice under this section shall not disentitle a woman to maternity benefit. Under Sec 7 if a woman entitled to maternity benefit dies before receiving such maternity benefit, such amount will be paid to the nominee or legal representatives. In Sec. 8. Every woman entitled to maternity benefit shall also be entitled to receive from her employer a medical bonus of Rs. 2500/- if no pre-natal confinement and post-natal care is provided for by the employer free of charge. In case of miscarriage, a woman shall, on production of such proof as may be prescribed, be entitled to leave with wages at the rate of maternity benefit, for a period of six weeks immediately following the day of her miscarriage (Sec. 9). A woman suffering from illness arising out of pregnancy, delivery, premature birth of child or miscarriage shall be entitled, to an additional leave with wages at the rate of maternity benefit for a maximum period of one month (Sec. 10.). Every woman delivered of a child who returns to duty after such delivery shall, in addition to the interval for rest allowed to her, be allowed in the course of her daily work two breaks of the prescribed duration for nursing the child until the child attains the age of fifteen months (Sec. 11). When a woman absents herself from work in accordance with the provisions of this Act, it shall be unlawful for her employer to discharge or dismiss her on account of such absence. Even if she is discharged her right to claim the maternity benefit will not be eliminated. Any woman deprived of maternity benefit or medical bonus or both, may, within sixty days from the date on which the order of such deprivation is communicated to her, appeal to such authority as may be prescribed (Sec. 12). No deduction from the normal and usual daily wages of a woman entitled to maternity benefit under the provisions of this Act shall be made. (Sec. 13). If a woman works in any establishment after she has been permitted by her employer to absent herself under the provisions of section 6 for any period during such authorized absence, she shall forfeit her claim to the maternity benefit for such period (Sec. 18). For any contravention of Act by employer shall be punishable with imprisonment which may extend to three months, or with fine which may extend to five hundred rupees, or with both (Sec. 21).

(9) THE WORKMEN'S COMPENSATION ACT 1923

The act extends to the whole of India. The act recognizes widow, unmarried legitimate or adopted daughter, or a widowed mother, daughter who has attained the age of 18 years and who is infirm, an unmarried illegitimate daughter or a daughter legitimate or illegitimate or adopted if married and a minor or if widowed and a minor, an unmarried sister or a widowed sister if a minor, A widowed daughter-in-law, A minor child of a pre-deceased daughter where no parent of the child is alive, as the dependents of the deceased to claim the compensation if wholly or in part dependent on the earnings of the workman at the time of his death. Amount of compensation depends upon the nature of the injury caused, The monthly wages of the workmen and The lum-sum equivalent of compensation amount as specified in schedule IV. Where death results an amount equal to 50% of the monthly wages or ceiling limit is upto Rs 1,20,000/- and where permanent total disablement an amount equal to 60% of the monthly wages or ceiling limit of Rs 1,40,000/-. In case of death for the payment of lum-sum to women or any person under disability shall be deposited with the commissioner and not allowed to be paid directly by the employer. Recent amendments has brought the following changes in the act like Sec. 4 (a) compensation for death is increased to Rs 1,20,000/-, Sec. 4 (b) compensation for Permanent Total Disablement is increased to Rs 1,40,000/-, the Wage ceiling limit is raised to Rs. 8000 and under Sec. 4(4) Funeral Expenses was raised to Rs. 5000/-

(10) THE EMPLOYEE PROVIDENT FUND AND MISCELLANEOUS PROVISIONS ACT, 1952

The act extends to the whole of India except the State of Jammu and Kashmir. Under Sec. 6A The Central Government may by notification in the Official Gazette frame a scheme to be called the Employees' Pension Scheme for providing Superannuation pension, retiring pension, permanent total disablement pension, widow or widower's pension, children pension or orphan pension. There shall be established a Pension Fund into which there shall be paid from time to time in respect of every employee who is a member of the Pension Scheme such sums from the employer's contribution not exceeding eight and one-third per cent of the basic wages, dearness allowance and retaining allowance if any of the concerned employees as may specified in the Pension Scheme. The Pension Fund shall vest in and be administered by the Central Board in such manner as may be specified in the Pension Scheme.

(11) STATE INSURANCE ACT 1948

The act extends to the whole of India. This is a Social Security Legislation in which the family of the insured person is covered in the benefit. The insured can take treatment from the Employee State Insurance Hospitals maintained by the Employee State Corporation. Under Sec. 3 Central Government may, by notification in the Official Gazette, constitute Employees State Insurance Corporation which is a artificial person created by law. Under Sec. 10 the Central Government constitute Medical Benefit Council consisting Three members, one shall be a woman representing the Medical Profession. The employee will contribute 1.75% of his salary towards the fund and the employer will contribute 4.75%. Sec. 20 defines "Sickness" as a condition, which requires medical treatment. The insured employee and his family can claim the sickness benefit, disablement benefit, and maternity benefit including miscarriage under this scheme. In case of death, of the insured person, the dependents covering widow, unmarried legitimate or adopted daughter, a widowed mother under Sec. 6A are eligible for the benefit under this scheme if wholly dependent on the earnings of the insured person at the time of his death.

(12) THE EQUAL REMUNERATION ACT, 1976

The act provides for payment of equal remuneration to men and women for the prevention of discrimination on the ground of sex. Sec. 4 says that no employer shall pay to any worker, employed by him remuneration payable in cash or kind at rates less favourable than those of which remuneration is paid by him to the workers of the opposite sex in such establishment for performing the similar job. No employer shall for the purpose of complying with this provision, reduce the rate of remuneration of any worker. No employer while making recruitment for the work of the similar nature, or during promotions, training or transfer, make any discrimination against women except where the employment of women in such work is prohibited under any law for the time being. However, no priority or reservation for Scheduled Castes or Scheduled Tribes, Ex-servicemen, Retrenched posts in an establishment or employment is affected by this provision (Sec. 5). An advisory committee is appointed to advise the appropriate government regarding the extent to which women may be employed in such establishments as the Central Government. The advisory committee shall consist of not less than ten persons to be nominated by the appropriate government, in which one-half in number shall be women. While advising it has to clarify number of women employed, the nature of work, hours of work, suitability of women for employment, the need for providing increasing employment and such relevant factors as the committee may think fit. In Sec. 7 the appropriate government may, by notification appoint such officers, not below the rank of a Labour Officer, to be the authorities for the purpose of hearing and deciding complaints under this act. Sec 10 if any employer omits or fails to maintain any register about the workers employed or fails to produce any register, muster roll or other document or refuse to give evidence shall be punishable with simple imprisonment for a term which may extend to one month or with fine upto Rs. 10,000/- or with both. If any employer recruits in contravention to this act, makes any payment of remuneration at unequal rates to men and women workers or makes any discrimination in contravention of this act shall be punishable with fine which shall not be less than Rs. 10,000/- but which may extend to Rs. 20,000/- or with imprisonment for a term which shall not be less than 03 months but which may extend to one year or with both for the first offence, and with imprisonment which may extend to 02 years for the second and subsequent offences.

(13) THE SEXUAL HARASSMENT OF WOMEN AT WORKPLACE (PREVENTION, PROHIBITION AND REDRESSAL) ACT, 2013

The Act applies to all woman who work in regular, temporary, ad hoc employees engaged on daily wage includes domestic workers, contract labours, coworkers, probationers, trainees, and apprentices, with or without the knowledge of the principal employer. India's economy had opened up in the early 90's. One of the effects of this was increase in women workforce. In 1997 the Apex Court pronounced a landmark judgment in Vishaka and others *Vs.* State of Rajasthan, an NGO by name Vishaka filed a Public Interest Litigation (PIL), after one Bhanwari Devi, a woman from Rajasthan who was allegedly gang raped seeking special measures to deal with sexual harassment inflicted in the course of employment. The Hon'ble Supreme Court in Vishaka Judgment laid down the guidelines that were mandatory for every employer to provide a mechanism to redress grievances pertaining to workplace sexual harassment and enforce the right of gender equity of working women. In the year 1993, India had ratified the United Nation Convention on Elimination of all Forms of Discrimination against Women where parties shall take all appropriate measures to eliminate discrimination against women in the field of employment[2]. Sexual harassment is considered as a violation of the fundamental right of a woman to equality as guaranteed under Article 14, right to life and to live with dignity as per Article 21 of the Constitution. It is also considered as a violation of a right to practice or to carry out any occupation, trade or business under Article 19(1)(g) of the Constitution, which includes a right to a safe environment free from harassment. The following acts are included to commit sexual harassment at workplace. Circumstances of promise of preferential treatment in employment, Threat of detrimental treatment in employment, Threat about employment, Creating an offensive work environment, interference with the work, humiliating treatment that affect the health or safety of women, unwelcome sexually determined behavior such as physical contact and advances, demand or request for sexual favors, sexually colored remarks, showing pornography, Any other unwelcome physical verbal or non-verbal conduct of sexual nature. The workplace also covers within its scope places visited by employees during the course of employment or for reasons arising out of employment including transportation provided by the employer for the purpose of commuting to and from the place of employment. The applicability of the act is shown in Fig. 1.

(a) Obligations of the Employer

Employer shall provide a safe working environment at the workplace which shall include safety from the persons coming into contact at

[2] MacKinnon and Catherine, (1979). Sexual Harassment of Working Women, New Haven, Conn: Yale University Press.

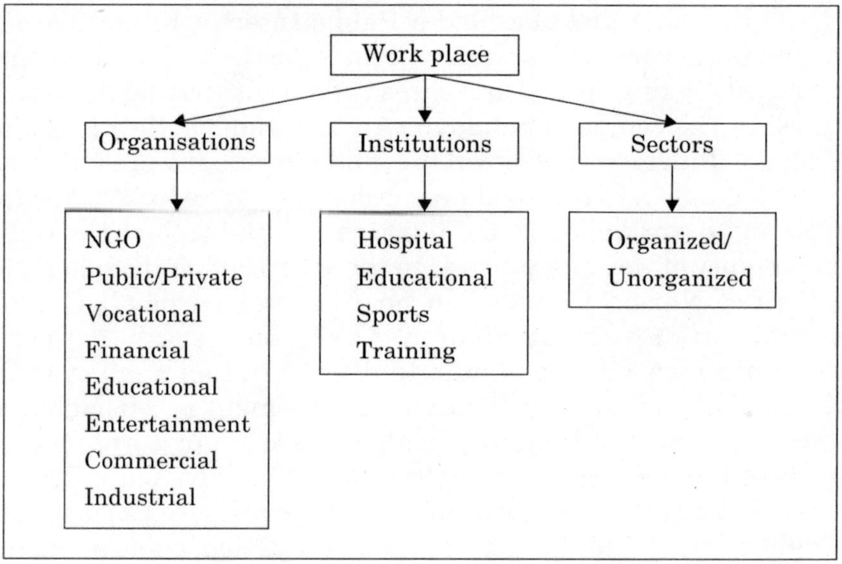

Fig. 1: Applicability of the Act the sexual harassment of women at workplace (Prevention, prohibition and redressal) Act, 2013

the workplace, treat sexual harassment as misconduct under the service rules and initiate action for misconduct, inform all employees of the penal consequences of indulging in acts that may constitute sexual harassment, penal action shall include termination and reporting the harassment incident to relevant Government authorities, and Constitute an Internal Complaints Committee ("ICC") to be headed by a woman, and half its members shall be women and include a third-party representative from an NGO or any other agency conversant in dealing with sexual harassment, organize workshops and awareness programmes at regular intervals for sensitising employees on the issues and implications of workplace sexual harassment and organizing orientation programmes for members of the Internal Complaints Committee, Monitor the timely submission of reports by the ICC. If an employer fails to constitute an Internal Complaints Committee or does not comply with any provisions contained therein, the Sexual Harassment Act prescribes penalty of up to Rs. 50,000/-. A repetition of the same offence could result in the punishment being doubled and / or de-registration of the entity or revocation of any statutory business licenses.

(b) Remedies available for the Aggrieved

The New Law stipulates certain measures for the aggrieved employee to address her grievance. The Government is also required to set up a 'Local Complaints Committees' (LCC) at the district level to investigate complaints regarding sexual harassment from establishments where the ICC has not been constituted on account of the establishment having less than 10 employees or if the complaint is against the employer. The Sexual Harassment Act also sets out the constitution of the committees, process to be followed for making a complaint and inquiring into the complaint in a time bound manner. The act empowers the ICC and the LCC to recommend to the employer, at the request of the aggrieved employee, interim measures such as Transfer of the aggrieved woman to any other workplace or granting leave to the aggrieved woman up to a period of 3 months in addition to her regular statutory/ contractual leave entitlement.

(c) Process for Complaint and Inquiry

Any aggrieved employee within 3 months from date of the sexual harassment incident should report the same, in writing, to the ICC or LCC. The law allows female employees to request for conciliation to the ICC or LCC in order to settle the matter. If the conciliation proceedings fail or if no conciliation was requested, the ICC or LCC shall conduct an inquiry and complete the same within 90 days from receipt of the complaint. Within 10 days from completion of the inquiry the ICC or LCC has to publish report with its recommendations. The employer shall act on the recommendations of the report within 60 days of publication of the report. If the allegation leveled is proved, and action for misconduct is taken as provided under the service rules of the organisation or if the harassment is grave, the organisation is bound to inform the relevant authorities to institute penal action under the Indian Penal Code, 1860, which has provided special provisions for crimes relating to sexual harassment. If the allegation leveled is not proved due to the inability of the complainant to prove the facts and in the absence of malicious intent, the organisation shall decide not to take any action. The allegation leveled is not proved and the allegation was made with a "false and malicious" intent, action can be against the complainant for misconduct under the service rules. An appeal to a court or tribunal is available to the complainant and the alleged against the recommendations of the ICC or LCC. The appeal has to be made within 90 days from the date of the recommendation. The Law provides the much needed grievance redressal process working women require at their workplaces.

5

Judicial Activism Protecting Women

Justice is the first virtue of civilized world. Social justice envisages an efficient social arrangement where the opportunity of leading dignified life with good things and amenities of life is available for all. In its essence, social justice means quality of being fair and just in social relations of human beings. The need for social justice to women is actually felt in a patriarchal society as the gender discriminations most often invade dignity of life and right to privacy of women contrary to the internationally ascribed moral vision of human rights norms. The variety of domestic violence, cruelties, sexual assaults, dowry harassments and oppressions in places of work make women, a deeply suffered lot when the minimum legal protection for a decent life is not forthcoming. The task of empowerment of women to have a real guarantee of dignified life lies at the threshold of social justice programming for women. Although special provisions, affirmative actions and reservations in education, employment and political life may have their own advantages, more fundamental than these are creation of a dependable legal framework for protection of their bodily integrity and personal autonomy. A multi-pronged approach for an all-round development of women by setting into service different provisions of the constitution might be more appropriate. The post emergency due process revolution, public interest litigation and judicial activism animating positive dimensions of right to life have made the right to life and due process jurisprudence interestingly more rewarding for women.

INTRODUCTION

Carving out positive rights like right to maintenance, right against sexual harassment, right of child prostitutes and children of prostitutes to rescue and rehabilitation reflects the peak of judicial activism through systematic and holistic application of several fundamental rights, directive principles, fundamental duties and constitutional remedies to redress individual and class grievances of women has assisted the cause of womans right to dignified life. Feminism symbolizes an awareness of oppression on domestic, social, economic levels, accompanied by a willingness to struggle against such subjugation. They have focused their attention on equalizing strategies, which represents attempts to improve womens access to existing education, employment, health care, credit and other opportunities, and ultimately to make resources more responsive to women's needs[1]. The social norm is different from legal system however, both are seeking justice. The concept of justice must be viewed through its relationship with law, morality and ethics. There is difference between ethics and system of values governing individual conduct and social morality as a system of norms which governs the social conduct of community. Definitions to the term law is between two extremes, one end law is defined on its cohesive nature which are based on the source of its authority and enforced by sanctions, and the other end its social acceptance[2]. Activist role shall be played by all the wings of government legislature, executive and judiciary in moulding the relevant law from the perspective of dignity of life, human rights and social justice to women which links democracy with feminism. Although the direction of development in the sphere is towards better protection of interests of women in the context of widely prevalent gender discriminations and oppressions. But it calls for consolidation of the past gains by an ongoing task of keeping the contours of dignified life sound and high by fruitfully using the means of constitutional litigation, activising the temaie organizations, spreading legal literacy and extending legal aid.

---

[1] Nelson, Barbara J. and Choudhry N, (1997). Women and Politics Oxford University Press, New Delhi.

[2] Shukla V.N., (2007). Constitution of India, Eastern Book Company, 10th Edition.pp. 451-52.

Equally significant is the determined efforts of aggrieved women, social activists and feminist organisations in applying the strategy or constitutional litigation.

(1) JUDICIARY BECOMING HYPERACTIVE THROUGH JUDICIAL ACTIVISM

In India Judicial activism is supported by check and balance principle based on "separation of powers' between the executive, legislature and judiciary. It has become inevitable for the judiciary to become a policy maker, policy implementer because of the lethargic attitude of the other two organs, there by sometimes overstepping its constitutional limits either consciously or unconsciously to save the democracy. Indian constitution has provided different powers to the apex court to uphold its objectives. Art 137 Supreme court is vested with power to review any judgement or order made by it subject to the provisions of any law made by the parliament or any rules under Article 145 on the grounds mentioned in Order 47, Rule 1 of the CPC[3]. Art 141 provides that law declared by the SC shall be binding on all courts is the law of the land. Article 32 and 142 enable supreme court to declare law and to give directions for complete justice. Judicial interventions by judicial review of the higher judiciary for ensuring the rights of individual and group. Article 13(2) the Union or the States shall not make any law that takes away or abridges any of the fundamental rights, and any law in contravention shall, to the extent of the contravention, be void. Feminine Perspective toward a pro-women policy focus on marginalisation of women in democratic participation their subordination in socio-legal regime should be countered. Free women through Empowerment against Patriarchal Social Construction to dictate freedom. The post emergency due process, revolution, public interest litigation and judicial activism animating positive dimensions of right to life is rewardful for women. Gender justice remedy is found to be more useful hence, constitutional strategy for feminine justice falls within Arts. 21 and 32 in the judicial emphasis. Constitutional litigations are the revolutionary means of desirable social transformation since last two decades.

---

[3] Kasibhatta Subramaniyam (1991). Women and Law, Asia Law House, Hyderebad, 3rd Edition, pp. 1–3.

(2) JUDICIAL APPROACH FOR LEGAL PROTECTION OF WOMEN

In India, positive rights like right to food, shelter, health, livelihood, education and good environment under Art. 21 evolved by the culmination of Directive Principles of State Policy with Fundamental Right. The judiciary should focus towards the social welfare goal in the constitutional jurisprudence. When the basic essentials of dignified life of women is deprived effecting their right to sustenance and shelter judiciary can protect women under Art. 21 by Suitable legislative and administrative actions, constitutional remedies, momentary compensation. Scrutiny of privacy through rehabilitative protection against immoral trafficking, dowry prohibition, sati, rape and other sexual offences, indecent representation of women, right to maintenance and maternity benefit. The inequalities of income, social position and access to good things of life result in exploitation in the society. The States power to make special provisions for women and children Article 15(3), Fundamental duty (Article 51(A), promotion of harmony and spirit of common brotherhood, renounce practices derogatory to the dignity of women, the whole legal system ought to secure fairness and reasonableness which shall stop gender bias. Art. 21 should be loaded with deprivation, rights and procedural safeguards for the protection of life and personal liberty. The Feminist human right perspective needs to percolate into various layers of procedure established by law and sensitize the judicial reasoning to bring out and apply positive rights to women. The judicial activism have to be channelized for the benefit of women.

(3) DIRECTIVE PRINCIPLES OF STATE POLICY AND JUDICIAL ACTIVISM

Our constitution in Part IV lays down a set of guiding principles which the state ought to follow both in framing laws and enforcing them. They confer no legal rights and create no legal remedies but still they provide a good guide in charting the path of the state in the governance of the country. Equal access to means of livelihood (Article 39(a)), equal pays for equal work (Article 39(d)), free legal aid (Article 39A) M.H. Hoskot *Vs.* State of Maharashtra[4], just and humane conditions of work (Article 42), protection from social injustice and all forms of exploitation (Article 46), maternity benefit, raising the living standard and levels of nutrition (Article 47), renounce practices derogatory to the dignity of women (Article 51(A)(e)), compulsory primary education, rural development and uniform civil code contain a great amount of gender justice value and add to the objective of dignified life with development. These directives linked rights of maintenance, succession, sexual harassment at workplace and primary education to right to life of women as they are the victims of such offences. The social justice influenced the decision was developed on the basis of Directive Principles of State Policy In Kishen Pattanayak *Vs.* State Orissa[5] long-drawn drought in Kalahandi had resulted in distress sale of girl child. The SC, issued guidelines for effective food distribution system through food camps saved women. Similarly, in Olga Tellis *Vs.* Bombay Municipal Corporation[6] had the effect of protecting right to privacy of women, who along with her family were dwelling on the footpaths of Bombay, being targets of peeping eyes. The judicial approach about right to maintenance is influenced by its consideration of dignified life. As held in Naurang Singh Chuni Singh *Vs.* Smt. Sapla Devi[7] the law of maintenance is aimed at prevention of vagrancy, and securing of right to food, clothing and shelter to the deserted wife and children. In Bai Tahira A *Vs.* Ali Hussain Fissalli Chothia[8] the Supreme Court applied Sec. 125 of the Criminal Procedure Code irrespective of the claims of Muslim personal law. In Madhl Kishwar *Vs.* State of Bihar a feminist challenged the constitutionality of Chota Nagpur Tenancy Act, 1908 which conferred right to intestate succession among tribal tenants only upon male heirs is violating right to equality (Art. 14) and right to life (Art. 21). The court held that the immediate female relatives of the last male tenant have the constitutional remedy to stay on holding the land so long as they remain dependent upon it for earning their livelihood.

---

[4] AIR (1978) SC 1548
[5] AIR (1989) 677
[6] AIR (1986) 180
[7] AIR (1968) All 412, 1968 Cri L J 1636
[8] AIR (1979) 362

(4) RIGHT TO LIFE AND PERSONAL LIBERTY (ARTICLE 21)

Right to dignified life is a precondition for the very human existence with all its attributes and potential activities, attaining of social justice through an activist jurisprudence of right to life has been demonstrated to be a rewarding constitutional strategy for women during the last two decades. This is complementary to the egalitarian means of attaining gender and social justice to women who were subjected to patriarchal oppressions from a long time. Art. 21, "No person shall be deprived of right to life and personal liberty except according to the procedure established by law" is a prescription against all deprivations hence, The term life as used in Article 21 means not merely the right for the continuance of a persons animate existence, but a right to the possession of each of his organs was highlighted in Kharak Singh *Vs.* State of U.P.[9]. Protection should be provided to all individuals against arbitrary or illegal action of the state except according to the procedure established by law which is just, fair, not arbitrary, fanciful or oppressive. It should confirm to the principles of natural justice in Maneka Gandhi *Vs.* Union of India[10]. In Kharak Singh *Vs.* State of U.P.[11], the Supreme Court held that the expression personal liberty is not limited to bodily restraint or to confinement in prison only. In Satwant Singh Sawhney *Vs.* A.P.O. New Delhi[12] it was held that right to travel abroad is included within the expression personal liberty hence, no person can be deprived of his right to travel except according to the procedure established by law. This point was highlighted in Maneka Gandhi *Vs.* Union of India[13] where it was further held that the fundamental rights conferred by part III of the constitution are not distinct and mutually exclusive hence article 21 has to stand along with 14 and 19. A new era has emerged which has given rise to many new fundamental rights. All these rights although not enshrined in the constitution specially found their root in article 21. Some of these

[9] AIR (1963) SC 1295
[10] AIR (1978) SC 597
[11] AIR (1963) SC 1295
[12] AIR (1967) SC 1836
[13] AIR (1976) SC 597

rights are Right to speedy criminal trial and more criminal courts Hussainara Khatoon *Vs.* Home Secretary, Bihar[14], Right to bail, right to human dignity, right to a prisoner not to be handcuffed except in very special circumstances, right against use of third degree methods by police, right of a detenue to have interview with his lawyer and family members, right against cruelty and unusual punishment, right of release and rehabilitation of bonded labour, right to compensation for violation of fundamental rights. Vishaka *Vs.* State of Rajasthan[15] a class action was brought under Right to Equality(Arts. 14), Right to Freedom (Art. 19) and Right to Life and Personal Liberty (Art. 21), for the enforcement of fundamental rights of working women and to prevent sexual harassment of working women in all workplaces. The Supreme Court referred Art. 15(3) The State to make special provisions for women and children, Art. 42 Directing the state to secure just and humane conditions of work and Art. 51A(e) Fundamental duty upon citizens to renounce practices derogatory to the dignity of Women and International Conventions. Sexual harassment includes Physical contact and advances; a demand or request for sexual favour; sexually coloured remarks; showing pornography; any other unwelcome physical, verbal and non verbal conduct of sexual nature. It shall be the duty of the employer to take preventive steps like publicizing about prohibition of sexual harassment, incorporation into the service rules, Rule 11 says the Central/State Governments are requested to consider suitable measures including legislation to ensure that the guidelines laid down by this order are observed by the employers in private sector. The court held that these directions would be binding and enforceable in law until suitable legislation is enacted.

(5) RIGHT TO PRIVACY OF WOMAN AS AN ASPECT OF DIGNIFIED LIFE

Right to be let alone without interference by others in the matters of intimate personal choices is considered since a long time as emanating from the concept of dignity of women personhood. Physical privacy, marital privacy and sexual privacy are influenced by the

[14] (No.1) AIR (1979) SC 1360

[15] AIR 1997 SC 3011

notion of dignified life and fair procedure. In State of Maharastra *Vs.* Madhukar Narayan[16] the Supreme Court sentenced the police inspector for attempt to commit rape and observed that even a women of easy virtue is entitled to privacy and no one can invade her privacy as and when he likes. In Nandini Satpathi *Vs.* P.L. Demi[17] that arrest of a women shall be done as far as possibly by a women police officer and investigation of a women detenue shall be done only in the presence of her lawyer without using third degree methods. In Sheela Barse *Vs.* State of Maharashtra[18] a PIL case, for redressing the grievances of custodial violence against women in police lock-ups, the Supreme Court directed for establishment of exclusively female lock-ups, separation of female arrestees from the male arrestees, investigation by female police constable and surprise visits to police lockups by sessions judge for inspection. In Harvinder Kaur and Saroj Rani's[19] the Delhi court and the Supreme Court respectively held that cohabitation after the restitution decree was not compulsory and the restituted marital life shall not force sex upon the wife. The provision was upheld by limiting the scope of restored marital life. In Air India *Vs.* Nargesh Mirza[20] the Supreme court invalidated a service regulation which requires Air Hostesses to retire upon their first pregnancy, the court considered the regulation as obstructing the ordinary course of human nature and a cruel instult on Indian womenhood by interfearing with her personal choice. In Neera Mathur *Vs.* LIC[21]. The petitioner had joined LIC as an assistant after medical examination and had not stated about pregnancy in the declaration. When she sought three months leave during probation period for delivery of child, LIC terminated her service on the ground of false declaration. The Supreme Court quashed the termination order as unfair and found the real mischief in the requirement of declaration about detailed aspect of personal life. In State of Maharashtra *Vs.* Madhukar

[16] AIR 1991 SC 207

[17] 1978 AIR 1025

[18] AIR 1983 SC 378

[19] [1984] AIR 1562, 1985 SCR (1) 303

[20] [1982] 1 SCR 438

[21] 1992 AIR 392

Narain[22] by holding that a women of easy virtue is also entitled right to privacy and cannot be compelled for sexual acts the Supreme Court infused the aspects of dignity into right to privacy.

(6) PRO-LIFE APPROACH TOWARDS SOCIAL JUSTICE

Womens right to dignified life will be better protected when, law and legal procedure are sensitized by a pro-life gender justice approach. The recent trend in the law relating to sati, dowry death, etc., by and large, reflects such a concern.

(a) Sati

The law relating to sati was made very stringent in 1987 with the passing of the commission of sati (Prevention) Act in response to an occurrence of sati event in Rajasthan. The offence of 'sati' is comprehensively defined to include all the possible situations of sati like burning or buying alive widow. Abetment of sati is also elaborately defined and is made punishable with death penalty or life imprisonment. Important provisions are made for punishing glorification of sati and empowering the collector or District Magistrate to prohibit sati and to remove temples or structures which commemorate sati and to seize property and funds.

(b) Dowry Death and Violence

Judiciary has shown sensitization to the problems faced by women especially in cases dealing with dowry related offences and dowry deaths (Sarkar L. 1987). The Dowry Prohibition (Amendment) Act 1986 inserted section 304B in the IPC provides "where the death of a women is caused by any burn or bodily injury if occurs within seven years of her marriage and before her death she was subjected to cruelty or harassment by her husband or his family in connection with any demand for dowry amounts to 'dowry death' punished with seven years imprisonment to life imprisonment. Iqbal Singh case, where a women committed suicide along with her three children

[22] AIR 1991 SC 207

because of dowry harassment, the trial court and Supreme Court relied on the evidences of neighbours and other circumstantial evidence and convicted the husband, the mother in law and sister in law to seven years rigorous imprisonment. Under section 498A Cruelty to married women includes willful conduct which may drive the wife to endanger her life, limb or health includes dowry harassments is punishable with imprisonment upto three years. Section 174 of Criminal Procedure Code investigation of death of women in suspicious circumstances within seven years of her marriage. The initial burden of proof is shifted upon the accused person and presumption against the husband or relative about abetment may be constituted under Section 13A of the Indian Evidence Act. In Lichamadevi *Vs.* State of Rajasthan the investigation had shown that the mother-in-law had poured kerosene on her daughter in law and ignited it while the trial court considered the evidences as inadequate, the High Court found them sufficient to convict the accused. The Supreme Court agreed with the High Court in relying on the evidence adduced by the doctor who treated the victim and heard the dying statement. On the whole, the entire procedure established by law brings with a pro-victim approach as a means of empowerment and justice.

(c) Female Infanticide

Innovations in medical science is assisting in determination of sex of the foetus which increased abortion of girl foetus thereby women population is reducing. According to Amartya Sen under the Medical Termination of Pregnancy Act 1971, the anguish caused by unwanted pregnancy because of failure of contraceptive device or method is an easy ground for termination of pregnancy during the first trimester of pregnancy. It seems, this provision is abused for termination of female foetus. No doubt this negates the right to life of female embryo. Female infanticide could be largely controlled by a bold reformatory legislation. The Parliament enacted the Pre-natal Diagnostic Techniques (Regulation and Prevention of Misuse) Act, 1994 to comprehensively deal with the evil practice. No Genetic Counselling or Genetic Laboratory or Genetic clinic shall conduct pre-natal diagnostic techniques including ultrasonography, for determining the sex of a foetus (Sect. 6). No person conducting pre-natal diagnostic procedures shall communicate to the pregnant or her relatives the sex of the foetus by words, signs or in any other manner (Sect. 5(2)). The act provides for supervision of genetic counseling centres, laboratories or clinics through registration, Central Supervisory Board and prohibition of pre-natal diagnostic techniques except for treating genetic abnormalities. In 2003 the Supreme Court issued directions to state to ensure strict compliance with the Act to control the decline in the ratio of female children and suggested to have a foolproof legal network and supervision for prevention of female foeticide.

(d) Rape and Compensation to the Victim

Law relating to rape, along with victim compensation principal, sensitizing of the rules of evidence owing to pro-dignified life approach is emphasised. In custodial rape, the legal assumption is against consent. The rule for requirement of circumstantial evidence is generally dispensed by the judiciary. Rape violates right to life hence it is the vicarious liability of the state to pay compensation to the victims of custodial rape is laid down in Rathnam *Vs.* State of Gujarat a tribal women was raped in police custody in the presence of her husband. Writ petition was filed by a Social Worker, the Supreme Court laid down a schedule for systematic enquiry and awarded a compensation of Rs. 50,000/- as an interim relief payable by the state government. In State of Punjab *Vs.* Gurmit Singh Supreme court held that rape destroys entire psychology of a women and pushes her into emotional crisis in addition to inflicting a much hated aggression on her privacy hence it violates the cherished right to dignified life. In State of Punjab *Vs.* Gurmit Singh held that minor contradictions in evidences and little delay in complaint did not obstruct conviction of the offender. In Prem Chand *Vs.* State of Haryana held that character, reputation or status of a raped victim was not a relevant factor for consideration by the court while awarding the sentence to a rapist.

(e) Rehabilitation of Prostitutes and their Children for a Dignified Life

It is remarkable development that Art. 21 and 32 are used to rehabilitate prostitutes and their children. In Upendra Baxi *Vs.* State of U.P. the Supreme Court invoked Art 21 and U.P. Suppression of Immoral Traffic in women and girls rules and issued several orders for improving the conditions of the inmates of the protective home. It asked a panel of doctors to check the state of health of inmates and ordered the superintendent to make medical treatment available. The court ordered for ensuring better hygienic conditions and sanitation, separation of minor girls from hardened prostitutes and providing of vocational training and guidance for self employment. In Vishal Jeet *Vs.* Union of India, a roving CBI inquiry was sought about the role of police and flesh traders and about rehabilitation of child prostitutes and destitute and destitute girls in protective homes. The court issued directions to the state governments to constitute advisory committee consisting of social workers for making suggestions about eradication of child prostitution, to provide adequate and well-equipped rehabilitation homes and to devise a machinery to ensure proper implementation of these suggestions.

(7) RIGHT TO CONSTITUTIONAL REMEDIES (ART. 32 TO 35)

Rights without remedies would be just abstract declarations without any real content in them and will be of no use. Art. 32 which guarantees. The Supreme court has been empowered to grant relief for the enforcement of fundamental rights. The supreme court has the power to issue directions, order or writs such as habeas corpus (to direct the release of a person detained unlawfully), mandamus (to direct a public authority to do its duty), quo warranto (to direct a person to vacate an office assumed wrongfully), prohibition (to prohibit a lower court from proceeding on a case) and certiorari (power of the higher court to remove a proceeding from a lower court and bring it before itself). Besides the Supreme Court, the High Courts located in the various States are also designated as constitutional courts and Article 226 permits citizens to file similar writs before the High Courts. The right guaranteed by article 32 cannot be suspended except as otherwise provided by article 359 of the constitution, where a proclamation of emergency is in operation. This remedial right is itself made a fundamental right, being included in part III (Kochunni *Vs.* State of Madras[23]). In Women's Resource Centre *Vs.* Commissioner of Police[24], the court ordered the state payment of Rs. 75,000/- as compensation for death caused of a 9 year old child due to police atrocities. This right has been described as the 'soul' of the constitution.

(8) PUBLIC INTEREST LITIGATIONS (PILS)

The locus standi that a petition under article 32 can only be filled by a person whose fundamental rights is infringed has now been considerably relaxed by the supreme court by permitting public interest litigations. Any public spirited citizens or organizations can file a PIL on behalf of individual or group who cannot approach the court due to poverty or social backwardness for the protection of constitutional rights. The court had developed new procedural norms to suit the requirements of the strategy. However no one are allowed to absue the process of law by initiating frivolus litigation for personal, political gains, publicity or other oblique reasons. PIL strategies were devised to assist relatives of victims in filing private complaint and later, this was extended to womens organizations to intervene in many bride burning cases the Sudha Goel Case[25], The Sathyarani Chadha and others *Vs.* State Delhi Administration[26], The Haryana Mahila Sansthan and others *Vs.* Devi Lal and others[27] by resorting to this device, womens organizations have been able to raise public consciousness, lobby for changes in dowry law, and prevent possible manipulation by unscrupulous and dishonest police officers and make the subordinate judiciary aware of the need for taking suffering seriously and disposing of cases expeditiously[28]. However drafting should be done by expert for issues of constitutional law. The apex court can issue guidelines and norms to fill up the

[23] AIR (1959) SC 75
[24] AIR (1990) SC 513
[25] AIR, 1986, SC, 250
[26] AIR, 1986, SC, 205
[27] Criminal Writ Petition No. 931-936 of 1988.
[28] Jethmalani, Ram (1985). Dowry and the Law Subversion of Human Right, in Gandhi P.K., (*ed.*), Social Action Through Law Partnership for Social Justice, New Delhi.

vacuum in existing legislation. In Injuint Women's Programme *Vs.* State of Rajasthan, a women's organization moved to apex court seeking investigation in dowry death. It was held that although IPC and Cr. P.C. normally cover dowry deaths, Art. 21 might be used to move to the High Courts, or Supreme Court directly. The court directed the state government to create special dowry cell with special investigation units and to include two leading women social workers named by the Social Welfare Ministry in such dowry cells. In Delhi Domestic Working Women's Forum *Vs.* Union of India. PIL to expose the cause of four domestic servants subjected to indecent sexual assault by seven army personnel. The victims were helpless tribal women, who were in need of rehabilitative quick and compensatory justice. The Supreme Court suggested that the National Commission for Women can formulate a scheme of victim compensation in case of rape and impress upon the union government to enact on those lines. Court shall award compensation as an ad hoc remedy.

(9) HABEAS CORPUS FOR THE PROTECTION OF RIGHT TO DIGNIFIED LIFE

In recent times Writ of habeas corpus penetrates not only through the stony walls of jail, but also into every issue of private detention and criminal justice system. Writ of habeas corpus ought to lie even against private detention shows the new path supported by judicial activism. It is making a mockery of the judicial process if a matter where a women complaint of illegal confinement is not placed and listed on priority before the court no other matter deserves to be listed. In Nasrin Case the case illustrates the significance of habeas corpus remedy in a society ridden with crimes like kidnapping, forceful confinement, keeping in brothel, etc. when the close relative like husband resorts to selling of wife to brothel, and with the connivance of police the brutal act is suppressed, it is remarkable that the remedy of Habeas Corpus comes as the solitary hope of dignified life. In Bahvant Singh two minor daughters of one birmati were kidnapped and detained by their cousin for pressurizing birmati who was in possession of some family land, so that she will not sell the land to persons other than him. With the help of Mahila Dakshatha Samiti, a voluntary organisation, Birmati petitioned for writ of habeas corpus before the Supreme Court. The court passed the order on the basis of which police recovered the kidnapped daughters. When subsequently, the secretary of the samiti was threatened by the kidnapper and village sarpanch, the court held them as guilty of contempt of court and fine was imposed. In addition to the role of writ of habeas corpus in rendering gender justice, the commendable role of feminist organisation is illustrated in this case.

CONCLUSION

On the whole, application of law with feminist perspective has added contents into women's right to dignified life. Women and feminist organisations are serious in pursuing the constitutional and legal means of attaining justice, both individual and social. The liberalization of writ procedure, which has enabled approaching the court through letters and legal aid programmes, has immensely helped the vulnerable section including women. The fact that feminist organisations like Saheli, Joint Womens Programme, All India Democratic Women's Association, Mahila Dakshatha Samiti and Delhi Domestic Women's Forum have been remarkably successful in lawyering for justice to women suggests the need for consolidating the gains of concerted efforts of women in future. It determined to take constitutional litigation as a sword of remedies with continuous, systematic and well coordinated efforts. Extension of legal literacy and legal clinical service for women with the assistance of lawyers and law teachers goes a long way in this direction.

6

Revolution towards Women Education

Education is never ending process. It starts with the birth of an individual and then it goes on till the death of the individual. Education makes an individual a real human being. It is an essential human virtue. Education equips the individual with social, moral, cultural and spiritual aspects and thus makes life progressive, cultured and civilized. The word 'education' is derived from the latin word 'Educatum' which means 'to bring up' or 'to nourish'. Rig Veda depicts "Education is something which makes a man self-reliant and selfless". Kautilya putforth, "Education means training for the country", Swami Vivekananda says "Education is the Manifestation of the devine perfection existing within". According to the western thinker Aristotle "Education is the creation of a sound mind in a sound body… it develops man's faculty, especially his mind, so that he may be able to enjoy the contemplation of supreme truth, goodness and beauty in which perfect happiness essentially consists."[1]

Women can be transformed as self-relient by encouraging their literacy by the mutual cooperation of family, government and non-govermental institutions. The University Grants Commission initiated different educational reforms for women education. The Central Education Department, the National Council of Educational Research and Training, National Adult Education Programme and

---

[1] Rao, R.K., (2005). Women in Education, Kalpaz Publications, Delhi, 2005, pp. 57-69.

other institutions have evinced greater interest in providing educational facilities for women. Women Study Centres have been established with the assistance of UGC to study their status, problems, issues and concerned with women. Other institutions like United Nation's International Children's Educational Fund (UNICEF), Indian Council of Social Science Research (ICSSR), United Nations Educational Scientific and Cultural Organisation (UNESCO), Council of Scientific and Industrial Research(CSIR) are also aiding educational reforms in India. Census 2011 revealed that Literacy rate of India stands at 72.99%. Overall Literacy rate has grown by 8.15% points in the last decade (64.84% in 2001 & 72.99% in 2011). The male Literacy rate has grown by 5.63% points (75.26% in 2001 & 80.89% in 2011) whereas female literacy rate 10.97% points (53.67% in 2001 & 64.64% in 2011). Number of illiterates (7+ age group) decreased from 304.10 million in 2001 to 282.59 million in 2011. Gender disparity in literacy rates declined by 5.34% points from 21.59% points in 2001 to 16.25% points in 2011. There has been a continuous decrease in gender gap in literacy since 1991 (24.84% point). The lack of education leads to lack of self-reliance, self-confidence among women hence, they are not able to come out of their problems. Social, economic and political empowerment to women through education is the need of the day. Education is one of the most important means of empowering women with the knowledge, skills and self-confidence necessary to participate fully in the development process. It helps to realize their rights and to gain confidence to claim them[2].

A. POLICY FRAMEWORK TOWARDS WOMEN EDUCATION

After independence, The Government of India adopted following initiations to promote the cause of women's education[3].

[2] Carol Chapnick Mukhopadhyay and Susan Seymour, "Women, Education and Family Structure in India, Westview Press, Boulder, pp. 37-57.

[3] Vijay Kaushik and Bela Rani Sharma, (1998). Indian Women Through Ages, Sarup & Sons, New Delhi, pp. 235-277.

(1) University Education Commission 1948-49

The recommendation insisted for more educational opportunities for women. It aimed at educational guidance against the social prejudice, equal pay for female teachers, separate schools for boys and girls upto 13 years and co-education after 18 years of age[4].

(2) Secondary Education Commission 1952-53

Recommended for equal education for both men and women related to home and community issues due to the lack of justification to have separate women's education. Four Regional colleges of education have been set up at Ajmer, Mysore, Bhubaneswar and Bhopal in order to prepare teachers for multi-purpose schools.

(3) The Central Social Welfare Board 1953

Constituted by the Planning Commission of India for promoting Social Welfare Schemes like housing for helpless women, establishing Centre for Social Education and Adult Education, starting Condensed and Vocational Training Courses in collaboration with Voluntary organizations for the benefit of women, children and handicapped. It gives financial subsidy of Rs. 50,000/- annually to voluntary organizations for providing services. Nearly 18,000 NGO's benefitted under the scheme.

(4) University Grants Commission 1956

It was constituted under the act of Parliament for promotion and coordination of University Education, Examination and Research in the universities in India. It undertakes 16 General Development Assistance Programmes to Central, State and Deemed Universities. Among them constitution of Day Care Centers, Special Scheme for Construction of Women's Hostel, Basic facilities for women, Equal Opportunity Cells, Guidelines for Development of Women's Studies

---

[4] Government of India, University Education Commission (1948-49), Vol. I, Manager of Publication, New Delhi.

in Indian Universities and Colleges, Research Fellowship in Humanities and Social Sciences Students will focus towards Welfare of Women.

(5) National Committee on Women Education 1958-59

The State shall frame Comprehensive Development Plan for the education of Girls and Women, Low fee for the low income groups in primary education and establishing co-education in middle and secondary education.

(6) Condensed Course for Adult Women 1958

The Central Social Welfare Board started two years Certification Course for the Primary/Middle/Metric level courses which increase the employability of beneficiary in the rural areas. The scheme aims to provide educational opportunities to girls above the age of 15 years by providing skill development and vocational training. This will increase confidence among the adult women through education to make them able citizens. The scheme is implemented through Voluntary Organizations and educational institutions, having requisite infrastructure and experience in the field of women education. The scheme is run issued with grants to conduct middle school or matriculation examination for women between 18-30 years. The residential candidates are paid with Rs. 200/- and non residential candidates with Rs. 60/- per month as stipend. About 1100 course were organized between 1958-1969. The programme secured 65% results in middle school and 36% for high school category and among them, 75% successful candidates are either employed or went for higher education. Budgetary requirement for this scheme under XII Plan would be Rs. 45 crores.

(7) Committee on Differentiation of Curriculum for Boys and Girls 1961

Recommended small reforms to eliminate inferiority hidden in women education, focus for self development, addition of topics relevant to women in the text books, appointing women teachers in schools.

(8) Correspondence School and Courses 1962

In Delhi a Directorate of Correspondence courses was opened to make higher education available to any citizen of the country.

(9) Committee to Study the Public Support for Women Education 1963

It recommended for the Special attention towards girls education in rural areas. Suggested to organize School Improvement Conferences throughout the states, emphasizing preference for the local candidates during recruitment to the schools and the provision of infrastructure to the schools shall be entrusted to the local bodies.

(10) Education Commission 1964-66

It recognized the role of women outside the home. It recommended separate schools for girls, girls hostels, provision for scholarships, part-time vocational courses, facility of education through correspondence courses, employment of women teachers in all sectors of education, etc. implementation of 10+2 & 3, 10 years of high school, two years of higher secondary & 3 years under graduate education was recognized as a National Pattern of Education and most of the states adopted the same in future days.

(11) Committee on Status of Women 1971-74

This Committee is constituted to examine the implications of constitutional, legal and administrative provisions to improve the social status of women and to assess the impact of women education and employment during the two decades. The committee recommon ded special focus for rural sectors with effective programmes, general policy framework on co-education in primary and secondary school, general education for both sexes till 10th standard, more relevant courses at university level and free education for girls in Secondary level.

(12) Integrated Child Development Services (ICDS) 1975

Pre-school education (PSE) has come under the purview of the Ministry of Women and Child Development (MWCD) along with pre-primary education. The Ministry will continue this scheme as planned under the ICDS scheme. The Non-formal education offered as per the Ministry of Human Resources (MHR) consists of providing a learning environment to children between the ages of 3-6. Pre School Education is supposed to be implemented through a medium of play to allow for social, emotional, cognitive and physical development of the child as well as prepare him for primary education in the formal system.

(13) Assistance to Voluntary Organisation 1982

The Scheme to control atrocities against women. Financial aid of Rs 81 lakhs was used under the IX Five year Plan by the Voluntary Organisations by constituting Women Study Centers of Higher Education for serving women, children, aged, infirm, handicapped and other special groups.

(14) Department of Women and Child Development 1985

The Ministry of Human Resources Development constituted a new department with the sole purpose of assisting Women and children to develop to their full potentials. This department prepared a National Policy of the Empowerment of Women in the year 2001.

(15) The Ministry of Human Resource Development (MHRD) 1985

All round development of the country is possible only through education. The Ministry was created through the 174th Amendment to the Government of India (Allocation of Business) Rules, 1961. It works through two wings like Department of School Education and Literacy aiming to develop school education and literacy in the country through the process of universalisation of education and Department of Higher Education takes care about the higher education system to bring world class opportunities of higher education and research in the country.

(16) National Policy on Education 1986

Education is a catalyst to bring changes in the status of women. In order to neutralize the accumulated distortions of the past, there should be a well conceived preference in favour of women. The National Education System will play a positive, interventionist role in the empowerment of women. It will foster the development of new values through redesigned curricula, textbooks, training and orientation of teachers, involvement of decision makers and administrators, and the educational institutions, this will be an act of faith and social engineering... It adopted the concept of a national system of education, implying that all students irrespective of caste, creed, language or sex have access to education of comparable quality. The policy lays special emphasis on removal of disparities and equalizing educational opportunities by attending to the specific needs of those who have educationally backward to bring gender equity. Encourage admission and retention of girl child in formal and informal schooling. This will enable them to transit to higher studies and also ensure quality in the national education system. Ensure women's participation in educational process, organizing nationwide gender sensitization programmes and parental awareness to create positive climate for girls education. It suggested strengthening of open school system at secondary level all over the country as an independent system with its own curriculum and examination leading to certification. Scheme for providing quality education in Madrasas by linking it with National Institute of Open Schooling (NIOS), as accredited centres for providing formal education, to enable children studying in such Madrasas to get certification for class 5, 8, 10 and 12. The scheme of area Intensive Development for ensuring an area intensive approach to education was launched in the IX Plan. The scheme for infrastructure development in private aided and unaided minority institutions providing elementary, secondary and senior secondary schools was introduced in XI Plan. As Education is the instrument for social change to improve the status of women. National Education system should empower through value based curriculum and text books.

Separate Schools and Colleges for Girls were constituted. The number of colleges was raised to 824 in 1992 from the prevailing 146 colleges during 1958-59. Some exclusive University specially for women University at Puna, Padmavati University at Tirupathi, Womens University Bijapur, Karnataka, etc. were constituted[5].

(17) National Literacy Mission 1988

To tackle the problem of illiteracy, Government of India constituted National Literacy Mission Authority with a council and Executive Committee and Director General of Literacy Mission. The intervention was focusing upon the fixed goals, clear time frame and age specific target groups. It lays stress on improvement in the content and process of teaching and learning on a continuous basis. Emphasis was not merely on enrolment of learners but on attainment of certain pre-determined norms and parameters of literacy, numeracy, functionality and awareness. It focused rural areas and particularly on women and persons belonging to SCs and STs. Peoples participation at village level was sought by constituting Village Education Committee which comprise one chairmen and other members selected among village Pradhan, School Teachers, Women Representatives of SCs and STs and other Development Functionaries. Adult Education aims at extending educational options to those adults, who have lost the opportunity and have crossed the age of formal education, but now feel a need for learning of any type, including literacy, basic education, skill development (Vocational Education) and equivalency. With the objective of promoting adult education, a series of programmes have been introduced since the 1st Five Year Plan, this scheme being the most prominent to impart functional literacy to non-literates in the age group of 15-35 years in a time bound manner. By the end of the 10th Plan period, NLM had made 127.45 million persons literate, of which, 60% were females, 23% belonged to Scheduled Castes (SCs) and 12% to Scheduled Tribes (STs). 597 districts were covered under Total Literacy Campaigns of which 502 reached Post Literacy stage and 328 reached Continuing Education stage.

---

[5] National Policy on Education (1986). Programme of Action, Ministry of Human Resource Development, New Delhi.

(18) Mahila Samakhya Programme 1988

It was launched to pursue the objectives of the National Policy on Education, 1986. It recognized that education can be an effective tool for women empowerment. The empowerment through education is possible by enhancing self-esteem and confidence, building a positive image in the society, developing critical thinking, helping decision making through collective interventions, autonomy to choose education, employment and reproductive health, encourage equal participation in developmental process, economic independence through gaining knowledge and skill. Finally, proving legal education to enrich women participation in all levels[6].

(19) Joint Council for Vocational Education (JCVE) 1990

For policy formulation and coordination at the national level this committee was constituted to monitor the vocational training courses and modules to increase mobility in self employment for the poor people.

(20) Programme of Action 1992 through Scheme of Support to Voluntary Agencies for Adult Education and Skill Development

To operationalise National Policy on Education, 1986, this scheme is initiated with the collaboration of Government and Non Government Organizations (NGOs) to promote Adult Education, among the age group between 15-35. Integrated efforts of voluntary sector, the Department of School Education and Literacy and The Ministry of Human Resource Development was sought in this regard. The Schemes like 'Jan Shikshan Sansthan (JSS)' for providing vocational education and skill development to those having no elementary education and assisting Voluntary Agencies in the field of Adult Education for encouraging innovation and creativity in literacy by way of continuing education were constituted. The

[6] Shramshakti, (1988). Report of the National Commission on Self Employed Women and Women in the Informal Sector, New Delhi, June.

Government have now merged both the schemes to make this scheme with revised parameters and enhanced financial assistance. This scheme aims to achieve, through voluntary efforts, the overall objectives of National Literacy Mission by achieving self reliance in literacy and numeracy, creating awareness upon the cause for the deprivation of education, acquiring skills to improve the economic status and general well being, imbibing the values of national integration, conservation of the environment, women's equality and observance of small family norms[7].

(21) Teachers Education 1995

National Council for Teachers Education was established as a statutory body for achieving planned and coordinated teacher education system came into existence in pursuance of the National Council for Teacher Education Act, 1993 (No. 73 of 1993) on the 17th August,1995. It has notified the revised regulations 2014 along with norms and standards for 15 programmes on November, 28, 2014 under the Government of India Gazette Notification by following the recommendations of the Justice Verma Commission (JVC) appointed by the Government at the instance of the Hon'ble Supreme Court of India. The JVC had suggested wide range reforms in Teacher Education like recognising for the first time three new programmes 4 year B.A, B.Sc. & B.Ed programmes, 3 year B.Ed. (Part-time), and 3-year B.Ed. & M.Ed. programme. The duration of B.Ed., B.P.Ed., M.Ed. has been increased to two years, providing more professional rigour and at par with best international standards comprising theory, practicum, internship along with 25% of the programme is developed to school based activities and internship. Information Communication and Technology, Yoga Education, Gender and Disability/Inclusive Education are integral part of each programme curriculum. Open and Distance Learning (ODL) has become more rigorous with built-in quality assurance mechanisms. Each teacher education institution to have compulsory accreditation in every 5 years from an accrediting agency recognized by NCTE. (An MoU has already been signed with NAAC in this regard)[8].

---

[7] Rao Y.V. and Francis C, Action Oriented Adult Literacy and Education in WCADL. Journal of Rural Development, Vol. 12, 6, pp. 651-655.

(22) The National Plan of Action for the Girl Child 1991-2000

It is a specially formulated action plan by the Government of India to protect and promote the Girl Child. This plan seeks to prevent female foeticide and infanticide, eliminate gender discrimination, provide safe drinking water and fodder near homes, rehabilitate and protect girls from exploitation, assault and abuse. The key measures planned under the National Plan include strengthening of the existing primary health care infrastructure, consolidation and maintenance of levels of immunization coverage, stepping up immunization where coverage is low, Polio eradication through immunization, ensuring essential supplies and drugs, training of doctors and para-medical health workers, educating women and girls on safe motherhood, providing primary education facilities in unserved areas, providing child care services, community mobilization and involvement.

(23) Sarva Shiksha Abhiyan 2000-2001

It tried to provide universal education by eradicating gender and social gap in elementary education and facilitated for the improvement of quality of learning. It focused on opening new schools, alternative schooling facilities, construction of schools, additional classrooms, toilet construction, building drinking water facility, provision for teachers, organizing periodic teachers training, academic resource support, supply of text books and support for learning. The Right to Education Act, brought holistic view of education, as interpreted in the National Curriculum Framework, 2005 was sought, equal opportunity was given to the disadvantaged sections of the society like SCs, STs, Muslim Minority, Landless agricultural workers and children with special needs. Gender concern was emphasized to enable girls to keep pace with boys in education. Centrality of teacher and creating inclusive environment for girls from oppressed and marginalized backgrounds, imposing moral compulsion upon the parents, teachers, educational administrations

---

[8] Website maintained by National Council for Teacher Education retrieved on 27th April, 2016 at 12.40 p.m.

and other stakeholders to create a integrating system of educational management in the country was sought.

(24) Kasturba Gandhi Balika Vidyalaya 2004

This scheme was launched by the Government of India for setting up residential schools at upper primary level for girls belonging to SC, ST, OBC and Minorities in Educationally Backward Blocks (EBBs). It was merged with the Sarva Shiksha Abhiyan programme with effect from 1st April, 2007. Priority was given to tribal community, girls and areas which have low female literacy rate and large number of small and scattered habitants that do not qualify for schooling. The National Resource Group (NRG) created under the Mahila Samakhya Programme at the National Level shall provide inputs on conceptual issues to advice Government of India on policy matters concerning to the education of girls. This group will provide the interface with research and training institutions, women's movement, educationalists, Non Governmental Institutions to bring in other experiences of educating girls.

(25) National Curriculum Framework 2005

It is one of four National Curriculum Frameworks published in 1975, 1988, 2000 and 2005 by the National Council of Educational Research and Training (NCERT) in India. It has ensured that irrespective of caste, creed, religion and sex all are provided with a standard curriculum. It prescribes the framework for making syllabi, textbooks and teaching practices within the school education programmes in India. This frame work focus on learning without burden by making learning a joyful experience by removing stress from children. It directs major changes in the design of syllabus. Insists upon developing a sense of self reliance and dignity among individual for bringing social relationships, sense of non violence and oneness across the society. It insists upon Child Centered Approach to promote Universal Enrollment and Retention until the age of 14 years. Creation of unity among students, Adopting three language formula covering Regional or Mother Tongue, Hindi and English, Mathematics, Computer Education, Social Science, Art, Health and Physical Education shall be imparted at school. Improve the skills like listening with patience, endurance, purity of mind to develop concentration, aptitude for cooperation and teamwork, acceptance of discipline, and a positive attitude to study among the students. Work related education is made as an integral component of the school curriculum. Teacher plays a role of a facilitator, supports and encourages learning, involves active participation of learners, develops multidisciplinary curriculum, focuses on education, bringing multiple and divergent exposure through continuous appraisal in educational system.

(26) Model School Scheme November 2008

The scheme aims to provide quality education to talented rural children through setting up of 6,000 model schools as benchmark of excellence at the rate of one school per block which are affiliated to Central Board of Secondary Education (CBSE). Under the State Government around 3500 schools were started in the educationally backward blocks (EBB) during 2009-10. Under the Public Private Partnership (PPP) remaining 2500 schools were constituted in blocks which are not educationally backward during 2012-13. Model schools infrastructure and facilities should be at par with the Kendriya Vidyalaya focusing towards physical, emotional and aesthetic development in addition to academics. The infrastructure should support teaching needs, sports and co-curricular activities. These schools will have adequate aids for using Information and Communication Technology, Internet connectivity with full time computer teacher. Schools will have Arts and Music Teachers besides subject teachers. The Teacher Pupil Ratio should not exceed 1:25 and the classroom will be spacious to accommodate 30 students at a ratio of 1:40. The curriculum include materials to develop leadership qualities, team spirit, participation abilities, development of soft skills and ability to deal with real life situations. Each school will have a counselor. The school should provide health education, health checkups, special teachers to cater to the need of special children, educational tours, NCC training to the students.

(27) Incentives to Girls for Secondary Education May 2008

This is a centrally sponsored scheme covering all girls who are coming under the SC/ST category who have passed class VIII who are between 14-18 years of age. Girls should be below 16 years of age on joining class IX. Married girls, girls studying in private un-aided schools and schools run by Central Government are excluded. A sum of Rs. 3000/- is deposited in the name of eligible girls as fixed deposit. The girls are entitled to withdraw the sum along with interest thereon on reaching 18 years of age and on passing 10th class examination.

(28) National Means cum Merit Scholarship Scheme May 2008

It is a centrally launched scheme aiming to award scholarship to meritorious students of economically weaker sections to reduce the drop out at class VIII to encourage them to the study at secondary stage. Every year for the selected students scholarship of Rs 6000/- per annum is awarded to study classes IX to XII in Government, Government Aided and Local Body Schools. The income limit of the parents from all source should be less than Rs. 1,50,000/-. The selection for the scholarship is done through a separate examination conducted by the State Government since 2013-14. Scholarships are disbursed by the State Bank of India directly into the accounts of the students on quarterly basis.

(29) Saakshar Bharat September 2009

According to 2001 Census male literacy was 75.26%, while female literacy remained at an unacceptable level of 53.67%, revealing that gender and regional disparities in literacy continued to persist. Hence, for encouraging Adult Education, and Skill Development among women, Government of India introduced two schemes like 'Saakshar Bharat' and 'Scheme for Support to Voluntary Agencies for Adult Education and Skill Development', in the 11th Plan. This is a new variant of earlier National Literacy Mission, a Centrally sponsored scheme from Department of School Education and Literacy (DSEL), Ministry of Human Resource Development (MHRD), Government of India (GOI) launched on the International Literacy Day, 8th September, 2009 to raise literacy rate to 80% and to reduce gender gap to 10% and minimize regional and social disparities focusing on Women, SCs, STs, Minorities and other disadvantaged groups. All those districts that had female literacy rate below 50% (as per census 2001) including Left Wing Extremism affected districts are covered under the programme. Government expects increase in female literacy to become a force multiplier for all other social development programmes. However, this is only the instrumental value of female literacy. Its intrinsic value is in emancipating the Indian woman through the creation of critical consciousness to take charge of her environment where she faces multiple deprivations and disabilities based on class, caste and gender[9].

(30) Right to Education April 2010

By The Constitution (Eighty-sixth Amendment) Act, 2002 Article 21-A was inserted to Indian Constitution to provide free and compulsory education of all children in the age group of 6 to 14 years as a Fundamental Right. The Right of Children to Free and Compulsory Education (RTE) Act, 2009 is the consequential legislation envisaged under Article 21-A came into effect on 1st April, 2010. 'Free education' means that no child is liable to pay any fee or charges which prevent him from pursuing and completing elementary education. 'Compulsory Education' impose an obligation upon the government, local authorities and parents to provide admission and ensure attendance of every child between the age of 6-14 years. The act prescribes norms and standards for the Pupil Teacher Ratios (PTRs), provision for building and infrastructure, working days for the schools, Teacher working hours, etc. It requires for the rational deployment of trained teachers for ensuring specified pupil teacher ratio. The act prohibits physical punishment and mental harassment of children during screening procedures for admission of children, elimination of capitation fee, prohibits private tuition by teachers and running of schools without recognition. It encourage the preparation of curriculum by keeping the values enshrined in the Constitution of India.

(31) Beti Bachao Beti Padhao 2016

According to the provisional figures of Census 2011, the child sex

[9] Saakshar Bharat Mission, Department of School Education and Literacy, Ministry of Human Resource Development, Government of India.

ratio for girls (0-6 years) has decreased from 976 in 1976 to 918 during 2011. This is an alarming indicator for women disempowerment. Simply putting ban on sex detecting technologies cannot change the traditional views of society thereby girl child still faces the problems of malnutrition and infanticide. It reflects both pre birth discrimination manifested through gender biased sex selection, and post birth discrimination against girls. The Government of India has introduced Beti Bachao Beti Padhao (BBBP) programme in 100 gender critical districts for preventing gender biased sex selective elimination, ensure protection of the girl child and her education. It involves Mass Communication Campaign aiming at ensuring girls are born, nurtured and educated without discrimination by interlinking National, State and District level interventions at community level by involving different stakeholders. Multi-Sectoral Intervention in 100 Gender Critical Districts covering all states and union Territories. The District Collectors lead actions under this scheme at the district level. Multi-sectoral interventions by Ministry of Women and Child Development by promoting registration of pregnancies in first trimester in Anganwadi Centres, undertaking training of stakeholders, community mobilization and sensitization, involvement of gender champions, reward and recognition of institutions and frontline workers. Ministry of health and Family Welfare monitor the implementation of Pre-Conception and Pre-Natal Diagnostic Techniques Act, 1994, to increase institutional deliveries, registration of births, strengthening PNDT Cells. Ministry of Human Resource Development undertakes the universal enrollment of girls, decrease drop out rate, girl friendly standard in schools, strict implementation of right to education, construction of functional toilets for girls.

B. EMPOWERMENT OF MINORITIES THROUGH EDUCATION

(1) National Institute of Open Schooling November 1989

The Ministry of Human Resource Development (MHRD), Government of India set up the National Open School(NOS) in November 1989 to cater to the needs of a heterogenous group of learners up to pre-degree level. The pilot project of Central Board of Secondary Education was amalgamated with NOS and vested with the authority to register, examine and certify students registered with it up to pre-degree level courses. In July 2002, the Ministry changed the nomenclature of the organisation as The National Institute of Open Schooling (NIOS) with a mission to provide relevant continuing education at school stage, up to pre-degree level through open learning system to prioritized client groups as an alternative to formal system for contributing to the universalisation of education, to bring great equity and justice in the society and to create evolution of a learning society. It provides opportunities to interested learners by making available the following courses/programmes of study through open and distance learning (ODL) mode. Open Basic Education, Secondary Education Course, Senior Secondary Education Course, Vocational Education Courses, Life Enrichment Programmes.

(a) Open Basic Education (OBE)

The National Institute of Open Schooling (NIOS) has launched the Open Basic Education (OBE) Programme, as an alternative educational programme, equivalent to the Elementary Education Programme of the formal Education system. The OBE Programme explores and makes use of the potentialities of Distance Education mode for reaching the unreached. There is a provision of separate OBE programme for children and adults. This programme is offered at three levels. OBE level A equivalent to class I-III, leval B equivalent to Class IV-V, and level C, equivalent to Class VI-VIII. For the implementation of the programme, NIOS has partnership with about 341 agencies providing facilities at their study centres. It is a sort of academic input relationship with partner agencies. The NIOS provides resource support such as adaptation of NIOS model curricula, study materials, joint certification, orientation of Resource persons and popularization to the voluntary agencies and Zila Saksharta Samitis etc. for implementation of the programme. At the secondary and Senior Secondary levels, it provides flexibility in the choice of subjects or courses, Pace of learning , and transfer of credits from CBSE. Board of School Education and State Open Schools to enable learners continuation. Within 5 years a learner is given about 9 chances to appear in public examinations. The credits gained are accumulated till the learner clears required credits for certification. The learning pedagogies like learning through printed self instructional material, audio and video programmes, participating in personal contact programme and Tutor Marked Assignments. Enrichment is also provided to the learners through half yearly magazine 'open learning'. The On-Demand Examination System (ODES) is in operation at secondary and senior secondary stage. The programme offers 26 subjects in the mediums like Hindi, English, Urdu, Marathi, Telugu, Gujarati and Malayalam for Secondary Examinations and 19 Subjects in Hindi, English and Urdu mediums for Senior Secondary Examinations.

(b) Vocational Education and Training (VET)

It is an important element of the nations education initiative. If India should enjoy the demographic dividend in the changing context it should redefine the critical elements of imparting Vocational Education and Training by making it flexible, contemporary, relevant, inclusive and creative. The Government is well aware of the important role of Vocational Education and has already taken a number of important initiatives in this area. School-based Vocational Education in India is currently covered by a centrally sponsored scheme of 1988 and was aimed at providing an alternative to the pursuit of higher academic education. One of the objective of the Vocational Education Programme of NIOS is to meet the need for skilled and middle level manpower for the growing sectors of economy, both organized and unorganized. The range of Vocational Education courses has been expanding over the years depending upon needs of learners and market demands. The present Vocational Education courses of NIOS are meant for both urban and rural sectors. Courses for the women is highlighted in the Table 1.

(2) National Commission for Minorities Educational Institutions (NCMEI) 2004

The Department of Secondary and Higher Education, Ministry of HRD, Government of India constituted the commission with its head quarters in Delhi. The genesis of the National Commission for

Table 1: Major vocational courses emphasizing women empowerment offered by the Institute of Open Schooling (NIOS)

Sl. No	*Title of the Course*	*Duration*	*Entry Qualification*
1	Secretarial practice	One year	Senior secondary
2	Certificate in rural health for women (Gram sakhi) a. Basics of health care b. Health and environment c. Health education d. Health extension activities	One year	IV class pass
3	Advanced certificate in rural health for women a. Communication skills in health education b. Medical, clinical and diagnostic skills c. Health management d. Emerging issues in health care.	One year	Passouts of certificate in rural health for women.
4	Certificate in care of elderly a. Basic life sciences b. Aspects of aging c. General care and specific needs of elderly	One year	Senior secondary
5	Certificate in computer applications a. Basic computing skills b. Computer applications	One year	Senior secondary
6	Diploma basic rural technology a. Home and health b. Agriculture c. Material, mechanics, energy and environment	One year	Not prescribed
7	Certificate in yoga	Six months	Secondary
8	Jan swasthya	One year	Senior secondary
9	Cutting and tailoring	Six months	No prescribed
10	Dress making	Six months	Below secondary
11	Poultry farming	One year	Senior secondary
12	Play center management	One year	Senior secondary
13	Paripurna mahila	One year	Secondary

Minority Educational Institutions can be traced to the UPA governments manifesto called 'National Common Minimum Programme'. A bill was introduced in the parliament in December, 2004 and both houses passed the bill to enact The National Commission for Minority Educational Institutions Act 2004 as amended by NCMEI (Amendment Act 2006). The commission is to look into specific complaints regarding deprivation or violation of rights of minorities to establish and administer educational institutions of their choice. Protection of rights of minorities are enshrined in Article 30 of the constitution which states that "all minorities, whether based on religion or language shall have the right to establish and administer educational institution of their choice". This is the first time that a specific commission has been established for protection and safeguard the rights of minorities to establish and administer educational institutions of their choice. This commission is a quasi-judicial body and has been endowed with the power of a civil court. It is headed by a Chairman who has been a judge of the Delhi High Court and two members to be nominated by central government. The commission was entrusted with adjudicatory function, advisory function and recommendary powers. The empowerment of the commission has provided a much needed forum for the minority educational institutions to highlight their grievances and get speedy relief. The subject matter of a complaint include non issue of no objection certificate (NOC) by the state government, delay in issue of minority status, refusal to allow to open new schools and colleges, refusal to permit additional courses, refusal to release grants in aid, refusal to give financial assistance, denial of permission to create new appointment of teachers, denying the approval of appointment of teachers, non equality in pay scales of teachers as compared to government school teachers, denial of teaching aids and other facilities like computers, library, laboratory, etc. By treating Minority Educational Institutions on par with government institutions, should investigate into the matters of non availability of books in Urdu in all subject for students of Urdu school, non appointment of Urdu knowing teachers, inadequate payment to Madrasa employees, non-release of grants to Madrasa, non payment of retirement benefit to teachers and non teaching staff of minority schools, extension of Sarva Shiksha Abhiyan facilities to Minority Educational Institution especially in the deprived rural areas.

(3) Nai Roshni The Scheme for Leadership Development of Minority Women 2012-13

Ministry of Minority Affairs has started this Scheme to cover women belonging to all minorities notified under Section 2(c) of the National Commission for Minorities Act, 1992 including Muslims, Sikhs, Christians, Buddhists and Parsis. To bring solidarity and unity through their own efforts to improve the scheme permits a representative mix of women from SCs/STs/OBCs, Women with disabilities and non-minority communities not exceeding 25% of a project proposal. The trainees shall be selected among the Elected Women Representatives (EWRs) from any community under the Panchayati Raj Institutions. The scheme aims to empower and build confidence among minority women, including their neighbours from other communities living in the same village by providing knowledge, tools and techniques for interacting with government systems, banks and other institutions at all levels. It also aims for empowerment of women from the minority communities to move out of the confines of their home and community and assume leadership roles and assert their rights, collectively or individually in accessing services, facilities, skills and opportunities beside claiming their due share of development benefits of the government for improving their lives and living conditions.

(a) Non-residential training in the Village/Urban locality

The training shall be conducted in the village by using existing facilities or rented permanent structure. The duration of the training shall be for six days and each day will be of six hours. Each batch of 25 trainees will be trained separately. Care should be taken to ensure that the dates for training are fixed in order to avoid festive occasions and demands of seasons. Printed training material in local language would be prepared by the organization within the framework of training modules. The training course, will be provided with stipend to partially compensate the loss of wage would be given to the beneficiary along with a meal and crèche arrangement for their children while the training is ongoing during the day. The implementing agency would open the account in the banks for those women trainees who do not have their own accounts and transfer the stipend amount to their bank accounts electronically. At least two third of the trainers engaged by the organization shall be women and they should be able to deliver their inputs in the local language of the area on the topics given in the training module.

(b) Residential leadership development training

Selected eligible women would be imparted leadership training in Residential Training Institutes. For approving residential trainings in training institutes, the institute concerned must have boarding/lodging arrangements for at least 25 women in a secured location. Printed training material in local language will be provided. Each batch of 25 trainees will be trained separately. The entire training fees, training materials, boarding, food, refreshment and travel expenses would be covered under the scheme. The trainees would be also given stipend for the duration of the training period. The implementing agency would open the account in the banks for those women trainees who do not have their own accounts and transfer the stipend amount to their bank accounts electronically. The organization carrying out training for leadership development of minority women would be responsible to select women who are capable of becoming trainers and assume leadership role to be trained in accordance with the criteria of the scheme.

(4) Maulana Azad National Fellowship for Minority Students

The objective is to provide integrated five years fellowship in the form of financial assistance to students from minority communities, as notified by the central government to pursue higher studies such as M.Phil and Ph.D. The fellowship will cover all the universities recognized by the University Grants Commission under section 2(f) and section 3 of the UGC Act and will be implemented by the Ministry of Minority Affairs. The total number of fellowships each year will be 756. In case of non availability of adequate number of candidates, the number of fellowships not availed during a year will be carried forward to the next academic session. 30% of the fellowship shall be for women and remaining 70% is for male. For M.Phil course the duration of fellowship is for 2 years and for integrated M.Phil and

Ph.D course fellowship for 2 years and admissibility of JRF and SRF for the remaining 3 years. Preference will be given to the candidates who deal with research topics pertaining to linguistic minorities, their language, protection of language, promotion of script, etc. in case the numbers of candidates exceed the number of available awards, UGC will select the candidates for the fellowships based on the percentage of marks obtained by them in their qualifying Post Graduation examination. The fellowships will be operated on the basis of a roster in which firstly given to Arts, then to Commerce, after which for Science and next for Engineering.

(a) Quantum of fellowship

The quantum of fellowship for JRF and SRF will be at par with the UGC fellowship as amended from time to time. Presently these rates are as follows. Fellowship at Rs. 12,000/- per month for initial two years as Junior Research Fellowship and at Rs. 14,000/- per month for remaining tenure under Senior Research Fellowship. Contingency for Arts and Commerce branches at Rs. 10,000/- per annum for initial two years and at Rs. 20,500/- per annum for remaining three years. Contingency for Sciences and Engineering branches at Rs. 12,000/- per annum for initial two years and at Rs. 25,000/- per annum for remaining three years. Departmental assistance for the host institution for providing infrastructure at Rs. 3,000/- per annum per student and Escort or Reader Assistance at Rs. 2,000/- per month in case of physically and visually challenged candidates. The fellowship holders under this fellowship will be known as Ministry of Minority Affairs scholars. Eligibility is restricted to only minority community notified under section 2(c) of the National Commission for Minorities Act, 1992. The candidate should have registered for regular and full time M.Phil/Ph.D Course in any university by fulfilling conditions of admission of that university, the minority students once considered eligible for the fellowship shall not be entitled to benefits under any other source, central or state government or bodies like UGC for the same study, Prior clearance of NET/SLET examination will not be a prerequisite for award of this scholarship. In order to qualify for the award of JRF/SRF the UGC norms would be applicable at pre-M.Phil and Pre-Ph.D stage, respectively, including the minimum score of 50% at the Post Graduate Level. UGC will select the candidates for award of this scholarship in a transparent manner. UGC shall disburse the fellowship amount to the candidates through electronic clearance system (ECS) wherever feasible. The decision of UGC in regard to awarding is final and no appeal would lie against any decision except provided under the law in force. The income ceiling of the parents/guardians of the candidate for this scholarship will be Rs. 2.5 Lakh per annum (Refer Tables 2 and 3).

Table 2: JRF/ SRF rates per candidate for arts and commerce branches*

Year	*Fellowship per month*	*Contingency per annum*	*Departmental assistance per annum*	*Total*
1(JRF)	Rs. 12,000 × 12 = Rs. 1,44,000	Rs. 10,000	Rs. 3000	Rs. 1,57,000
2(JRF)	Rs. 12,000 × 12 = Rs. 1,44,000	Rs. 10,000	Rs. 3000	Rs. 1,57,000
3(SRF)	Rs. 14,000 × 12 = Rs. 1,68,000	Rs. 20,500	Rs. 3000	Rs. 1,91,500
4(SRF)	Rs. 14,000 × 12 = Rs. 1,68,000	Rs. 20,500	Rs. 3000	Rs. 1,91,500
5(SRF)	Rs. 14,000 × 12 = Rs. 1,68,000	Rs. 20,500	Rs. 3000	Rs. 1,91,500
Total	**Rs. 7,92,000**	**Rs. 81,500**	**Rs. 15,000**	Rs. 8,88,500**

*Ministry of Minority Affairs, Government of India, 2016.

***Note*: Escort/Reader Assistance is provided @ Rs. 2000 per month in cases of physically and visually challenged candidates.

(5) Maulana Azad National Scholarship Scheme for Meritorious Girl Students of Minority

Maulana Azad Education Foundation was established on the occasion of Maulana Abdul Kalam Azad's birth centenary. The foundation is registered under the Societies Registration Act, 1860, on 6th July, 1989. The foundation is a voluntary Non Profit Social Service Organisation. It was established to promote education among the educationally backward sections of the society. It is funded by the Ministry of Minority Affairs, Government of India. It introduced National Scholarship Scheme to recognize, promote and assist

Table 3: JRF/ SRF rates per candidate for science and engineering branches*

Year	*Fellowship per month*	*Contingency per annum*	*Departmental assistance per annum*	*Total*
1(JRF)	Rs. 12,000 × 12 = Rs. 1,44,000	Rs. 12,000	Rs. 3000	Rs. 1,59,000
2(JRF)	Rs. 12,000 × 12 = Rs. 1,44,000	Rs. 12,000	Rs. 3000	Rs. 1,59,000
3(SRF)	Rs. 14,000 × 12 = Rs. 1,68,000	Rs. 25,000	Rs. 3000	Rs. 1,96,000
4(SRF)	Rs. 14,000 × 12 = Rs. 1,68,000	Rs. 25,000	Rs. 3000	Rs. 1,96,000
5(SRF)	Rs. 14,000 × 12 = Rs. 1,68,000	Rs. 25,000	Rs. 3000	Rs. 1,96,000
Total	**Rs. 7,92,000**	**Rs. 99,000**	**Rs. 15,000**	Rs. 9,06,000**

*Ministry of Minority Affairs, Government of India, 2016.

***Note*: Escort/Reader Assistance is provided @ Rs. 2000 per month in cases of physically and visually challenged candidates.

meritorious girl students who cannot continue their education without financial support. The Scholarship is given to student passing S.S.L.C. Exam and taking admission in 11th in the year after declaration of 10th standard result. Applications received in subsequent years is not considered. Only girl students belonging to National Minorities, *i.e.* Muslims, Christians, Buddhists, Sikhs and Parsis who have secured not less than 55% aggregate marks in the tenth standard. Family income of the student from all sources should be less than Rs. 1,00,000 in the preceding financial year. She should have confirmed admission to Class XI. The institution offering admission should be recognized by the Government or other competent authority. A student getting a scholarship from any other source would not be eligible for this scholarship, the last date of receiving the application by the foundation is 30th September which must be adhered to and the amount of scholarship will be Rs. 12,000/- (Rupees Twelve Thousand Only) which will be released in two installments of Rs. 6000/- each. The first installment will be released after sanction of scholarship and the second installment will be released when the student submits proof of passing class 11th and admission to class 12th is sought.

(6) Educational Loan from National Minorities Development Finance Corporation

The NMDFC extends educational loans with an objective to facilitate job oriented education for the eligible persons belonging to Minorities. Under the scheme a maximum amount of Rs. 10 Lakhs is available at the rate Rs. 2 Lakhs per annum for technical and professional courses of durations not exceeding five years. An amount of Rs. 3 lakhs is available for short duration cost intensive skill development training having duration upto 01 year. Further for courses abroad, a maximum amount of 20 lakhs is available at Rs 4 lakhs per annum for a course duration of maximum 5 years. Funds for this purpose are made available to the State Channelizing Agencies at an interest of 1% per annum for on lending to the beneficiaries at 3% interest per annum. The loan is payable in maximum five years after completion of the course.

C. WOMEN EDUCATION: NEW CONSISTENT LEARNING MODEL[10]

Adults do not learn for the sake of learning, they learn to be able to perform a task, to solve a problem, or live in a more satisfied way. Hence there is a need for organizing learning experiences around life situations rather than sticking on to the syllabus of study. A climate conducive to learning is important in this approach, which would be characterized by mutual respect between teacher and students, encouragement for collaboration and cooperation among students, openness and authenticity on the part of the teacher. The teacher should help to design and execute their learning plans. Initially the teacher should give a skeleton over the subject by lecture,

[10] Pradeep M.D., Aithal P.S., (2015). Learning Through Team Centric Exercise & Key Point Pedagogy-An effective Learning Model for Slow Learners in Social Work Education Training in International Journal of Multidisciplinary Research and Development bearing, Volume 2, Issue 9, Sept, Impact Factor 4.342, e-ISSN No 2349-4182, pp. 265-270.

encourage group work over the topic delivered and individual support and guidance to get deep understanding (Toohey, 1999)[11]. It is the joint responsibility of learner, teacher and community through negotiation seek empowerment. The educator should be a facilitator of learning rather transmitter of information (Hokenstad and Rigby, 1977)[12]. According to the critical pedagogical ideology, the educator is not the pre-eminent possessor of knowledge. Learners also bring their own interpretative powers to life experiences. Both are co-sharers in the creation of what is known. When no particular interpretation deserves to have a privileged status, then the intellectual skill of critique is essential. Students must learn how to approach whatever content is presented with means for critically assessing its virtues and shortcomings. To prepare students as reflective practioners, there is a need for expanded ways for them to appreciate their own wisdom and creativity (Weick, 1994)[13]. According to Heany (1995)[14]. The process of liberatory education, which is dialogical, affirms the mutual and co-equal roles of teachers and learners and, therefore, appropriate for women education and training. The dialogical approach to learning is characterized by cooperation and acceptance of inter-changeability and mutuality in the roles of teacher and learner, demanding an atmosphere of mutual acceptance and trust. In this method, all teach and all learn. Without dialogue, there is no communication, and without communication there can be no liberatory education. Team centric learning exercise & key point pedagogy model is named as 'Pradeep Consistent Learning Model" developed by Mr. Pradeep after observing the learning pattern of slow learners in social work education since past 7 years. This model will inter-link learning environment, Pedagogy,

---

[11] Toohey S, (1999). Designing courses for Higher Education, Buckingham: Open University Press, 1999.

[12] Hokenstad M.C. and Rigby B.D., (1977). Participation in Teaching and Learning an Idea Book for Social Work Educators". New York- International Association of Schools of Social Work.

[13] Weick A., (1994). Reconstructing Social Work Education. J. Laird (Ed.) Revisioning Social Work Education-A social Reconstructionist Approach, New York, The Haworth Press, pp. 11-30.

[14] Heaney, T. Issues in Freirean pedagogy. Thresholds in Education/"Freire Issues" Section 1995, Retrieved on August 7, 2008 from: http://www3.nl.edu/academics/cas/ace/resources/Documents/FreireIssues.cfm.

and Interest of learners thereby improve learning abilities of the students average and slow learners systematically. Hence this model works in facilitating progressive learning of slow learners in the class. According to this model each class of one hour/ one and half hour duration is organized as follows. The Process of Consistent Learning in which each student is asked to paste a chart sheet near to his bed in his room/hostel for oriented learning. The planned topic for the class will be discussed/presented using suitable teaching method by choosing appropriate pedagogy for 45 minutes. After teaching, all groups will be guided to simplify the taught concepts into 'key points'. Within 5 minutes by group exercise. This will encourage group participation and create a healthy inter group competition among the students. This enrich analytical skills and motivates each student to listen to the lecture attentively. Teacher will guide the students to supplement 'key points' with innovative and easy Flowcharts, graphs, pictures, diagrams, formulas which facilitate for easy learning. Any 2 to 3 students are randomly picked by the teacher from any group and asked to briefly present the gist of 'Key Points' to the whole class. This briefing opportunity will make the students to be alert during the group discussion and even improves the confidence and gradually eliminates their stage fear. All the students are oriented to update the 'Key Points' on the chart pasted by them at their room/hostel and motivated to read every day before they go to bed. Day by day the chart will assure confidence about awareness on the subject. Next day the teacher conducts the 'Entry Test' in which a set of questions on the topic discussed in the previous class will be displayed on the board. While the teacher is taking attendance the student get time to memorise the concepts from the chart what he studied in the previous day and Students will be randomly picked to answer the entry test questions from each group. The students who answer the entry test will be appreciated which motivates others to improve themselves and answer in next class (P.S. Aithal 2015). It is a mutual learning method which not only improves the analytical and memorizing capacity of the students but also improves the mentoring, supervision and follow up skills of a teacher. This method can be adopted in any institution of higher education because it is cost worthy, easy to adopt. Hence, this can be considered to be a best practice in Teaching (Refer Fig. 2).

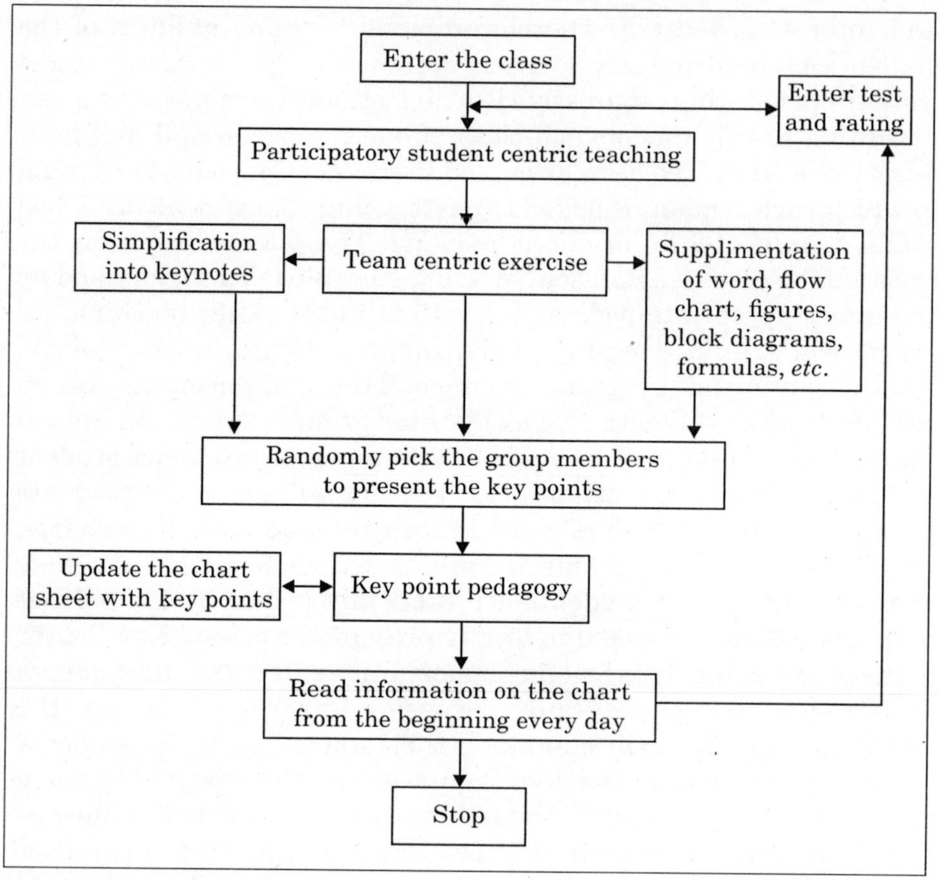

Fig. 2: Flow chart diagram of 'Pradeep Model of Consistent Learning': An Innovative Pedagogy for Women Higher Education.

CONCLUSION

Information collected by the human mind will be correlated with the aware concepts and skills to satisfy the desired purpose. Knowledge guide to assume, use, adopt and control physical, societal changes. Application of knowledge encourage critical or experimental understanding to constitute wisdom. The potentiality and usage of knowledge depends upon the utilization of information. Education institutions have to ensure transmission and dissemination of information among students who aspires to take up women education.

In a participatory method of teaching, it is assumed that knowledge and education are never neutral and the trainers role is to help the participants understand where their own views have come from, to challenge pre-conceptions and to encourage them to consider other possibilities. It assumes that society can be transformed by the engagement of critically conscious persons, through a process of deconstruction, reconstruction and transformation. Participants life experiences are the major source of knowledge in this method. The trainers are not teachers, but facilitators, and partners with the participants in this process of social change.

7

Revolution towards Protection of Women Health

The World Health Organisation defines health as "A state of complete physical, mental and social wellbeing which is essential for leading a productive life, and it is not merely the absence of disease or infirmity". Women Health Status is the foundation for all the success stories in every fields of endeavour. Any serious attempt to improve the health of women must deal with biased social customs, culture, and social norms which will affect their health. There is a need for more comprehensive integrated approach towards health issues to foresee a significant impact over the present conditions of Indian Women[1].

A. POLICY FRAMEWORK FOR WOMEN HEALTH IN INDIA

(1) Integrated Child Development Services (ICDS) 1975

It is the world's largest and unique Scheme designed for protecting the health of pregnant, lactating women and children below 6 years of age for the early childhood care constituted under The Ministry of Women and Child Development (MWCD). It involve integrated package of services covering supplementary nutrition to Mother and

[1] WHO (2004). Voluntary HIV Counselling and Testing Manual for Training of Trainers.

the Child, immunization, medical check-ups, recommendation services, pre-school non-formal education, nutrition and health awareness. It is a centrally funded scheme implemented through the states and union territories. Another modification in the financial responsibility of State and Central has been that instead of 100% support in non-supplementary expenses the Central Government is now only responsible for 90% in all States and Union Territories. In the financial year 2009-2010 the sharing pattern of Supplementary Nutrition for North-eastern States between Centre and States has been changed from 50:50 to 90:10 ratio. In other States and UTs, the pattern continues to be a 50:50 ratio sharing. Anganwadi's are set up according to the population in a given area. ICDS also outlines the amount of calories that the beneficiaries should receive. Anganwadi tries to bridge the gap between the nationally recommended calorie level and average intake of children and women among low income or disadvantaged communities through providng supplementary feeding. A child between the ages 6-72 months should receive 500 calories of food containing 12-15 grams of protein at the cost of Rs. 4 and a child severely malnourished on medical advice after health check-up should receive 800 calories of food containing 20-25 grams of protein at the cost of Rs. 6/- per child/ per day. Every pregnant and lactating mother's should receive 600 calories of food containing 18-20 grams of protein at the cost of Rs. 5/- per beneficiary/ per day. Immunization of pregnant women and infants protects them from diseases like poliomyelitis, diphtheria, pertussis, tetanus, tuberculosis and measles. These are major preventable causes of child mortality, disability, morbidity and related malnutrition. The state is responsible for registering the beneficiaries who are below poverty line. Under the third phase of the ICDS scheme The GOI sanctioned 792 additional Projects, 2,13,286 additional Anganwadi Centres and 77,102 Mini-Anganwadi Centres. To cover SC/ST and minority population in remote rural areas. The eleventh Five Year Plan has set aside Rs. 51,400 crores for ICDS which includes Rs. 9,000/- Crores for Conditional Maternity Benefit Scheme. The ICDS scheme receives aid from Cooperative for Assistance and Relief Everywhere (CARE), UNICEF and the World Food Programme (WFP)[2].

---

[2] Jai Shree Chandra, (1993). Women and Child a Paradigm for Rural Development, Rawat Publications, Jaipur, pp. 37-45.

(2) National Health Policy 1983

Network of comprehensive Primary Health Centres which were linked with expansion in health education emphasising upon the elementary health problems to be resolved by the health volunteers. A referral system was set up at the Community Health Centre. The morbidity and mortality of women in the country were very high. Diseases like malaria and Tuberculosis was widespread. Many more cases of drug resistance came up. The infection got linked with HIV/ AIDS. Undernutrition also continued to be a severe problem with high incidence of macro and micro nutrition deficiencies among women and children resulting in low birth weight babies[3]. The country was far short of meeting the goals set for the year 2000 A.D. under the 'Health for All' pledge taken at Alma Ata because of decline in the public health expenditure. Instead of an increase, both in the central sector as well as in the state sector, in the year 2002, the per capita health expenditure in the country was around Rs. 200/- only. Ever since independence, health which is a state subject under the Indian Constitution, has continued to depend heavily on the provisions under the Central Government Budget.

(3) National Nutrition Policy 1993

Till the end of the IV PIan, India's main emphasis was on the aggregate growth of the economy and reliance was placed on the percolation effects of growth. In the face of continuing poverty and malnutrition, an alternative strategy of development comprising a frontal attack on poverty, unemployment and malnutrition became a national priority from the beginning of' the Fifth Plan. This shift in strategy has given rise to a number of interventions to increase the purchasing power of the poor, to improve the provision of basic services to the poor and to' devise a security system through which the most vulnerable sections of the poor (*viz.* women and children) can be protected.

[3] Srinivasan S. and Natrajan V.K., "Voluntary Health Services in Rural Areas: A Study, Kurukshetra, Vol. XXXV, 2-3, pp. 15-18.

(4) National AIDS Policy 1997

The Government of India adopted the policy to prevent the spread of HIV infection by reducing the social impact and bring collective national efforts from the Government, Non Government, Participatory Rural Institutions. It aims to mobilize support of Non Governmental Organisations and Community Based Organisations for initiating community interventions against AIDS. It sought supportive socio-economic environment for the prevention. The scheme tried to prevent women, children and other socially weak groups from vulnerability to infections by generating Public Health Rationale to overcome the stigma and discrimination against the victims. It created general awareness about the transmission and adoption of safe behavioural practices to prevent the disease from spreading. It ensured proper health care in hospitals and at homes for the care and to have consistent discussions with international agencies for support and cooperation in the field of research, vaccine, drugs for the prevention of AIDS in the country[4].

(5) The Population Policy 2000

Development can be achieved through improving the standard of life of the people by protecting welfare and well being. It is very essential to meet the needs of contraception to keep control over the growing population. The Population policy focus for medium term target to bring the fertility rate to replacement level by 2010. Long term target of achieving stable population by 2045. The panchayats was choosen to promote gender sensitive population stabilization issue with the national support along with the main task of empowering women for improved health and nutrition[5].

(6) New National Health Policy 2002

The role of Central Government and Responsibilities by the State Governments has become the key factors of this plan. Proper usage

---

[4] Sudhir Varma, (2010). Gender, HIV and Social Work, Rawat Publications, New Delhi, pp. 135-136.

[5] Population Policy of India, Government of India, Ministry of Health and Family Welfare.

of Out Patient Departments of the Government hospitals was encouraged. It encouraged the Indian Medicines including Homoeopathy. But the policy could not compel the doctors to work in rural areas hence there was a heavy shortage of lady doctors in the Rural Health Care Institutions. Very few Anaesthetists were available in Primary Health Centres or Community Health Centres. The policy had not given much importance to women health. The poor health status of women was due to the social, cultural and economic factors. The policy was considered to be gender neutral. Even thought it focus on reducing Infant Mortality Rate (IMR) and Maternal Mortality Rate (MMR) there was no improvement in general health status of women. No efforts are channelized towards the Nutrition and access of women to general health care facilities. There were no Gender Budgeting for the medicines which are given free of cost or no travel reimbursement of travel cost to women who seek health care facility. It has not targeted women who cannot reach the health facilities. No quotas to women in the Village, Block and District level Management Boards. Women were kept out from the decision making bodies of health programmes. Being an health care policy it should have been finalized after deliberations with the community at large but failing to which it presumed to be a bureaucratic document. The policy has not done anything to control the population growth, to reduce the prices of essential drugs, to raise the overall quality of medical education and research by private sectors. It simply shifted the main burden of health care to the Private Health Care Sector. Government should take the responsibility to provide basic health care, specialty services, immunization to prevent diseases, maternity services, ambulance, contraceptives and health education. There is a need to strengthen the health systems supported by government for the rural areas and regulate the growing private sector in the urban areas. In the country as a whole many health staff were absent from the duty without intimation on many days. India adopted The Drug Policy in 1986, The National Nutrition Policy in 1993, The National Population Policy 2000, The Policy on Indian System of Medicine in 2002, The Pharmaceutical Policy in 2002 and The Universal Health Insurance Scheme for the Poor in 2003. Announcing more policies will not improve the health conditions of women without proper convergence[6].

[6] National Health Policy (2002). Government of India, Ministry of Health and Family Welfare.

(7) National Rural Health Mission (NRHM) April 2005

It is an initiative undertaken by the Government of India to address the health needs of under served rural areas launched by then Prime Minister Manmohan Singh. Initially this scheme targeted the health needs of 18 states which had weak public health indicator. The Union Cabinet headed by Dr. Anbumani Ramadoss approved the launch of National Urban Health Mission (NUHM) and National Rural Health Mission as the sub missions of National Health Mission. Accredited Social Health Activists (ASHAs) were engaged for establishing a link between the community and the health systems. They will assist women and children of deprived sections of the population to avail health services this increased the utilization of outpatient services, diagnostic facilities, institutional deliveries and inpatient care. The Rogi Kalyan Samiti (Patient Welfare Committee) and Hospital Management Society acts as a group of trustees for the hospitals affairs. United Grants to sub centers have been used to improve the efficacy of Auxiliary Nurse Midwives (ANMs) and their capacity is build for better antenatal care and other health care services, Village Health Sanitation and Nutrition Committee (VHSNC) for increasing their involvement in their local communities to address the needs of the poor households. It supported co location of AYUSH Services in Health facilities in PHCs, CHCs and District Hospitals. The initiatives include Janani Suraksha Yojana (JSY) to control Maternal Mortality among pregnant women by encouraging them to deliver using government health facilities through cash assistance. National Mobile Medical Units (NMMUs) covered many unserved areas. National Ambulance Services Free services in every place in the country connected with a toll free number and assured service within 30 minutes of the call. Janani Shishu Suraksha Karyakram (JSSK) to provide free to and fro transport, free drugs, free diagnostic, free blood, free diet to pregnant women who come for delivery in public health institutions and sick infants up to one year. Rashtriya Bal Swasthya Karyakram (RBSK) Child Health Screening and Early Intervention Services has been launched in February 2013 to screen diseases specific to childhood, developmental delays, disabilities, birth defects and deficiencies covering 27 crore children between 0–18 years of age along with the free treatment including surgery. Mother and Child Health Wings (MCH Wings) to reduce maternal and child mortality, dedicated Mother and Child Health Wings with 100/50/30 bed capacity have been sanctioned in high case load district hospitals and CHCs which would create additional beds for mothers and children. Free Drugs and Free Diagnostic Service to lower the out of pocket expenditure on health. District Hospital and Knowledge Center (DHKC) to provide Multi-specialty health care including dialysis care, intensive cardiac care, cancer treatment, mental illness, emergency medical and trauma care, etc. These hospitals would act as the knowledge support for clinical care in facilities below it through a tele-medicine center located in the district headquarters and developed as centers for training of paramedics and nurses. National Iron+ Initiative to look at Iron Deficiency Anaemia in which beneficiaries will receive iron and folic acid supplementation irrespective of their Iron/Hb status[7].

(8) Prevention of HIV/AIDS

By the early 90s of the 20th Century HIV was not a worry for the health professionals. The concept of stigma, discrimination filled with hate, violation of human rights should be brought within the perview of the law to safeguard an HIV infected person. According to UNICEF, during 2000-2006, only 24% of females in the age group 15-24 had comprehensive knowledge of HIV/AIDS and only 22% women used condom in high risk sex. With a growing number of women infected with the virus, it is very important to know whether the existing programmes are reaching them in the remotest and the poorest areas of the country or not. The test of the success of an existing programmes is not a survey in the urban or semi-urban areas but in the far-flung rural areas where women are becoming a prey to the virus in large numbers. As it is necessary to explain to the target group the exact nature of transmission of the virus. As most of these women are illiterate the only way to explain is by audio methods or by illustration, both of which are yet to be accepted by the orthodox and self proclaimed protectors of Indian culture[8].

---

[7] Manual of Integrated Management Information System for NRHM (2005). Department of Women Welfare, Ministry of Human Resource Development, Government of India, New Delhi.

[8] National Federation and Social Programmes (2001). Social Work Manifesto on HIV/AIDS. January.

(9) Health Conditions of Women Since 1990

The National Family Health Survey (NFHS) was initiated in India in the early 1990s. This was conducted under the stewardship of the Ministry of Health and Family Welfare (MoHFW), Government of India, with the International Institute for Population Sciences (IIPS) as the nodal agency, and technical assistance of United States Agency for International Development (USAID) through ICF Macro (presently known as ICF International). USAID has been the primary funder of the NFHS surveys, but for the most recent survey (NFHS-3) DFID, the Bill and Melinda Gates Foundation, UNICEF, UNFPA and the Government of India have also provided funds. NACO and the National AIDS Research Institute (NARI) provided technical assistance for the HIV component of NFHS-3. The major objective of the NFHS has been to strengthen India's demographic and health database by providing information that are reliable to strengthen the survey research capabilities of Indian institutions to dissiminate high quality data to meet the country's needs for data on emerging health and family welfare issues[9].

(10) Sexually Transmitted Infections (STIs)

According to the WHO, more than one million new cases of sexually transmitted bacterial infections occur worldwide every day. Health protection from Sexually Transmitted Diseases (STDs) can be more severe in women as compared to men. There is an increased risk of infertility, pelvic inflammatory disease (PID), Still births, etc. in spite of massive investments in maternity care, family welfare, mother and child immunization and nutrition, the planners have lost sight of the prevention and treatment of STDs. It is not widely known that unlike HIV, STDs can be transmitted through simple kissing also. Pregnant mothers can transmit these infections to the child also. The India Health Report on Nutrition 2015 offers a critical analysis of the current situation with nutrition at the national and state levels in India. It provides easy-to-understand, state-wise data dashboards for 28 states and Delhi that give a comprehensive view

[9] National AIDS Control Organisation, (2008). Government of India, Mainstreaming gender in HIV Programmes. Draft for Review. March 19.

of nutrition and its determinants. It looks at disparities in these outcomes and their multiple determinants across geographical regions, socio-economic classes, and demographic groups and helps identify strategic choices for policy-making at the state level[10].

(11) Initiation by Voluntary Organisation

Many voluntary organizations which are either self financed or aided by the government are working for improving the health standard of the country. Prominent role is played by Swami Vivekananda Youth Movement (1984) a voluntary organisation belonging to state of Karnataka aims to provide equitable, high quality healthcare through sustainable mechanisms, with active community involvement and in line with the organizational interpretation of core values. From a modest beginning with basic health care clinics at Chinnadagudihundi and Thumnerale villages in Nanjangud Taluk of Mysore District in Karnataka State, to the well equipped multi-speciality hospital at Saragur. It has developed a multitude of programs and projects that comprehensively address the health needs of the community. Rural Health initiatives now are grouped under a program named Rural Oriented Health Initiative (ROHINI) aiming to improve the health and well being of the rural population through improved quality and access to health services. The programme has been conceptualized and structured to holistically meet the needs of the rural and tribal communities and to create maximum impact. Through this initiative, the organization is evolving a novel, sustainable and replicable model in rural health care. Reproductive & Child Health (RCH) Program (2000) with an aim to improve the health status of women and children of tribal and rural communities in H.D. Kote Taluk and to empower women to take decisions regarding their health and well being. The programme is striving towards achieving the relevant Millennium Development Goals, Reduction of Under-5 Mortality Rate and HIV prevalence covering issues like ante-intra-post natel care, family planning, immunization, reproductive track infections in women, fertility, childhood diseases and adolescent health. According to NACO, Karnataka is a high risk

[10] National Institute of Allergy and Infectious Disease and NIH, USA HIV Infection in Women. May (2006).

state, having one of the highest Antenatal Clinic HIV and General Population HIV prevalence rates in the country. In order to target this population, SVYM works not only to treat the medical and psychosocial needs of people living with HIV/AIDS, but also targets populations at risk for contracting the disease, trains physicians, counselors and other health care professionals across the state on specific issues and partners with other NGOs as well as the government to make policy changes at the state and national level.[11] The XI Plan recognized women as heterogenous category with special consideration for the vulnerable women belonging to scheduled castes, scheduled tribes, religious minorities, single women, elderly, victims of HIV/AIDS, Migrant Labour, Disables, etc.

B. NATIONAL FAMILY HEALTH SURVEYS (NFHS) IN INDIA

(1) NFHS Survey-1 (1992- 93)

The NFHS covers the population of 24 states and the National Capital Territory of Delhi containing 99% of the population of India. This is a household survey with an overall sample size of 89,777 covering ever married women between the age of 13-49. The following are the highlights of the survey. The age for marriage among women range between 25 to 49 years. It was 21.7 years in Goa, 15 years in Madhya Pradesh, Rajasthan, Uttar Pradesh, Bihar, Andhra Pradesh. The legal age of marriage of 18 years was not followed. 28.7% was the Crude Birth Rate (CBR), Total Fertility Rate (TFR) in rural was 3.7% and in urban it was 2.7% and among High school educated women it was 2.2% and illiterate women it was 4%. The highest TFR was recorded in Uttar Pradesh with 4.8%. The knowledge of family planning is nearly universal in India with 99% in Urban area and 94% in Rural. In contrast to widespread knowledge of sterilization, knowledge of the three officially sponsored temporary methods like IUD, Pill and Condom is much less widespread. One forth of the currently married women do not know any of the modern

[11] Annual Report of Swami Vivekananda Youth Movement, April 2008 to March (2009).

temporary methods. Well known modern method was pill (66%), IUD (61%), Condom (58%) and injection was least known to (19%). Female sterilization was frequently used method and very few couples used condoms. The contraceptives among SC and ST women were very low. The contraceptives were offered from the Primary Health Centres. Level of knowledge increased with age through age 30-34 and stays very high between the age of 45-49 years. Religious differences in the use of contraceptives are even more substantial than the differences by education. The prevalence rate is high among Jains (63%), lowest among Muslims (28%). As The Government projected the use of female Sterilization and IUD, many women voluntarily choose to undergo Sterilization. ORS Therapy was known to only 15% mothers but they have not availed it. Infant Mortality Rate (IMR) was 52% in rural areas and the death of children born to illiterate mothers was 250% greater than the mothers with high school education hence, the mothers education was very important to improve child health. The Maternal Mortality Rate (MMR) was 437. Nearly lakhs of women died due to the illness arising out of pregnancy and childbirth. Nearly 37% did not received antenatal care. The universal immunization programme was a partial failure with only 35% beneficiaries. Chronic under nutrition prevailed with more than half of the children below 5 years of age resulted in under weight. Majority women do not know about HIV/AIDS.

(2) NFHS-2 (1998-99)

The survey showed major problems with the implementation of health and family welfare policies. The sex ratio improved slightly from 944 to 949. Inspite of the expansion of health facilities, there was many inherent lacunas in the government health services hence only 29% people used it and others depended on the private sector. Nearly 50% of women married before attaining the age of 18 years. Crude birth rate was declined by 4% from 29 to 25. Total Fertility Rate in rural areas was high with 3.1%. It was concluded that mere rise in the literacy rate without realizing the importance of reducing fertility will not be so significant. Women are exploited sexually as they were getting pregnant without their desire. Although the preference of son syndrome in the society, still women did not wanted to keep producing once they had two sons or two sons and one daughter. The government of Uttar Pradesh, Rajasthan, Bihar and Madhya Pradesh did not bothered to control the alarming state with high fertility rate. Between 1992-1999 the knowledge about contraceptive methods had grown tremendously. The use of condom and pill was not familiar as the government projected only female sterilization. After many measures by the government the contraceptive prevalence was only raised to 7% from 41 to 48%. Women in Andhra Pradesh, Karnataka, Maharashtra, West Bengal and Tamil Nadu got sterilized at an age lower than 24 years due to the higher literacy rates. The supply of contraceptives by the hospitals in the day time was not effective as all the couples used to go for work in the days. The government also failed to organize discussions on family planning in general with women. The need is felt for awareness generation before and after the marriage about contraception, need for spacing of children, possibilities of HIV/AIDS and STDs after sterilization. The crude death rate was remained at 9.7% 1000. At 540 deaths of women per one lakh live births primarily due to severe anaemia resulting in bleeding, low institutional deliveries, child marriages. The poor health lead to easy victimization of women to HIV. By 1999 the states like Mizoram, Tamil Nadu, Andhra Pradesh and Karnataka knew about adverse affects of AIDS[12].

(3) NFHS-3 (2005-06)

It is the largest survey on health in the country. It found that dropping out of students from the education is very high. The number of Girls who were encouraged to education was remarkably less. In the educational status of women there is a huge gap between the rural and urban sectors. Among adults 40% of women have never been to schools and only 20% passed out from the schools among the enrolled. The median age at marriage for women in the country continued below to 17.2%. High rate of fertility rate was observed. As majority women were married during their teenage between 15-19 years, 16% of them already delivered their first child. The intervals between

[12] National Family Health Survey, NFHS-2, (1998-99). Key findings. International Institute for Population Sciences.

the two births was observed to be 31 months. The knowledge about contraception like pill, IUD and condom has increased but the easiest method of female sterilization continued to be common. Most of the women get sterilized before they reach the age of 26 years. Girls have higher child mortality rate because of indifference from the families. There found a greater relationship between the education level of mother and infant mortality rate. Only 55% of just born children are put to breast feeding hence, many were put away from the colostrums and antibodies of mother, hence given way for more susceptible infections and early death. Higher risk sex was found among SCs and STs. Only 61% of women were heard about AIDS. The NACO has revised the HIV estimate to 2.4 million persons which is 0.36% in the national average in India[13].

(4) NFHS-4 (2014-15)

National Sample Survey designed to provide information on population, family planning, maternal and child health, child survival, HIV/AIDS and sexually transmitted infections (STIs), reproductive health, and nutrition in India. The survey will involve interviewing randomly selected women ages 15-49 years and a sub-sample of men ages 15-54 years. It is implemented by a group of Field Agencies and Population Research Centres (PRCs). These Field Agencies will be selected by following a rigorous selection procedure. Technical assistance is provided by ICF International, USA. It is funded by the United States Agency for International Development (USAID), DFID, the Bill and Melinda Gates Foundation (BMGF), UNICEF, UNFPA, the Mac Arthur Foundation and the Ministry of Health and Family Welfare (MoHFW), Government of India. This survey is conducted to provide essential data on health and family welfare needed by the Ministry and other agencies for policy and programme purposes. It will provide estimates of the levels of fertility, infant and child mortality, family welfare and health indicators background characteristics at the national and state levels. It will measure welfare and health indicators over time at the national and state levels. Information on several other emerging issues including

[13] National Family Health Survey, NFHS-3. (2005-06). Reports. International Institute for Population Sciences, Mumbai.

prenatal mortality, Adolescent reproductive health, high-risk sexual behaviour, safe injections, tuberculosis, and malaria, non-communicable diseases, use of emergency contraception and HIV prevalence for adult women and men at the national level and for 11 State/UTs including high HIV prevalence states. It was found that more than half of the children in 10 out of 15 states are still anaemic. It also showed that more than half of women were anaemic in eleven states. 13 States like Andhra Pradesh, Bihar, Goa, Haryana, Karnataka, Madhya Pradesh, Meghalaya, Sikkim, Tamil Nadu, Telangana, Tripura, Uttrakhand, West Bengal and two Union Territories of Andaman and Nicobar Islands and Puducherry show promising improvements in maternal and child health and nutrition. 15 States/Union Territories indicate that fewer children are dying in infancy and early childhood. After the last round of National Family Health Survey in 2005-06, infant mortality has declined in all first phase States/Union Territories for which trend data are available. All 15 States/Union Territories have rates below 51 deaths per 1,000 live births, although there is considerable variation among the States/Union Territories. Infant mortality rates range from a low of 10 in Andaman and Nicobar Islands to a high of 51 deaths per 1000 live births in Madhya Pradesh[14].

CONCLUSION

The cultural norms pertaining to the attitude towards marriage, age of marriage, the value attached to fertility, importance to sex, the pattern of family structure, and the ideal role expectation from women through social conventions definitely affects women health. Traditional Society confines women life to the family, specifies the degree of her access to medical care, education, nutrition and other accessories of health. Societal gender bias resulted in malnutrition and low priority for health services of women. Presently women are facing high risk of malnutrition, retardation in growth and development, disease, disability and even death during infancy, early childhood, adolescence, the reproductive age and during old age, they

[14] National Family Health Survey, NFHS-4. (2014-15). Reports. International Institute for Population Sciences, Mumbai.

are exposed to the threats of breast and uterus cancer. Hence, the improvements in female health status depends upon a number of non health components such as education, skill development, income generation, opportunities for decision making and the availability of basic support services to carry out her multiple roles. Thus, it is essential to address the causes of women's ill health by identifying the measures to improve the social and health situation through the multi-sectoral package. Rural Primary Health Centre and Family Welfare Centres are working to create health consciousness among the marginalized. The Institutional Deliveries are initiated in The National Rural Health Mission (NRHM) and Janani Suraksha Yojana (JSY). International aid is also granted by The World Health Organisation, World Bank and Ford Foundation. Domestic empowerment focus upon her reproductive rights to decide the number, timing and spacing of her children.

8

Political Empowerment of Women

It is the fundamental right of every citizen to contribute to the decision making process. The New Delhi Document on Women in Development (1985) recognized that despite the rapid growth of informal political activity by women, their role in the formal political structure had virtually remained unchanged. This recognition has resulted in a serious debate on the concepts and indicators for political participation. Under National Plan of Action for Women 1976 The Government of India and United Nations gave importance for the issues of health, education and employment. Subsequent National Documents prepared at the time of the Nairobi Conference of 1985, the Non Aligned Meet of 1985 and The Forward looking strategies afterwards, have recognized the issues related to the nature of political participation of women, the problems faced therein and the strategies to be evolved for empowerment. The political participation of women does not merely include the electoral and administrative processes but the bearing on the political processes in voting, supporting the political groups, communication with the legislators, dissemination of political views and opinions among the electorates and other allied activities. Political participation always involve an organized activity that affects the power relationships in the society. political participation not only include the activities which formally empower the women to make decisions but also the intension to influence the attitudes and behaviour of those people who have powers for decision making. In fact, protests and demonstrations against those in power also form part of political participation.

Women participation has covered a range of activities including movements, protests and support meetings on all issues connected with labour, dowry, rape, domestic violence, price rise, food adultration, deforestation, etc. creating awareness about political issues are the urgent requirement for the present days which may remove the obstacles in the way of political empowerment of women and enrich their political participation. Democracy being the system for the people, by the people and off the people will get public acceptance at genuine spirit only when men and women contributes equally in the process of decision making. Political parties being at the core of democracy should promulgate for more incorporation of women into decision making positions. Self Help Group (SHG) Movement have accelerated the phase of women centric activities covering income generation, training, leadership development, social service, self employment, micro credit, etc. at the local and community levels. Women Associations and Clubs are motivating the members to be active in the society by building confidence which helped in sharing information and knowledge in the grossroot levels. Women are actively participating in Gram Sabhas, conduct frequent visits to the panchayat office, participate in the public meetings and try to understand about the various schemes and programmes for them. Still low self-esteem, ignorance and lack of awareness about the political ideologies are the major cause for low rate of mobilization among women in local governance. Encouraging women to participate in political decision making process is a great challenge due to the lack of civic consciousness, problem of illiteracy, lack of political education and lack of knowledge about the working system of government. Due to the domestic constraints and social restrictions most of the women are not allowed to participate in Gram Sabhas hence, they are not getting any opportunity to project their domestic problems before the local self government hence the gross root development has become steady. The following initiatives are sought as a remedy for all the problems pertaining to women in political field like organizing Mass Awareness Programmes about gender equity and positive discrimination for women, promotion of more women through the field level executives in the village levels into public domain, organizing Skill up gradation through various training, Imparting political education to rural women by the Government Agencies and Voluntary Organisations and sensitization about women role and responsibility in the decision making process. According to Prof. Mohannarayana K.S. (2010) The political awareness programmes to women organized by NGO's and government agencies should aim to raise the knowledge of members of self help groups towards political ideologies, should motivate them to play positive role in grossroot politics for strengthening the democracy, enriching democratic culture through sensitization, should mainstream gender in the local governance, capacity building to participate in decision making process, to impart political education to the rural mass.[1] Political participation of women is limited due to a nexus of traditional factors like dominance of Indian politics by considerations of caste, class, religion, feudal and family status, etc. mainly the patriotical forces that work in favour of men against women. Consequently, women are still left on the periphery of the political process, and political participation remains a day dream to most of the women. Hence, political participation seeks to reorganize the lives of people and ensure that the participation by women is not underestimated by being branded 'non-political' instead it shall be considered as 'social' in nature[2].

(1) WOMEN IN GOVERNANCE

The true spirit of democracy cannot be realized if marginalized women is kept outside the perview of political system. Gender equity is a pre-requisite for effective participation of women in strengthening the institutional structure of democracy. Women have been marginalized because of several socio-economic constraints. It is also found that the average representation of women MPs (12.15%) is higher than the women MLAs (9%) in state assemblies. Even though the number is rising the representation by women is not up to the expected level, especially when the ideal number should be at least 33 percent. The number of women in leadership positions at the local, village, district, state and national level is still not proportionate

[1] Mohannarayana K.S. (2010). Mobilisation of Women for Local Governance through Political Empowerment Programmes for SHGs, Shodha, Biannual Bilingual Research Journal, Experimental Journal, July.

[2] Neeta Tapan (2000). Need for Women Empowerment, Rawat Publications, Jaipur, pp. 53-57.

with their numbers in society. Political participation is not the mere right to vote but to be a part of decision making process. Unfortunately, women are under represented in the organs of Government like legislature, executive and judiciary. The number of Women MPs increased at the three fold ratio from 22 with 4.50% (1st election) to 66 with 12.15% (16th election) shown a remarkable journey of women to the lower house of the parliament. Even though the increase was found to be steady, exceptions were sought in 6th Election held in 1977 with only 3.51%, 9th Election of 1989 with 5.48% and 14th Election of 2004 with 8.29%. (Refer Table 4).

Table 4: Women representation in Lok Sabha in the General Election.

General election	*Year of election*	*Total women members*	*Percentage*
First	1951	22	4.50%
Second	1957	22	4.45%
Third	1962	31	6.28%
Fourth	1967	29	5.58%
Fifth	1971	28	5.41%
Sixth	1977	19	3.51%
Seventh	1980	28	5.29%
Eighth	1984	43	7.95%
Ninth	1989	29	5.48%
Tenth	1991	39	7.30%
Eleventh	1996	40	7.37%
Twelfth	1998	43	7.92%
Thirteenth	1999	49	9.02%
Fourteenth	2004	45	8.29%
Fifteenth	2009	59	10.87%
Sixteenth	2014	66	12.15%

Source: Data compiled by factly team from the statistical reports of the Election Commission of India.

(2) WOMEN CONTESTING IN THE GENERAL ELECTIONS

The representation of women in politics is highly depending upon education, political knowledge, public support and confidence to grab the challenging task to involve with the political affairs of the country.

They should be encouraged and supported to contest confidently in the elections either along with or against the male candidates through getting tickets from recognized political parties. In 1957 there were only 45 women contestants, in 1996 this hike to 599 and finally in the 2014 it came to 668. Women contestation was peek with 599 contestants in 1996 and 668 contestants during 2014 elections and it found a downfall in 1977 with 70 from the 1971 election contestants of 83 and drastic downfall during 1998, 1999 and 2004 with 274, 284 and 355 contestants respectively. The 15 fold increase in the number of women contestants depics the political empowerment of women which lead for the increased participation in the social welfare and decision making process (Refer the Fig. 3).

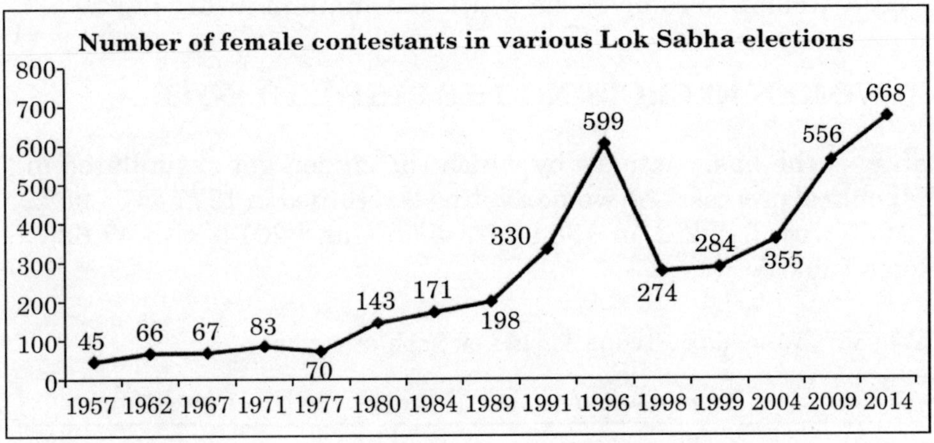

Fig. 3: Women contestants in elections to the Lok Sabha
Source: Data compiled by Factly team from the statistical reports of the Election Commission of India.

The pattern of political behavior varies from region to region as it is influenced by the factors like social status of women, their economic position, the cultural norms, the regional outlook towards women participation in the wider society. For example, in Kerala, which has a record of rapid growth in women literacy, also has a record of electing very few women members to the legislature. In contrast, Uttar Pradesh, with its general low profile of women, has elected a large number of women to the legislature. The number of women contestants in parliamentary elections has not increased significantly over the years. The high cost of electioneering is another deterrent factor to most women candidates. Hence, there is an increasing tendency among women to contest elections as independent candidates.

(3) SUCCESS RATE OF WOMEN *VS.* MEN

Consistently the success rate of women was higher than the male candidates in all the elections. In 1971, the success rate for men was 18%, but women achieved twice the rate by 34%. In the 2014 Lok Sabha election women achieved success of 9.3% over the men who achieved 6.4%. This rise in the numbers will increase the confidence of many women to come to the political domain in future days.

(4) WOMEN EXERCISING THE RIGHT TO VOTE

Voting is the basic activity by which the citizen get assimilated in the political process. The women voting is recorded in 1977 as 54.96%, in 1980 with 51.22%, in 1984 with 58.6% and 2014 with 47.62%. (Refer Table 5).

Table 5: Womens participation in Lok Sabha elections

Year	*Women voted*	*Voters*	*Percentage*
2014	38,79,11,330	81,45,91,184	47.62

Source: Delhi Policy Group, 2014

Women participation in formal elections is to a great extent dependent on the mobilization efforts of the political parties, general awareness among the community of the importance of exercising franchise, and the overall political culture. Political participation of women covers initiatives on political activities, work for the parties and performance in political process including voting. Women political power is limited in its application inspite of the reservations in the local authorities. They are facing many social and economic constraints to enter and render the service in the power domain. It can be faced by training and skill development of elected women to execute their roles and responsibilities by enhancing administrative caliber to perform better in their positions. According to Study commissioned by the Ministry of Panchayati Raj (2008) 50% of the Elected Women Representatives in the country had not received any training after being elected and 45% of former women Pradhans has not contested for the second time due to the lack of efficiency and results in their positions. The Committee on the Panchayat Raj Institutions, 1978 recommended the reservation of two seats for women in panchayats and to co-opt women in case they did not come through elections. A committee of women to be constituted within panchayats to operate specific programmes for women and children. But the co-option of two women member has not brought any impact on womens participation as this remained only on paper and not in the spirit of getting the women involved in panchayat activities. The 73rd and 74th Constitutional Amendment Act (1993) assure 33.3% of seats for women belonging to scheduled castes and tribes in Panchayati Raj Institutions to cover Grama Panchayath, Taluk Panchayati and Zilla Panchayat and also urban self–government covering Municipal Corporations and Municipalities. Not less than one-third (including the number of seats reserved for women belonging to the Scheduled Castes and the Scheduled Tribes) of the total number of seats to be filled by direct election in every Panchayat to be reserved for women and such seats to be allotted by rotation to different constituencies in a Panchayat under (Article 243 D(3)), Not less than one- third of the total number of offices of Chairpersons in the Panchayats at each level to be reserved for women under (Article 243 D (4)), Not less than one-third (including the number of seats reserved for women belonging to the Scheduled Castes and the Scheduled Tribes) of the total number of seats to be filled by direct election in every Municipality to be reserved for women and such seats to be allotted by rotation to different constituencies in a Municipality under (Article 243 T (3)), Reservation of offices of Chairpersons in Municipalities for the Scheduled Castes, the Scheduled Tribes and women in such manner as the legislature of a State may by law provide under (Article 243 T (4)). Government accelerated women political participation in Participatory Rural Institutions by resource allocation for capacity building of members, inclusion of poor and excluded women, allocating funds for evaluation of effects and decentralization of power. The participation of women in Panchayat Raj Institutions, which were considered to be the most effective instruments for realizing the goals of economic betterment and social justice for the least privileged, was felt essential. It is considered as a step towards equality.

CONCLUSION

There is no equal representation of women in Parliament, State Legislatures and local self government bodies like Municipalities and Panchayats. After much hue and cry, the constitution has been amended to include Articles 243-D and 243-T which provided for reservation of seats in Panchayats and Municipalities respectively. But even then, the elected women are mere puppets of their husbands and it is the liking or choices of the husbands which prevail in these local bodies when it comes to real political execution at Panchayats and Muncipality levels. In India, limited adult franchise was granted to women in 1937. Since then, women have been participating in political processes, as voters, as candidates contesting for the elections, involved in deliberations both in the State Assemblies and Parliament through holding pubic office at different levels and in the judiciary where women perform watchdog roles in the protection of sanctioned rights. No serious efforts have been made to moblize women as a political pressure group by any political parties. Caste, personality and families of candidates appears to be more important to voters than party ideology or affiliations. Factors like education, religion, class and tradition also seem to affect womens participation. Despite the general depressed picture of womens role in Indian democracy, there has been a rise in the number of women in key positions of power. We can list few achievers in the political sphere by claimbing to the highest cadre in the political ladder like Mrs. Indira Gandhi who become India's Prime Minister at the helm of affairs, Mrs. Jayalalitha become the Chief Minister for the State of Tamil Nadu, Mamta Banerjee become The Chief Minister of the West Bengal, Smt. Sushma Swaraj is the Minister for External Affairs, Government of India at present in the NDA Government, Smt. Sonia Gandhi is the President of Congress Party, Smt. Smriti Irani was the Minister for Human Resource Development in present Central Government. The concept of participatory development by Voluntary

Action Groups and Educational Institutions were recognized as important instruments to achieve the developmental goals for women. Apart from subjects of direct relevance to them like welfare, child development, removal of dowry and controlling social malpractices other subjects related to education, health, security, civil supplies have been given priority for empowerment. Political parties in their manifestos promise to women all opportunities for increased participation in social, economic and political life yet, the record of most of the parties is poor so far as inclusion of women in their party is concerned. Many women MPs have participated actively in the debates on dowry and influenced the government to make changes in the existing dowry laws. They have also given useful suggestions to have a National Commission to Women to appoint Women Judges in the Family Courts and Special Courts for hearing cases of dowry deaths. On various occasions, they have raised questions regarding the Common Civil Code, Immoral Traffic in Women and Children, Dowry Death and Rape Issues. Recently Smt. Smriti Irani, Minister for Human Resource Development had argued for the extension of additional two years period for the women scholars to submit the thesis for doctoral degree. On the whole, the women decade has forced all political parties to be alert towards women empowerment. The women problems will get solved only after establishing classless society. However, under the pressure of women members, at least the inclusion of women issues in their manifestos has been feasible. Subordination of women in society acts as a structural constraint to their participation in political activities. Owing to the gender based division of labour in family, women have to bear the full responsibility of household chores. It is the women's duty to bring fuel, fodder, water and to cook. They have to look after the rearing and education of children besides socializing. These constraints operate more or less for all classes and communities of women. There has been more positive action on the part of the government to integrate women in the decision making process. Women through constitution have been allowed to enter politics, but women's real active political participation will necessitate changes both in values and in the social structure. The number of women in the upper cader of power continues to be very low despite the reservation at PRI levels. Women's Political Power has not been fully harnessed. They continue to face social, economic and other forms of institutional barriers to entering PRIs and while performing as Elected Representatives. According to a Study commissioned by the Ministry of Panchayati Raj (2008), 50% of the EWRs in the country had not received any training after being elected and 45% of former women Pradhans did not contest elections the second time partly because they did not feel competent in executing their responsibilities. Even though the situation, however, differs from State to State, giving training to Elected Women Representatives (EWR) to develop administrative, technical and financial knowledge for more effective functioning is the best strategy to enrich women participation in the political sphere. They can better understand their roles and responsibilities and build confidence to contribute equally to the development of the country. It is very proud to quote that Mrs. Maneka Gandhi being the Cabinet Minister for Women and Child Development, Government of India has initiated to frame National Policy for Women with special emphasis upon education, empowerment and security.

9

Social Empowerment of Women

Social empowerment is a process in which awareness is created about the status to build self-confidence through critical thinking. The Department of Women and Child Development under the Ministry of Human Resource Development has implemented the following schemes for women empowerment.

A. POLICY FRAMEWORK FOR SOCIAL EMPOWERMENT

(1) Central Social Welfare Board 1953 (CSWB)

An autonomous organisation funded by the Ministry of Women and Child Development for promoting social welfare activities for women, children and differently abled through the financial assistance to voluntary organizations on the recommendation of State Boards. The board has developed networking with more than 8,000 voluntary organisations through the State Social Welfare Board located in the states and union territories across the country. It gives support to Voluntary organizations under a variety of programmes in order to facilitate and strengthen their role in empowering women through education and training. It provides collective mobilization, awareness creation and income generation facility by the provision of support services[1]. Nearly 33 State Boards and field office establishments

[1] Nanavatty, Meher C. "Role of Central Social Welfare Board in the Changing Social Context. The Indian Journal of Public Administration, Vol. XXXIII, 3, pp. 501-511.

are proposed during the XII plan. It initiates assistance to needy, destitude and disadvantaged women and children through Integrated Scheme for Women Empowerment for North East Region, Condensed Courses for Women, Awareness Generation Projects for Rural and Poor Women, Family Counselling Centres and Short Stay Home.

(2) Short Stay Home for Women and Girls 1969

Grants are given to Voluntary Organisations which have engaged in fulltime women and community related activities, to set up Short Stay Homes for women and girls, with a view to protect and rehabilitate who are facing social, economic and emotional problems. They may be the victims of family problems, mental stress, social obstracism, exploitation or forced into prostitution and are in moral danger. Such homes will locate in District, Block Headquarters or a Town having population not less than 50,000 approximately. The scheme provides temporary shelters to the needy women and girls for the duration of six months to three years having option for case work, medical care, psychiatric treatment, occupational therapy, skill development, training provisions, rehabilitation services, educational, vocational and recreational activities. Counseling services are given to those women who have left the homes and facility is given for their well being and safety. Child accompanying the mother or born in the Short Stay Home may be permitted to stay there up to the age of seven years. The grant will be paid upto Rs. 7,00,000/- and above for maintenance, honorarium for staffs, rent of building, contingencies, medical, rehabilitation and one time grant of Rs. 50,000/- for non-recurring items such as furniture, bedding and other skill development equipments under the Scheme.

(3) Working Women Hostels (1972-73)

This scheme is introduced to provide safe and cheap accommodation to working women belonging to lower income groups who live away from home and to increase mobility of employment. This is made available to all working women without any distinction with respect to caste, religion, marital status, etc. Women under training for job may also be accommodated in such hostels subject to the condition that taken together, provided to maximum limit of 30 per cent of the total capacity. Children of working women, upto the age of 18 years for girls and up to the age of 5 years for boys may be accommodated in such hostel with their mothers. Working women, who are single, widowed, divorced, separated, married but whose husband or immediate family does not reside in the same city. Women who are under taking training for job can stay if total training period does not exceed one year. Since inception, 891 hostels have been sanctioned under the scheme with the intake of 66,299 women and 8532 children in 323 Day Care Centres. Financial assistance can be availed by the state government agencies like Women Development Corporations, Women Finance Corporation, Urban Municipal Bodies, Panchayati Raj Institutions and Self Help Groups.

(4) Family Counselling Centres 1983 (FCC)

It is introduced with a view to provide counselling, referral and rehabilitative services to women and children who are victims of atrocities, family maladjustment, social ostracism, natural disasters, etc. Family Counselling Centres have been recognised as service providers under the Protection of Women against Domestic Violence Act in several States. Moreover, in some States, Counsellors have been designated as Protection Officers. In view of its continuing relevance, the scheme is proposed to be continued in the XII Plan. The scheme, which has 787 FCCs at present, is yet to cover all districts. The honorarium of the Counsellors is also proposed to be reviewed under the next plans.

(5) The Central Rural Sanitation Programme 1986 (CRSP)

India's first nationwide programme for rural sanitation was introduced by the Ministry of Rural Development with the objective of improving the quality of life of rural people and to provide privacy and dignity to women. The programme provided large subsidy for construction of sanitary latrines for BPL households. The programme was supply driven, highly subsidized, and gave emphasis on a single construction model. Based on the recommendations of the National Seminar on Rural Sanitation in September 1992, the programme was again revised. The revised programme aimed at an integrated approach to rural sanitation. The Total Sanitation Campaign (TSC) under the restructured CRSP was launched from April 1999 by converting 'community led' project approach to 'people centered' approach as demand driven project. The programme lays emphasis on Information, Education and Communication (IEC) for generation of effective demand for sanitation facilities. It also lays emphasis on school sanitation and hygiene education for bringing about attitudinal and behavioral changes for adoption of hygienic practices from an early age. As per the latest data of Census 2011, in rural areas, 32.7% families have access to sanitation facilities.

(6) National Commission for Women 1992

Statutory body at national level to safeguard the rights and interests of women by investigations into atrocities, sexual harassment at work place, conduct Lok Adalats, Legal Awareness, Camps, review of women specific legislations with appropriate authorities and undertakes suo-moto cases regarding deprivation of rights. It has investigated 24,025 complaints which includes more cases of dowry deaths and dowry harassments. It will participate and advice on the planning process for socio-economic welfare. State commissions are constituted by respective states also. Out of the 41 legislations having direct bearing on women, the Commission reviewed and suggested remedial legislative measures in 32 Acts and forwarded the same to the government for necessary action. Drafted Bill on Sexual Harassment at the Work Places and Bill on SAARC Regional Convention for Prevention and Combating Trafficking in Women and Children.

(7) Awareness Generation Projects for Rural and Poor Women

This scheme is introduced to create awareness in the community on issues relating to the status, rights and problems of women. Its main objectives are to identify the needs of rural and poor women, to increase their active participation in decision making both in the family and community. To tackle issues including atrocities on women and children. This is meant for the women between the age group of 20-25 years. The voluntary organizations can undertake a survey to understand area where, they need awareness programmes. The board will impart training to the organizers through the identified Training Institute. It also encourages to organizing camps for the duration of eight days and takes a feed back within six months after completion of the camp. The awareness is created on the topics like status of women, women and law, women and health, community health and hygiene, technology and environment, women and the state government, religion, culture and women, women and economy, women and social action, panchayats and Gram Sabhas, National integration and communal harmony and legal literacy. The voluntary organizations should involve participation of local bodies like Panchyat Raj Institution, Medical Officers, Child Development Project Officers (CDPOs), Legal experts, Social Workers, Public Representatives etc for organizing the camps. It has to prepare information, education and communication materials like banners, charts and kits to be displayed during the camps.

(8) Rashtriya Mahila Kosh (March 1993)

A registered society was constituted under the Societies Registration Act, 1860 as National Credit Fund for Women for micro-finance to start dairy, agriculture, ship keeping, vending and handicrafts. RMK support through voluntary organizations, women development corporations, womens cooperative societies, block samitis under the swayamsidha programme. Taking the Principal corpus to Rs.100 crore. The Governing Board has decided to convert it from existing society to a government owned Non-Banking Finance Company (NBFC) u/s 617 of the Companies Act, with corpus of Rs 500 crores with a Pan-India office network for the financial inclusion of more than 2 lakh women from the disadvantaged sections annually. The process for restructuring and expansion is focused in the XII Plan.

(9) Swa-Shakthi Projects (October 1998)

A Central Scheme for Rural Women's Development and Empowerment for the states of Bihar, Chhattisgarh, Gujarat,

Haryana, Jharkhand, Karnataka, Madhya Pradesh, Uttaranchal for five years with a budget of Rs 186 crores.

(10) Swayamsidha

Integrated project for constituting Self Help Groups for service, facilitate micro-credit and promote micro-enterprises. 650 Block Projects for four to five years are formed, implemented and monitored by Appropriate Government or Non Governmental Organizations nominated by the State Government. Around 69,803 SHGs have been formed with 10.2 lakh beneficiaries. 56% SHG's have availed bank loan and 85% involved in income generation activities under the 650 Block Projects.

(11) National Policy for the Empowerment of Women 2001

It is to bring about the advancement, development and empowerment of women. The Scheme aims to create an environment through positive economic and social policies for full development of women to enable them to realize their full potential. The de-jure and de-facto enjoyment of all human rights and fundamental freedom by women on equal basis with men in the political, economic, social, cultural and civil sphers. Equal access to participation and decision making of women in social, political and economic life of the nation. Equal access to women to health care, quality education at all levels, career and vocational guidance, employment, equal remuneration, occupational health and safety, social security and public office, etc. Strengthening legal systems aimed at elimination of all forms of discrimination against women. Changing societal attitudes and community practices by active participation and involvement of both men and women. Mainstreaming a gender perspective in the development process. Elimination of discrimination and all forms of violence against women and the girl child and Building and strengthening partnerships with civil society, particularly women's organizations. It suggested to introduce gender perspective in the budgeting process by developing "Gender Development Indices" (GDI), by networking with specialized agencies, undertaking "Gender auditing and development of evaluation mechanisms", undertaking the collection of "Gender-disaggregated data" by all primary data collecting agencies of the Central and State Governments as well as research and academic institutions in the Public and Private Sectors.

(12) Swadhar Greh Scheme (2001-02)

Department of Women and Child Development launched for the Temporary accommodation, Maintenance and Rehabilitative services to women and girls rendered homeless because of family discord, crime, violence, disasters, mental stress and forced sex work. Short Stay Home scheme launched in 1969 had 271 Short Stay Homes benefitting more than 6700 women which was implemented by Central Social Welfare Board. As profile of inmates, admission procedure, component of counseling, vocational training, rehabilitation and follow up procedures in both schemes were same hence, Centre for Market research and Social Development, New Delhi and Department of Parliamentary Standing recommended to merge the schemes with new name "Swadhar Greh" with revised financial norms to cover all the districts of the country.

(13) Swalamban (2003-04)

Nearly 463 Training Proposals were approved to Generate Substantial Employment to women. Training in Computer Programming, Consumer Electronics Mechanic, Garment Making, Handloom Weaving, Handicraft and Embroidery were provided to 71,240 people.

(14) Nirmal Gram Puraskar 2005 (NGP)

To encourage the Panchayat Raj Institutions to take up sanitation promotion this incentive award scheme was introduced. The award is given to those Participatory Rural Institutions which attain 100% open defecation free environment. This award publicized the sanitation programme significantly all across the country. Encouraged with initial success of Nirmal Gram Puraskar and looking into the need to upscale the sanitation interventions, the Total Sanitation Campaign was renamed as the Nirmal Bharat Abhiyan, (NBA) in 2012, with the objective to accelerate the sanitation coverage in the rural areas so as to comprehensively cover the rural community through renewed strategies and saturation approach and to transform rural India into Nirmal Bharat. While the programme has been successful to some extent, the fact that there are still a large number of rural households without access to safe sanitation facilities.

(15) Rajiv Gandhi National Creche Scheme (2006)

The scheme will provide assistance to NGOs for running crèches for infants (0-6 years) and would provide assistance to ensure sleeping facilities, health care, supplementary nutrition, immunization, etc. The Center must have clean toilet and sanitation facility that caters to the need of small children. All times be equipped with a basic First Aid Kit containing paediatric medicines for common ailment and adequate cooking facility, cooking utensils, food provided to children must have adequate nutritional value. A crèche worker and helper will undergo a mandatory short term training which is organized by the state board through the identified training institute. nearly 33.11 lakh children were benefitted with the scheme.

(16) The National Environment Policy (2006)

The policy recognises that a diverse developing society such as ours provides numerous challenges in the economic, social, political, cultural, and environmental arenas. All of these coalesce in the dominant imperative of alleviation of mass poverty, reckoned in the multiple dimensions of livelihood security, health care, education, empowerment of the disadvantaged, and elimination of gender disparities. The National Environment Policy seeks to extend the coverage, and fill in gaps that still exist, in light of present knowledge and accumulated experience. It does not displace, but builds on the earlier policies.

(17) National Mission for Empowerment of Women March 2010 (NMEW)

Constituted by the Ministry of Women and Child Development for integrating various schemes of various departments. The mission focus to achieve consistency at all levels of governance by a participatory way. A new model called 'Convergence Model' has been launched in Pali District, Rajasthan. The demand and supply of service through the scheme is met by Scientific forecasting, Initiating awareness, Connecting women with services. Establishment of Convergency Cum Facilitation Centers for Women at District, Ward, Taluks, and Village levels. Estimated budget for the scheme was Rs 141 crore for 2 years. Inclusive growth through identifying the vulnerabilities of women by referring to age, caste, abilities, ethnicity, education, income level, religion, marital status, region, etc. It also studies the offences against women, health and nutrition level.

(18) Priyadarshini (April 2011)

Central scheme for Livelihood Programme in Mid Gangetic Plains in 13 Blocks spread over 5 Districts in Uttar Pradesh and 2 Districts in Bihar. The programme aims at holistic empowerment of vulnerable women and adolescent girls in the project area through formation of women's Self Help Groups and promotion of improved livelihood opportunities. Over 1,00,000 households are to be covered under the project and 7,200 SHGs would be formed during the project period ending 2016-17.

(19) Ujjawala (December 2007)

It is a Social Security scheme initiated by Ministry of Women and Child Development for Prevention of Trafficking for Rescue, Rehabilitation and Re-Integration of Victims of Trafficking for Commercial Sexual Exploitation. The new scheme has been conceived primarily for the purpose of preventing trafficking on the one hand and rescue and rehabilitation of victims on the other. Social mobilization and involvement of local communities, awareness generation, workshops, to rescue the victims and place them in safe custody, to provide rehabilitation services both immediate and long term by providing shelter, food, clothing, medical treatment, counseling, legal aid and vocational training, reinforce the victim into the family and society. Presently, 160 Projects with 79 Protective and Rehabilitation Homes have been sanctioned.

(20) Gender Budgeting Scheme (2007-12)

To ensure adequate budgetary commitments by building capacities of functionaries and stakeholders at all levels a gender budget scheme was launched in XI Plan. The Ministry will sponsor workshops, develop training materials, organize direct interactive session with ministries, provide technical support to gender budgeting of other organizations. The Scheme also had a component for setting up a Gender Budgeting Cell (GBC) in the Ministry of Women and Child Development for meeting the requirement of capacity building and technical support to conduct Gender Audit.

(21) Media Initiatives

The Media Division of the Ministry of Women and Child Development looks after media and publicity affairs through other Departments of the Government namely DAVP, Song and Drama Division, Prasar Bharati, Doordarshan, etc. It looks after print advertisements, broadcasting of audio spots, telecasting of video spots, scroll messages on important themes, organization of an annual event called Vatsalya Mela, etc. In the coming years new schemes are likely to be launched and existing schemes likely to be expanded leading to increased media activities both in print and audio visual fields. A comprehensive multi-sectoral communication strategy for gender would be introduced in the XII Plan.

(22) Grant-in-Aid Scheme for Research, Monitoring and Publication

Ensuring efficient implementation of policies and programs is the most important aspect of any intervention. The tools and strategies to assess these aspects are Research, Monitoring and Evaluation. One of the core priorities of the XII Plan should be to commission qualitative and quantitative research and impact evaluation studies and establish reliable sex disaggregated data collection processes. The Planning, Research, Evaluation and Monitoring (PREM) Division of the Ministry of Women and Child Development is operating a GIA (Grant-in-Aid) Scheme for research and evaluation works since

1986-87 under which it provides financial support to eligible academic institutions/research organisations and NGOs for research and evaluation on subjects relating to women and children. It is proposed to include a number of areas as priorities for research/evaluation on women related issues during the XII Plan.

(23) Widow, Handicap and Old Age Pension Scheme

The Government has initiated provisions for the Monthly Pension of Rs. 500 to the Widows, disabled and older people. The Proof of death of her husband, disability or old age is made mandatory to avail this benefit. The Applications for these pensions are available in the Taluk Panchayats, Social Welfare Departments and NGOs Working for the women. The eligible candidates can apply through filling the available application along with submission of the necessary documents like Death Certificate in case of widow pension, Age or Disability Certification through the specified Government Medical Practitioner.

(24) Swachh Bharat Mission (Gramin) October, 2014

This scheme aims to attain 100% open Defecation Free India by 2019. The focus is given to bring improvement in the general quality of life in the rural areas, to accelerate sanitation coverage for achieving Swachh Bharat by 2019 with the cooperation of all Gram Panchayats in the country, encourage cost effective and appropriate technologies for ecologically safe and sustainable sanitation, to motivate communities and Panchayati Raj Institutions to promote sustainable sanitation by awareness and health education, to develop community managed environmental sanitation systems focusing on solid and liquid waste management for overall cleanliness in the rural areas. The scheme provides Incentive of Rs. 9000/- and Rs. 3000/- for each toilet and Rs. 10800/- and Rs. 1200/- belonging to North Eastern States, Jammu and Kashmir and Special category states is given by Central and State Government respectively to BPL households and Identified Above Poverty Line (APL) households after they construct and use toilets respectively. Other APL households are motivated to construct toilets with their own funds or by taking loans from SHGs, banks, cooperative institutions, etc. Upto 2 Lakh per community

Sanitary Complex is granted. Upto 35 lakh is granted to each district to production centres of sanitary materials and rural sanitary marts. For knowing the financial contribution (Refer Table 6).

Table 6: Financial contribution for Swachh Bharat Mission (Gramin)

Sl. no	*Component*	*Amount ear-marked as percent of the SBM (Gramin) project outlay*	*Contributions* GOI	*State*	*Benefi-ciary*
A	Information Education and and Communication Start Up Activity and Capacity Building	Up to 8%	75%	25%	0%
B	Revolving Fund	Upto 5%	80%	20%	0%
C	(i) Individual Household Latrines	Actual amount required for full coverage	Rs. 9000 (Rs. 10800 in case of North Eastern States, Jammu & Kashmir and Special category States)	Rs. 3000 (Rs. 1200 in case of North Eastern States, Jammu & Kashmir and Special category States)	
	(ii) Community Sanitary Complexes	Actual amount required for full coverage	60%	30%	10%
D	Administrative charges	Up to 2%	75%	25%	0%
E	Solid/Liquid Waste Management (Capital Cost)	Actual amount as per SLWM project cost within limits permitted	75%	25%	0%

Source: Website hosted & maintained by National Informatics Centre, Contents provided by Ministry of Drinking Water and Sanitation, Government of India.

Only about 22% of the rural families had access to toilets in 2001. With the efforts put into the Total Sanitation Campaign/Nirmal Bharat Abhiyan (NBA) this has gone up to 32.70% as per Census 2011. Further as per NSSO 2012, 40.60% rural households have toilets. All rural households are planned to be covered with sanitary facilities by 2019 (Refer Table 7) for the progress of the scheme from 2012.

Table 7: Achievements made under SBM (Gramin) from 2012-2015

Component	***2012-13***	***2013-14***	***2014-2015 (Upto 31.10.2014)***
Household toilets	45,59,162	49,76,294	13,70,347
School toilets	76,396	37,696	8,748
Anganwadi toilets	36,677	22,318	3,325

Source: Website hosted and maintained by National Informatics Centre, Contents provided by Ministry of Drinking Water and Sanitation, Government of India.

(25) Pradhan Mantri Jan-Dhan Yojana (PMJDY)

It is a National Mission for Financial Inclusion of all the people of the country to ensure access to financial services like Savings Bank Accounts and Deposit Accounts, Remittance, Credit, Insurance, Pension in an affordable manner. Account can be opened in any bank branch or Business Correspondent (Bank Mitr) outlet with Zero Balance unless the account holder wishes to get cheque book. To open this account the account holder if has Aadhaar Number then, no other documents are required and in case he do not have it, then, any of the officially valid documents like Voter ID Card, Driving License, PAN Card, Passport and NREGA Card can be used. If a person does not have any of the officially valid documents but if it is categorized as 'low risk' by the banks, then she can open a bank account by submitting any one of the documents like identity card with applicants photography issued by Central or State Government, Statutory Authorities, Public Sector Undertakings, Scheduled Commercial banks and Public Financial Institutions. This scheme provides special benefits of interest on deposit, accidental insurance cover of Rs. 1 lakh, no minimum balance need to be maintained, life insurance cover of Rs. 30,000/-, Easy Transfer of money across India, Beneficiaries of Government Schemes will get Direct Benefit transfer in these accounts, after satisfactory operation of the accounts for 6 months, an overdraft facility will be permitted upto Rs. 5000/- in only one account per household, preferably for lady of the household, access to pension, insurance products, accidental insurance cover, RuPay Debit Card must be used at least once in 45 days. For total number of accounts opened under this Scheme (Refer Table 8)

Table 8: Description of total number of accounts opened under PMJDY as on 06.04.2016 (Summary)

Types of bank	*Rural*	*Urban*	*No. of accounts*	*No. of rupay card issued*	*Balance in account (in Lakhs)*	*No. of accounts with zero balance*	*Adhaar seeding*
P.S. Bank	94544725	74604177	169148902	143328907	2884820.19	45381167	80748258
R.R. Bank	32664245	5366097	38030342	26989510	635960.24	8741146	11632967
P. Banks	4900162	3058433	7958595	7505878	139223.87	3164979	3032385
Grand total	132109132	83028707	215137839	177824295	3660004.30	57287292	95413610

P.S. Bank: Public Sector; *R.R. Bank*: Regional Rural and *P. Bank*: Private Bank

Source: Department of Financial Services, Ministry of Finance, Government of India.

(26) Pradhan Mantri Suraksha Bima Yojana (May 2015)

This is a government backed accident insurance scheme in India. It was originally mentioned in the 2015 Budget speech by Finance Minister Arun Jaitley in February, 2015. It is formally launched by Prime Minister Narendra Modi. As till the day only 20% of the people of India had insurance and this scheme aims to increase the number. This scheme is available to people between the age group of 18 to 70 years of age with bank accounts. It has an annual premium of Rs. 12/- per annum excluding service tax which is about 14% of the premium. The amount will be automatically debited from the savings bank account of the subscriber. In case of accidental death or full disability, the payment to the nominee will be 2 lakhs and in case of partial permanent disability 1 lakh. Full disability has been defined as loss of use in both eyes, hands or feet. Partial Permanent Disability has been defined as loss of use in one eye, hand or foot. This scheme will be linked to the bank accounts opened under the Pradhan Mantri Jan Dhan Yojana Scheme. Most of these account had zero balance initially. The government aims to reduce the number of such zero balance accounts by using this and related schemes. The cover is subject to exclusions of the policy like intentional self injury, suicide or attempted suicide whilst under the influence of intoxication liquor or drugs, any loss arising from an act made in breach of law with or without criminal intent.

(27) Pradhan Mantri Jeevan Jyoti Bima Yojana (June 2015)

The account holders between 18 years and 50 years who have given the consent to join the scheme. The scheme has the premium of Rs. 330/- per annum. The premium will be directly auto-debited by the bank from the subscribers savings bank account. Sum assured amount is Rs. 2/- Lakh it will be paid to the nominee on the death of the insured member. The term of assurance will be terminated if the account holder attains the age of 55 years.

(28) Scheme of Housing for All

This scheme is a vision of Prime Minister Narendra Modi. The government has identified 305 cities and towns in 9 states for beginning construction of houses for urban poor. The project is aimed for urban areas with following components like slum rehabilitation of Slum Dwellers with participation of private developers using land as a resource, promotion of afforadable housing for weaker section through credit linked subsidy, affordable housing in partnership with public and private sectors and subsidy for beneficiary led individual house construction or enhancement, 2 lakh crore over the next six years central grant of 1 lakh per house on an average will be available under the slum rehabilitation programme. State Government or Housing Boards can take up project of affordable housing to avail the Central Government grant. The scheme will be implemented as a Centrally Sponsored Scheme except the credit linked subsidy component, which will be implemented as a Central Sector Scheme. The Mission also prescribes certain mandatory reforms for easing up the urban land market for housing, to make adequate urban land available for affordable housing. Houses constructed under the mission would be allotted in the name of the female head of the households or in the joint name of the male head of the household and his wife. Under PMAY, it is proposed to build 2 crore houses for urban poor including Economically Weaker Sections and Low Income Groups in urban areas by the year 2022. This Mission has four components *viz.*, *In-situ* Slum Redevelopment with private sector participation using land as resource, Affordable Housing through Credit Linked Subsidy, Affordable Housing in Partnership with private and public sector and Beneficiary led house construction/ enhancement.

(29) Skill India (July 2015)

It is an initiative of the Government of India which is launched by Prime Minister Narendra Modi with an aim to train over 40 crore people in different skills by 2022. The scheme includes National Skill Development Mission, National Policy for Skill Development and Entrepreneurship 2015, Pradhan Mantri Kaushal Vikas Yojana (PMKVY) scheme and Skill loan scheme. United Kingdom will be contributing to this programme. Virtual partnerships will be initiated at the school level to enable young people of either country to experience the school system of the other country and develop an understanding of the culture, traditions, social and family systems. A commitment to achieve mutual recognition of UK and Indian qualifications was made.

(30) Atal Pension Yojana 2015 (APY)

For every contribution made to the pension fund, The Central Government would also co-contribute 50% of the total contribution or Rs. 1,000/- per annum, whichever is lower, to each eligible subscriber account, for a period of 5 years. The minimum age of joining APY is 18 years and maximum age is 40 years. The age of exit and start of pension would be 60 years. Therefore, minimum period of contribution by the subscriber under APY would be 20 years or more. Aadhaar would be the primary KYC document for identification of beneficiaries, spouse and nominees to avoid pension rights and entitlement related disputes in the long-term. The subscribers are required to opt for a monthly pension from Rs. 1000/ - Rs. 5000/- and ensure payment of stipulated monthly contribution regularly. The subscribers can opt to decrease or increase pension amount during the course of accumulation phase, as per the available monthly pension amounts. However, the switching option shall be provided once in year during the month of April. This scheme will be linked to the bank accounts opened under the Pradhan Mantri Jan Dhan Yojana scheme and the contributions will be deducted automatically. Most of these accounts had zero balance initially. The government aims to reduce the number of such zero balance accounts by using this and related schemes.

(31) Pradhan Mantri Ujjwala Yojana (PMUY) 2016

Prime Minister Narendra Modi launched a Rs. 8000 crore scheme to provide 5 crore free LPG connections in the name of the women members of BPL households. In the first year, 1.5 crore connections will be released and the target of 5 crore will be completed in three years. It is a good scheme compared to the just 13 crore LPG connections provided in last 60 years of Independence[2].

[2] The Times of India. "Modi Launches Rs. 8 k-cr LPG for poor Scheme", Monday May 2, (2016).

10

Economic Empowerment of Women

The contribution of the voluntary organisations has been considered significant in demonstrating the effectiveness of participatory development for empowering women by facilitating their needs, enabling them to take part in decision making to move in their own vision. Economic empowerment of women is possible by developing their vocational and technical skills by providing training to enable them to take up income generating activities according to their interest. The opening up of the economy and rapid economic growth in the last five years has increased the existing structural barriers by introducing furthermore new challenges. As Economic development creates more jobs in the industrial and service sectors it attracts, workers from the traditional agricultural sector. It resulted in migration of men moving away from the less remunerative agricultural sector for better earnings leaving behind women who are compelled to become the prime agriculturists in the absence of the men even without basic benefits like land titles, severely limited resources, less access to credit, seeds, fertilizers, debt burden left behind by men and other extension services[1]. The 12th Five year plan adopted 'Rights Based Approach' to empower them with the provisions of services, skill development and control over entitlements. For women generating employment opportunity is a mile stone to compete with their counterparts. Chopra J.K. (1980) in

[1] Gadgil D.R. (1965). Women in the Working Force in India, Asia Publishers, Bombay.

urban India, the female work participation rates have increased from 8.31% in 1981 to 9.19% in 1991. According to census report 2011 this rate has been increased to 25.6% (Refer Table 9).

Table 9: Work participation in India

Total work participation in India as on 2015			
Sl. no	***Category***	***Number***	***Rate***
1	Total persons	402,234,724	39.1
	Males	275,014,476	51.7
	Females	127,220,248	25.6
	Main workers		
2	Persons	313,004,983	30.4
	Males	240,147,813	45.1
	Females	72,857,170	14.7
	Marginal workers		
3	Persons	89,229,741	8.7
	Males	34,866,663	6.6
	Females	54,363,078	11

Source: Census Survey Report 2011.

A. POLICY FRAME WORK FOR ECONOMIC EMPOWERMENT OF WOMEN

Inclusive Growth visualize that every women should explore to their fullest potential and contribute to the economic growth and prosperity of the country by addressing the differential needs of women. Main streaming gender in all sectors is focused by the Ministry of Women and Child Development through the following targeted interventions. According to Hate C.A. (1969). The status of women is changing very gradually towards the positive efforts. There is a need for employment to enjoy the identity in society[2].

[2] Hate C.A. (1969). Changing Status of Women in Post Independence India, Allied Publishers Pvt. Ltd, Mumbai.

(1) Women's Vocational Training Programme 1974

This aims at skill development for increasing women employment in organized and self employments. Women's Occupational Training Directorate constituted 10 Regional Vocational Training Institutes (RVTIs) in India apart from the National Vocational Training Institute (NVTI) at NOIDA to conduct basic, advanced and post advanced levels. State Governments provided exclusive training facilities to women by creating network of 231 Women Industrial Training Institute (WITI's) and 534 Women wings in general ITI's with 46,750 training seats.

(2) The Support for Training and Employment Programme (STEP) 1986-87

As per the situational review of women in informal sector by The National Commission for Self Employed Women in the Informal Sector (1988) had suggested introduction of protective measures which would ensure guarantee of employment for income generation, minimum wages, welfare and support services, training and upgrading skills. The scheme covers traditional sectors of employment like agriculture, small animal husbandry, dairying, fisheries, handlooms, handicrafts, khadi and village industries, sericulture, social forestry, waste land development. This project was launched in 19 states. Nearly 60% of the projects is carried in dairy sector. About 8,000 women's dairy co-operatives with more than 4 lakh members have been organised throughout the country by the initiative of State Cooperative Milk Federations. Under the XI plan 1,60,560 beneficiaries were covered under the STEP scheme. This linked vocational courses under National Skill Development Programme to increase the employability of trained SHG members. The beneficiaries under the project will be poor or assetless marginalized women with special focus on SC/ST households, women headed households and families below the poverty line.

(3) The National Minorities Development & Finance Corporation (NMDFC) 1994

It works under the control of Ministry of Minority Affairs,

Government of India. This aims to promote the economic and developmental activities for the benefit of the backward minorities like Muslims, Christians, Sikhs, Buddhists and Parsis who are notified under the National Commission of Minorities, Act, 1992. It provides concessional finance to the families having annual income less than Rs. 81,000/- per annum in rural areas and Rs. 1,03,000/- per annum in urban areas for self employment and income generation activities. The vocational Training Schemes aims at imparting skills to the targeted individual beneficiaries for self employment. The scheme is implemented through State Channelizing Agencies (SCA) with the help of government recognized institutes. The cost of training is Rs. 2000/- per candidate per month for the courses of maximum duration of 6 months. Stipend at Rs. 1000/- per month will be paid during the training. 90% of the training cost is met by the NMDFC and remaining by SCA's.

(4) Design Development and Skill Up-gradation

As per the changes in the perception, liking and tastes of the people, handloom and handicraft items produced by the crafts person have to be in line with the latest designs and aesthetics as well as competitative in terms of cost. Crafts person may require exposure to new designs and training to upgrade their skills to meet this challenge. National Minorities Development Finance Corporation considers proposals furnished by the State Channelising Agencies and NGOs to provide grants for organizing design skill development training programmes for the benefit of crafts persons belonging to the Minority Communities.

(5) Schemes After 2000

The eleventh five year plan initiated SABLA, for empowering adolescent girls, Indira Gandhi Matritva Sahyog Yojana (IGMSY) for maternity benefits, Mahila Kisan Sashaktikaran Pariyojana for women farmers, a scheme for leadership training of Minority women, Ujjawala for combating trafficking and Dhanalakshmi to tackle the issue of declining child sex ratio. National Mission for Empowerment of Women (NMEW) 2010 will facilitate every women to access all governmental programmes. Around 16 States/UTs have already established State Mission Authorities for empowerment of women and 11 States are in the process of setting up of State Resource Centres for Women. Inclusion and mainstreaming of women also received special attention under programmes such as the MGNREGA, the Right to Free & Compulsory Education, National Rural Health Mission, National Rural Livelihood Mission and National Skill Development Mission. Gender Budgeting initiatives led to development of new schemes for Department of Telecommunications and Ministry of Petroleum and Natural Gas. Gender Responsive Budgeting is done by 56 ministries by the Gender Budgeting Cells by scanning existing policies and schemes which utilize public resources by a gender lens to reduce existing gender disparity. After revision of the guidelines of the scheme in 2009, Programme Implementation Manual has been issued. Training for skill upgradation, organisation of women into cooperative groups and provision for credit by linking Rashtriya Mahila Kosh (RMK), National Bank for Agriculture and Rural Development (NABARD), and Council for Advancement of People's Action and Rural Technology (CAPART) or other financial institutions for agriculture, animal husbandry, dairying, fisheries, handlooms, handicrafts, khadi and village industries, sericulture, waste land development and social forestry sectors.

(6) Grant in Aid on Women Labour

Ministry of Labour and Employment will protect and safeguard the interest of workers by creating healthy working environment for higher productivity. It promotes welfare, safety, industrial relation, social security and environmental measures for the workers. Many acts are enacted by the central and state governments. The ministry has undertaken Grant-in-aid scheme for the welfare of women labour. This scheme, which is working since Sixth Five Year Plan (1981-82) through the grants sactioned to Voluntary organizations. It facilitate for creating awareness on the women right, provision for legal aid through organizing seminars and workshops. It also create consciousness among women about various schemes of Central and State governments. Upto 75% of the total cost of the project will be assisted through the grants.

(7) Micro Units Development and Refinance Agency Bank (MUDRA Bank)

It is a new institution setup by the Government of India for development of micro units and refinance of Micro Finance Institutions (MFIs) to encourage entrepreneurship in India and provide the funding to the Non Corporate Small Business Sector (NCSBS). MUDRA Yojana had announced by the Finance Minister in Parliament during Union Budget for the year 2016. It need two types of products like refinance for the micro units having loan requirement from Rs. 50,000/- to Rs. 10,000,00/- lakhs and support MFIs for lending. The bank will refinance to micro business under the scheme of Pradhan Mantri MUDRA Yojana. The Bank has launched its three initiative products like SHISHU, KISHOR and TARUN to signify the stage of growth and funding needs of the micro units or entrepreneur. It refinance through state level institutions. MUDRA will deliver the loan through NBFCs, MFIs, Rural Banks, District Banks, Nationalised Banks, Private Banks, Primary Lending Institutions and other intermediaries. There is no fixed Interest rate in MUDRA loan it charges a base rate between +1% to 7% minimum. Any Indian Citizen who are involved in income generating activity such as manufacturing, processing, trading or service sector and whose credit need is less than 10 lakh can approach Banks, MFIs, Financial Institutions or NBFC for availing of MUDRA loans. MUDRA Bank is not refinancing agriculture sector under this scheme but traders of vegetables and fruits are covered under this scheme. Recently Central Government decided to provide an additional fund of One Lakh crore to this scheme and Rs. 40,000/- crore for Mudra Bank Shishu Loan Scheme, Rs. 35,000/- Crore for Mudra Bank Kishor Loan Scheme and remaining Rs. 25,000/- crore for Mudra Bank Tarun Loan Scheme.

B. WOMEN WELFARE INITIATED IN THE FIVE YEAR PLANS

Social welfare services as conceived in Five Year Plans therefore, mean services for the weaker and vulnerable sections of the community who cannot take advantage of existing social and other services because of certain physical, mental and social handicapness or whose needs require the organisation of special services for their development and well being[3].

(1) The First Five Year Plan (1951-56)

This plan to envisage welfare measures to women, The Central Social Welfare Board (CSWB) was established in 1953 which symbolized the welfare approach to women problems. The CSWB used community development approach, by which recognized for the first time the need for organizing women into 'Mahila Mandals' or 'Women Clubs'. Community Development worker, perceived more as a harmonizer of interests rather than a stimulator of awareness working closely with the rural elite. Moreover, although rural women came within the purview of the CD programmes, they did not specifically catered to as a target population based on economic or other specific class related criteria. A large majority of poor rural women thus remained untouched.

(2) The Second Five Year Plan (1956-61)

This plan closely linked with the overall approach of intensive agricultural development. The welfare approach to women issues persisted. The plan recognized the need for organisation of women as workers. It also perceived the social intensity of various prejudices and disabilities affecting women. The plan stated that women should be protected against hazardous work, receive maternity benefits and crèches for children. It also suggested speedy implementation of the principle of equal pay for equal work and provision for training to enable women to compete for higher jobs.

(3) The Third Five Year Plan (1961-1966)

It pointed female education as a major welfare strategy. In Social Welfare, the larger share was provided for expanding rural welfare services and condensed courses of education. The health programme

[3] Reports of the Planning Commission of India, New Delhi.

concentrated mainly on the provision of services for maternal and child welfare, health education, nutrition and family planning.

(4) The Fourth Five Year Plan (1969-1974)

It continued the emphasis on women's education. The basic policy was to promote women's welfare within the family as the base of operation. The outlay on Family Planning was stepped up to reduce the birth rate from 40 to 25 per thousand through mass education. High priority was accorded to immunization of pre-school children and supplementary feeding for children, expectant and nursing mothers.

(5) The Fifth Five Year Plan (1974-1978)

It emphasized the need to train poor women to generate income and ensure their protection. It also recommended a programme of functional literacy to equip women with skills and knowledge to perform the responsibilities as a housewife including child care, nutrition, health care, home economics, etc. This plan coincided with the International Womens Decade and the submission of the Report of the Committee on the Status of Women in India (CSWI). The overall task committed was to undertake a comprehensive examination of all the questions relating to the rights and status of women in the context of changing social and economic conditions in the country and problems relating to the advancement of women.

(6) The Sixth Plan (1980-85)

This Plan aimed a shift from welfare approach for women to development approaches for women. Influenced by the era that heralded concepts of social justice, the sixth plan recognized womens lack of access to resources as a critical factor impending their development. Among others, the programme providing joint pattas (Titles) to men and women was initiated. However, though the plan defined the magnitude of women problems and suggested development strategies, the 'Family' rather than the 'Women' remained the basic unit of development programmes. Special

Component Plan was introduced to facilitate the monitoring of the development programmes meant for scheduled caste population.

(7) The Seventh Five Year Plan (1985-1990)

It operationalised the concern for equity and empowerment articulated by the International decade for women. For the first time, the emphasis was qualitative, focusing on inculcating confidence among women, generating awareness about their rights and training them for economic activity through employment. In keeping with the spirit of decade which aimed at integrating women into the mainstream of national development. The plan emphasized the need to open new avenues of work for women as they were considered as crucial resource for the development of the country. The access of women to critical inputs and productive resources such as land were expanded to include support through credit, marketing, training in skills, management and technology. It was emphasized that technology that causes unemployment or displacement of women must be resisted. Another sailent and crucial recognition was the need for organisation of women workers and unionization that could demand for improved legal services to safeguard their rights and reduce occupational health hazards. The plan acknowledged the long hours spent by women in the family farm or family business activities within the household services especially in the collection of fuel, fodder, water, etc. but womens contribution are not included in computing Gross National Product. For Complementing the productive endeavour certain supportive service were offered to women like maternal and child care facilities.

(8) Eighth Five Year Plan (1992-1997)

The plan was launched immediately after the initiation of structural adjustment policies and macro stabilisation policies which were necessitated by the worsening balance of payments and inflation during 1990-91. To reorient some of the development programmes, it was realised that the problem of poverty could not be tackled by estimating growth alone as it was low over a long period of time. Hence, direct intervention through poverty alleviation programmes became necessary. It was a plan for managing the transition from a centrally planned economy to a market led economy through indicative planning. The plan aims to generate adequate employment, controlling population growth through peoples cooperation, universalization of elementary education and complete eradication of illiteracy among who are between 15 to 35 years, provision for safe drinking water, Primary Health Care including immunisation programmes at villages and complete elimination of scavenging. Growth and diversification of agriculture to achieve self sufficiency in food and generation of surplus for exports. The level of national investment proposed was Rs. 7,98,000/- crore and the public sector outlay, Rs. 4,34,100/- crore. Consistent with the expected resources, the size of the plan of the States and Union Territories was projected at Rs. 1,86,235/- crore and of the central plan at Rs. 2,47,865/- crore. The average rate of growth of the economy rose from 6% per annum in the seventh plan (1985-90) to 6.8% in the Eighth Plan (1992-97). Growth averaged a high rate of 7.5% per annum in the last three years of the Eighth Plan (1994-95 to 1996-97). According to Economic Survey, 1998 there is evidence that various employment generation and anti-poverty programmes have started showing positive results. However, the problems of poverty alleviation and human resource development are large and complex. Sustained and serious efforts are required to reduce wide disparity between states and regions, rural and urban and men and women respectively. The survey also points out the necessity of ensuring adequate budgetary allocation to social sectors. Financial resources have to be mobilised by both the centre and the states. Furthermore, available resources need to be better targeted and effective safety nets need to be designed to protect poor and vulnerable sections against income fluctuations and market failures. Public efforts and resources need to be supplemented by private sector participation and support from non-governmental organisations (NGOs) for the development of social sectors.

(9) Ninth Five Year Plan (1997-2002)

Adoption of Women's Component Plan (WCP) to ensure that benefits from other developmental sectors do not by pass women and not less than 30% of funds flow to them from all the women related sectors.

Review of the progress of WCP during the Ninth Plan reveals that funds flowing from one of the women-related Departments (*viz.* Family Welfare) was as high as 70% of its Gross Budgetary Support of the Ninth Plan (1997). Launching of 'Swa-Shakti' to create an enabling environment for empowerment of women through setting up of self-reliant Self-Help Groups (SHGs) and developing linkages with lending institutions to ensure women's access to credit facilities for income generation activities (1998). 'Stree Shakti Puraskars' instituted for the first time in the history of women's development to honour 5 distinguished women annually for their outstanding contribution to the upliftment and empowering women (1999). Setting up of a Task Force on Women under the Chairmanship of Shri K.C. Pant, Deputy Chairman, Planning Commission to review the existing women specific and women related legislations and suggest enactment of new legislations or amendments, wherever necessary. The Task Force also suggested a thematic programme for celebrating the year '2001' as Women's Empowerment Year, besides reviewing 22 existing legislations (2000). Introduction of Gender Budgeting to attain more effective targeting of public expenditure and to offset any undesirable gender-specific consequences of previous budgetary measures (2000-01). Adoption of a National Policy for Empowerment of Women to eliminate all types of discrimination against women and to ensure gender justice, besides empowering women both socially and economically (2001). Celebration of the Year 2001 as 'Women's Empowerment Year' to create awareness generation, remove negative thinking, besides building up confidence in women through the process of conscientization to take their rightful place in the mainstream of the nation's social, political and economic life (2001). Recasting of Indira Mahila Yojana as 'Swayamsidha', an integrated programme for empowerment of women through a major strategy of converging the services available in all the women related programmes besides organising women into SHGs for undertaking various entrepreneurial ventures (2001). Launching of 'Swadhar' to extend rehabilitation services for 'Women in Difficult Circumstances' (2001). Introduction of a Bill on Domestic Violence against Women (Prevention) to eliminate all forms of domestic violence against women and the girl child (2002).

(10) Tenth Five Year Plan (2002-2007)

To adopt a Sector specific 3-Fold Strategy for empowering women, based on the prescriptions of the National Policy for Empowerment of Women.

(a) Social empowerment

To create an enabling environment through various affirmative developmental policies and programmes for development of women besides providing them easy and equal access to all basic services to enable them to realize their full potentials. Providing easy and equal access to Primary Health Care and family welfare with a special focus on the under-privileged segments of population through universalising Reproductive and Child Health (RCH) services. Achieving the goals set by the National Population Policy (2000) with regard to reducing Infant Mortality Rate (IMR) to 30 per thousand and Maternal Mortality Rate (MMR) to 100 per lakh live births by 2010. Supplementing health care and nutrition services through the Pradhan Mantri Gramodaya Yojana (PMGY) to fill the critical gaps in the existing primary health care infrastructure and nutrition services. Tackling both macro and micro-nutrient deficiencies through Nutrition Supplementary Feeding Programmes with necessary support services like health check-ups, immunisation, nutrition, education and awareness. Consolidating the progress made under female education and carrying it forward for achieving the set goal of 'Education for Women's Equality' as advocated by the National Policy on Education, 1986 (revised in 1992). Providing easy and equal opportunity for free education for women and girls at all levels in the field of technical and vocational education for job oriented trades. Increasing enrolment rates and reducing drop out rates through the support services of mid day meals, hostels and incentives schemes of free supply of uniforms, textbooks, transport charges, etc. There is a need to extend network of Regional Vocational Training Centres to all the states and Women's Industrial Training Institutes and Women's Wings with General Industrial Training Institutes with residential facilities in all districts and sub-districts. Encouraging the media to project positive images of women and the Girl Child to change the mind-set of the people for the balanced portrayals of women and men. Gender sensitization at administrative and enforcement machinery to ensure the protection of rights and interests of women to involve them in planning, implementation and monitoring of processes.

(b) Economic empowerment

To ensure Training, Employment and Income generation among women to make them economically independent and self-reliant through Organising them in Self-Help Groups under various poverty alleviation programmes like Swarnajayanti Gram Swarozgar Yojana (SGSY), Swarna Jayanti Shahari Rozgar Yojana (SJSRY), Rashtriya Mahila Kosh (RMK), Support for Training and Employment Programme (STEP), Training-cum-Production Centres for Women (NORAD), etc. Ensuring that women in the Informal Sector who account for more than 90% are given special attention with regard to improve their working conditions as they are deprived of minimum or equal wages and other legislative safeguards. Making concerted efforts to ensure that the benefits of training and extension in agriculture and allied activities like horticulture, small animal husbandry, poultry, fisheries, etc. Reach women in proportion to their numbers by granting Joint *Pattas* for husband and wife under the Social Forestry and Joint Forest Management programmes. Ensuring that the employers fulfil their legal obligations towards Child care facilities, maternity benefits, special leave, protection from occupational hazards, allowing formation of women workers' Unions, legal aid and protection, etc. Upgrading the skills of women displaced from traditional sectors due to advancement of technology so that they can take up jobs in the new and expanding areas. Formulating appropriate policies and programmes to promote alternative opportunities for self-employment in traditional sectors like khadi and village industries, handicrafts, handlooms, sericulture, small scale and cottage industries. Initiating affirmative action to ensure at least 30% of reservation for women in the Public Sector as their representation in 1999 was only 14.5% which require a upward mobility. Increasing access to credit for women either through the establishment of new micro-credit mechanisms and micro-financial institutions or strengthening existing arrangements in these areas along with an expansion of the limited coverage of Rashtriya Mahila Kosh.

(c) Gender justice

To eliminate all forms of gender discrimination by allowing women to enjoy not only the de-jure but also the de-facto rights and fundamental freedom on par with men political, economic, social, civil, cultural spheres of live. Complete eradication of female foeticide through effective enforcement of both the Indian Penal Code, 1860 and the Pre-Natal Diagnostic Technique (Regulation and Prevention of Misuse) Act, 1994 with most stringent measures of punishment so that a very harsh path is set for the illegal practitioners. Adopting measures that take into account the reproductive rights of women to enable them to exercise their reproductive choices. Working out strategies, in close collaboration with the Ministry of Labour, to ensure extension of employment opportunities and thus, remove inequalities in employment both in work and accessibility. Initiating interventions at the macro-economic level to amend existing legislations to improve women's access to productive assets and resources. The value added by women in the Informal Sector as workers and producers is recognised through re interpretation of conventional concepts of work and preparation of Satellite and National Accounts. Defining the Women's Component Plan (WCP) clearly and identifying the schemes and projects under each Ministry to ensure the adoption of women-related mechanisms through which funds flow to women from these sectors. Initiating action for enacting new women specific legislations, amending the existing legislation to inculcate gender justice. Expediting action to legislate reservation of not less than 1/3 seats for women in the Parliament and in the State Legislative Assemblies and thus ensure women in proportion to their numbers reach decision making bodies so that their voices are heard. Arresting the increasing violence against women and Adolescent girls on top priority with the strength and support of a well-planned Programme of Action prepared in consultation with the strength of the Law and Order Authorities. Standardisation of a Gender Development Index based on which the gender segregated data will be collected at National, State and District levels to assess the progress made in improving the status of women at regular intervals to achieve equality on par with men. Accelerating the process of societal reorientation towards creating a Gender Just Society.

(11) Eleventh Five Year Plan (2007-2012)

The Eleventh Five Year Plan aimed at inclusive development. Its vision was that every woman in the country should be able to develop to her full potential to contribute for the economic growth and prosperity. It recognized the differential needs of women and children as a heterogeneous category. It also acknowledged the need for inter sectoral convergence as well as the need for focused measures by the Ministry of Women and Child Development (MoWCD) for the development of women and children. It recognized the need for partnership with civil society to create permanent institutional mechanisms that incorporate the experiences, capacities, and knowledge of Voluntary Organisations and women's groups in development, planning, and implementation. Towards this end, the approach adopted was to empower women by recognizing their Agency to develop them. This it sought by mainstreaming gender in all sectors and targeted interventions. The Working Group on Feminist Economists, constituted in the Eleventh Plan to review gender equality across sectors, suggested many of the strategic recommendations of the Plan and has been reconstituted to provide recommendations for the Twelfth Plan. The Plan period saw the introduction of many new schemes and programmes targeted at particular groups or aimed at addressing specific issues. These included SABLA, for empowering adolescent girls, Indira Gandhi Matritva Sahyog Yojana (IGMSY) for maternity benefits, Mahila Kisan Sashaktikaran Pariyojana (MKSP) for women farmers to impart leadership training of Minority women, Ujjawala for combating trafficking and Dhanalakshmi to tackle the issue of declining child sex ratio. Existing schemes are modified to make them more effective and to plug identified gaps. Implementation of Legislations such as Prohibition of Child Marriage Act, 2006, Protection of Women from Domestic Violence Act, 2005, and Hindu Succession (Amendment) Act, 2005 are monitored by the States to provide women a safe working environment, Protection against Sexual Harassment at the Workplace Bill was introduced in Parliament. Several other policy decisions are made in the sector of women and children. The National Mission for Empowerment of Women (NMEW) was launched on March 8th, 2010 for strengthening inter sectoral convergence at the Central, State, District and Field levels of governance by creating awareness among women about all Government schemes and programmes. The National Mission Authority, Supporting Committees and the National Resource Centre for Women are established. The first pilot convergence project was launched in Pali district of Rajasthan in September 2011 and similar pilots are planned in other States/UTs. The State Governments also establishing parallel structures at the State level. 16 States/UTs have already established State Mission Authorities and 11 States are in the process of setting up of State Resource Centres for Women. The Mission stands testimony to the commitment of the Government to the empowerment of women in the country. A landmark step initiated is the restructuring of the Rashtriya Mahila Kosh (RMK) into a systemically important Non-Banking Finance Company with an enhanced corpus of Rs 500 crores. The restructured RMK will have a Pan India office Network and in its new and expanded form, it would facilitate the financial inclusion of more than 2 lakh women from the disadvantaged sections of society on an annual basis towards the fifth year of its working. The XI Plan document and its Mid Term Appraisal also emphasized the need for capacity building and enablement of the Panchayat for effective delivery of policy and programmes. Further, it enunciated the measures to accelerate the process of women's political empowerment and participation in PRIs by increasing resource allocation for capacity building of all PRI members, including poor and other excluded womens, granting funds for time-series evaluations of the impact of women on PRIs, and acceleration of the State Governments' process of devolution of powers. Inclusion and mainstreaming of women also received special attention under programmes such as the MGNREGA, the Right to Free & Compulsory Education, National Rural Health Mission, National Rural Livelihood Mission and National Skill Development Mission. Gender Budgeting initiatives led to development of new schemes in the gender neutral sectors like Department of Telecommunications and Ministry of Petroleum and Natural Gas. Gender Outcome assessment would be encouraged in all Ministries at Central and State levels as Gender Budgeting helps assess the gender differential impact of the budget and takes forward the translation of gender commitments to budgetary allocations. Gender

Responsive Budgeting is well recognized as an important tool for enabling gender mainstreaming. It seeks to view each activity that uses public resources through a gender lens in order to ensure that budgeting reduces existing gender disparities. Importance of Gender Audits of public expenditure, programmes and policies at national, state and district levels. In 2004-05, the Ministry of Finance mandated the setting up of Gender Budgeting Cells (GBCs) in all Ministries as focal points for mainstreaming gender. So far 56 Ministries have set up the Gender Budgeting Cells. One of the key tasks of the GBCs is to undertake a gender scan of all existing policies, programmes and schemes of their respective Ministries. Furthering the process, the Ministry of Finance issued a Gender Budgeting Charter on 8th March 2007 which specifies the composition of Gender Budgeting Cells and their functions. However, the implementation of the charter remains a challenge. To build the capacities of functionaries and stakeholders at all levels, a Gender Budgeting Scheme is launched by MWCD in the XI Plan, through which more than 1000 persons have been trained. Another major initiative was the introduction of the Gender Budget Statement in the Union Budget in 2005-06, which serves as an important tool for reflecting budgetary allocations for schemes that substantially benefit women. The magnitude of the gender budget reflected in the Gender Budgeting Statement increased from 2.79 percent of the total union budgetary allocations in 2005-06 to 6.22% in 2011-12.

(12) Twelfth Five Year Plan (2012-2017)

The Ministry of Women and Child Development was constituted to empower women to contribute as equal partners in development in an environment free from violence and discrimination. Promoting social and economic empowerment of women through cross cutting policies and programmes, mainstreaming gender concerns, creating awareness about their rights and facilitating institutional and legislative support for enabling them to realise their human rights and developing to be potential. In accordance with the requirements of the Performance Monitoring and Evaluation System (PMES) of the Government of India, The Ministry is responsible for the specific Results Framework Document (RFD) for implementing Five-Year

Strategic Plan (FYSP) framed for 2011 to 2016 with the culmination with The Millennium Development Goals (MDGs) targeted upto 2015. Rajiv Gandhi Scheme for Empowerment of Adolescent Girls provides nutritional food, life skill education, health education, home based skills to adolescent girls. Emphasize on legislative framework by the protection of children against sexual abuse by enacting new legislation and the promotion of child centred jurisprudence. Preventing and combating trafficking of women and children by protection from all forms of violence and discrimination. Mainstreaming gender concerns in policies, programmes and schemes of Government of India and State Governments through gender budgeting. Enabling economic empowerment of marginalized women with relief and rehabilitation to the vulnerable women who lack either with family or societal support and independent income. Promoting the rights based approach in the formulation of policies, programmes, schemes and legislation for women and children. Improving Internal efficiency, responsiveness and service delivery, Policy coordination, advocacy and education relating to nutrition. The Ministry shall Implement the Integrated Child Development Services Scheme (ICDS) by building capacities of anganwadi workers and helpers. SABLA scheme provides compensation for the wage loss, provision for health care of mother and infants by supporting pregnant and lactating women. Indira Gandhi Matritva Shayog Yojana provides the Maternity Benefit Scheme. In Integrated Child Protection Scheme (ICPS) institutional mechanisms and structures aided by state governments and Child Helpline by Childline Foundation are provided. Rajiv Gandhi Creche Scheme for the children of working mothers will be reviewed based on the demand assessment in the current context covering children who are in need of care and protection, starting short stay homes for women in distress and working women hostel through the intervention of NGOs and Government. Rashtriya Mahila Kosh (RMK) will improve the access of women to micro finance, skill upgradation for employment to the asset-less and marginalized women. Advocacy and legal aid provision for women for preventing trafficking of women and children and setting up of rehabilitation homes for trafficked victims through NGOs. Capacity building of officers of Central and State Government for institutionalized Gender Budgeting process. Filling the gaps in legislative framework by coordination with other Ministries for convergence of policies, legislation, schemes and programmes relating to women and children. Providing various support services to women and children through the Central Social Welfare Board and its network of voluntary organizations and bilateral and multilateral cooperation with UN Organisation for gender equity. Compleying obligations under international conventions relating to women and children. Conducting research to find new facts of women and child development. For Highlights of Five Year Plan in India (Refer Table 10).

CONCLUSION

Women's right is enshrined in the constitution, but Gender bias, discrimination, confinement of women in domestic works, social restriction, poor access to health services, malnutrition, lack of education and employment, exclusion from political sphere, low status, violence, migration, changes in labour market, need for new skills, changing technology are the challenges to fulfill the constitutional commitment. Inspite of ensuring mandated rights to women through various legislations like right to residence under the Protection of Women from Domestic Violence Act (DVA) or inheritance rights in ancestral property, they are not able to access these rights. Reforms are needed in enhancing Personal Income Tax exemption limit to women having dependent aged family members, exemption of Tax for child care, Self Help Groups and Women's Cooperatives, review of Pension schemes and post retirement benefit schemes are the need of the day. In spite of the progress made over the years, Gender sensitivity should be attained in public finance, trade and fiscal policies. Possibilities of denial of registration of cases by the police, inadequate investigations, delays in judicial process acts as barriers to access justice by women. Hence, extensive reforms in judicial mechanisms for responsive, sensitive and accountable administration of justice has to be focused. Inclusive growth demands all sections to join hands as partners in the process of development. Efficient implementation of policies and programs by the government can be supported with assessing need of public identified through research, monitoring and evaluation systems. Government should

Table 10: Highlight of the five year plans in India.

Sl. no.	*Five year plan and year*	*Initiatives*	*Effect*
1	First plan (1951-56)	Central social welfare board established in 1953	Mahila mandals or women clubs
2	Second plan (1956-61)	Organising women as workers	Protection against hazardous work, Maternity benefit, Creches for children.
3	Third plan (1961-66)	Female education	Expansion of rural welfare services, Condensed courses, Health education, Nutrition and family planning.
4	Fourth plan (1969-74)	Education	Family planning
5	Fifth plan (1974-78)	Functional literacy	Child care, Nutrition, Health care, Home economics
6	Sixth plan (1980-85)	Women development	Multi-disciplinary approach in health, Education and employment.
7	Seventh plan (1985-1990)	Economic and social development	'Beneficiary Oriented Schemes' (BOS)
8	Eighth plan (1992-1997)	Human development	Enable women to function as equal partners and participants in the development process
9	Ninth plan (1997-2002)	Empowerment of women	'Women's Component Plan' (WCP) - 30% of funds/benefits flow from all the general development sectors.
10	Tenth plan (2002-2007)	Empowerment of women	Social empowerment, Economic empowerment and gender justice
11	Eleventh plan (2007-2012)	Empowerment and gender equity	Heterogeneous intervention considering diversity in castes, Classes, Communities, Economic groups, Geographic and development zones.
12	Twelfth plan (2012-2017)	Dignity and equality of women	Creating structural and institutional mechanisms.

Source: Planning Commission, Government of India.

build Transparent legal system to evaluate the impact of policies, setting up required infrastructure, appoint dedicated personnel, and further strengthen the support services like shelter homes, medical facilities, counseling services, tackle cost of legal representation and delay in judicial proceedings, unplug the loopholes of related laws by creating enabling environment for women in the country to live so as to find remedies for inclusive growth[4].

[4] Savara, Meera (1982). Changing Trends in Women's Employment, Himalaya Publishing House, New Delhi.

11

Domestic Empowerment Through Self Help Groups

INTRODUCTION

Organizational base, pool of resource and technology has lead to generation of employment and income. Empowerment is a process of creating awareness about social realities and available rights, to build capacity through education, knowledge and skills to initiate participation for change. Participation of women in savings and economic attainment will improve their status and gives power for decision making. It changes the nature and direction of systems affecting marginalized women and other disadvantaged sections in the society. Self help groups (SHGs) are small voluntary association of people from the same socio-economic background with a purpose of solving their common problems through self help and mutual help. It is a tool to promote rural savings and provide gainful employment. This collective actions introduce leadership and strength among women by reducing the risk from external threat. It enables women to overcome the oppression of patriarchy by realizing their true potentials which reflects total well being. The micro credit is one of the solution to promote the quality of life which accelerate the socio-economic development by reducing the rural poverty considerably. Self Help Groups play important role of ensuring good health and empower women within the household as well as in the society. This chapter discuss about constitution, scope and credibility of Self Help groups, the Governments initiatives towards its promotion, Women Empowerment initiatives in rural areas for rural development.

Self Help Groups (SHGs) are mostly informal groups which follow the framed rules to satisfy common perceived aims by collective activity. These groups are known by different names in different places like sangha, samooh, mandal, dangham, samiti, etc. The basic principle of the SHGs are group approach, mutual trust, organisation of small and manageable groups, group cohersiveness, spirit of thrift, demand based lending, collateral freeness, women friendly loan, peer group pressure in repayment, skill development, training, capacity building and empowerment[1]. The rules and regulations of SHGs vary according to the preferences of the members and promoters. It is not formed for charity and group members are not volunteers even though the work is usually unpaid, members work to change their own life situation with the mutual support. The members pool savings as a thrift deposit. Many such groups are formed for production activities, promote saving among members and use the pooled resources to meet their various credit needs. When fund generation is low in the initial phases due to low saving capacities, it will be supplemented by external resources. Hence, it provides primitive banking service to its members which is cost effective, flexible and without defaults based on local requirement. These groups meet regularly to collect the savings from members, select members for granting loan, provide training and mitigates conflicts that arises. In the meetings they discuss common village problems by sharing information and try to find solutions, efforts are made to improve members health and literacy. According to Sheela J and Jayamala M (2003) Non-governmental organizations started sponsoring micro finance based SHGs after nineties by the mutual coordination of National and International donors. Encouraging policies of Government of India and Reserve Bank of India ensured economic self- reliance of rural poor women who are unnoticed in social structure to fight against exploitation[2].

---

[1] Lalitha N., (1995). Rural Women Empowerment and Development Banking Kanishka Publication and distributors, New Delhi.

[2] Sheela J. and Jayamala M. (2003). Social Welfare, Vol. 55, No. 06, Role of Self Help group women in value base emancipation.

(1) HISTORY AND DEVELOPMENT

The origin of Self Help Groups (SHGs) is from the brain child of Gramin Bank of Bangladesh which used to provide micro finance to rural women as a most powerful instrument to tackle poverty. Which was founded by the economist, Prof. Mohammed Yunus of Chittagong University in 1975. Even though in India, SHGs started in the year 1975, was initiated by National Bank for Agriculture and Rural Development (NABARD) during 1986-87 and real effort was taken during 1991-92 by linking it with banks. In Tamil Nadu, SHGs was started in 1989 at Dharmapuri District. At present in India approximately, 1.50 lakh groups are functioning with more than 30 Lakh members. Number of rural financing micro-credit schemes have been introduced in the form of "cooperatives" and "loan melas". Targeting women-specific programmes started much later by NGOs such as SEVA (Sustainable Agriculture & Environment Voluntary Action) of Tamil Nadu. PRADAN (Professional Assistance for Development Action) formed its first SHG in Alwar, Rajasthan, in 1987. A savings and credit SHG is a simple yet effective way of reaching out and connecting with rural poor women. The SHGs in India were formed by Mysore Resettlement and Development Agency (MYRADA), a NGO in 1985 due to breakdown of the large cooperatives organized by MYRADA. By 1986–87, there were nearly 300 SHGs in MYRADA projects. Its programs reach to people in various districts of Karnataka, Tamil Nadu and Andhra Pradesh. The objective of helping the poor to help themselves is achieved by forming SHGs by Self Affinity Groups (SAGs) by partnership with NGOs and other organisations. MYRADA then approached NABARD for funding an action research project on self-help groups. Asian and Pacific Regional Agricultural Credit Association (APRACA) weighed options and agreed on further action for effectively increasing credit access for the poor. In India, NABARD and a member of APRACA, carried out an elaborate study which gave useful insights into the dynamics of group organization, saving potential and repayment ethics of the poor. Encouraged by the results of the study and action research project of MYRADA, NABARD, in consultation with the Reserve Bank of India (RBI), Commercial Banks and NGOs, launched a pilot project in 1991–92 for linking of SHGs with banks. Thus, the micro finance activity is the result of NABARD that started in

February 1992 through an initial pilot project promoting 500 SHGs. RBI had advised Commercial Banks in July 1991 to extend finance to SHGs guidelines. Subsequently, the linkage project was extended to Regional Rural Banks and Cooperative Societies. The government entered this arena through Rashtriya Mahila Kosh, India Mahila Yojana, and The Ministry of Women & Child Development launched a Central Sector scheme named Support to Training & Employment Programme for women (STEP) in the year 1986-87 with an objective of extending training for up-gradation of skills and sustainable employment for women in large numbers through a variety of action oriented projects. The scheme was revised in the year 2009-10 to cover 10 traditional sectors of employment besides the option of supporting the locally appropriate sectors. Rural Women Development and Empowerment Project known as "Swashakti" has reached a take off stage in nine states by involving NGOs fully for its delivery of various components. This project lead to holistic empowerment by making them stakeholders along with state government departments, banks and beneficiaries. Loan funds were sourced increasingly from apex level NGOs and developmental banks like NABARD, SIDBI, Cooperative banks and Commercial banks. Reserve Bank of India monitored the financing of SHGs and small micro-enterprises without demanding collateral securities and other bureaucratic red-tapism. SHG enhance the quality of women as participants, decision maker and beneficiaries in the democratic, economic, social and cultural spheres of life. It also plays a large role in achieving Millenium Development Goals in developing countries[3].

(2) WORKING OF SHGs

SHGs comprise maximum of 20 members among them one is selected as an 'Animator' for two years and two members are selected as representatives. The group members meet every week to discuss about the group savings, rotation of funds, bank loan, terms to repayment of loan, social and community action programmes, etc. SHGs democratic way of functioning is explained below.

---

[3] Rao V.M. Women Self Help Groups, Profiles from Andhra Pradesh and Karnataka, Kurukshetra, Vol. 50, No. 6, pp. 26-32.

(a) Formation

SHGs are formed only for the sake of savings and credit activities. Motivation for the group formation and the profile of the leader is a major determinant of its strength. Women groups are better able to address the specific needs and problems of the members. The role of facilitator is critical in strengthening group process and truly instilling the concept of Self Help. Most SHGs have an elected chairperson, a deputy, a treasurer and other office holders. Their effectiveness is disseminating information, upgrading skills and facilitating linkages, contribute towards the extent of self-reliance of the group. Forming, storming, norming and performing being the stages of group formation, full participation of all members, quality of leadership, homogeneity among members, transparency in operations are the factors affecting group formation[4].

(b) Functions of SHGs

It creates a common fund by the members through their regular savings which will be pooled in a democratic way. It conducts periodical meetings to take needed decisions. It provide small and reasonable loan with affordable interest rate varying from group to group which helps easy repayment on time. Usually the interest fixed will be little higher than the bank Rate but lesser than the money lenders.

(c) Scope of SHGs

Many organizations in India, including Non Governmental Organizations (NGOs), Community Based Organizations (CBOs), Local and National Government Bodies, now recognize the enormous potential of SHGs. SHG movement is known for the rapid growth of rural bank and SHG linkage to support borrowings. The emphasize on capacity building helped to address the dynamic and multifaceted nature of poverty, lack of skills, building knowledge and confidence

---

[4] Lalitha N. "Women Thrift and Credit Groups-Breaking the barriers at the gross roots" Peninsular Economist. Vol. XII, No. 2, pp. 188-195.

for using finance to exploit opportunities, manage life cycle events and cope with crisis. Indian micro finance scene is dominated by SHGs linkage to banks. The Indian development is unique by useing formal institutions in providing finance to SHGs instead of creating parallel non-formal channels of outing finance to poor.

(d) Gender Equity

Through resources and agency support rural women should be guided to join the SHGs to encourage formation of micro enterprises according to their interest, skills and need which empowers them to exhibit better roles as entrepreneurs, wife, mother, etc. to measure their development[5]. Focus more on enriching their capacity instead of providing welfare to improve their financial, social and political status by making them an agent for social change to enjoy joyful life. Women have developed abundant self-confidence and self-esteem through SHG movement which tackles poverty, social and gender discrimination and makes them self sustainable[6].

(e) Entrepreneurship Development

Andhra Pradesh experienced critical financial conditions due to the existing hindrences to women entrepreneurship like less cooperation from family, ignorance about the DWACRA, IRDP, TRYSEM initiatives, insufficient managerial skills among women, apathy, sense of fear, illiteracy, outdated custom, etc.[7]. SHGs have obtained the necessary skills to produce a product, manage funds, organize the operations of enterprises which linked them to the market and government departments has improved members position at home and community. It enable the rural poor to earn their own livelihood by promoting micro enterprises in the regions of poverty by comprehension of market dynamics where the entrepreneurs

---

[5] Sathish P., (2001) Mainstreaming of India, Micro-Finance, Economic and Political Week. Vol. XL, No. 17, pp. 1732-1738.

[6] Chiranjeevulu T., (2003). Empowering Women through self help groups-Experiences in Experiment, Kurukshetra, March.

[7] Debry, Bibek *et al.* (1991). Energizing rural development through Panchayats Academic Foundation, New Delhi.

equipped to face the changing market behavior and competition[8]. The enterprise were under constant risk due to the ease entry and exit policies of the groups hence, the sustainable development depends on internal and external factors. New empowerment agenda was initiated through the intermediation of banks by bringing strategies to move up in the socio-economic ladder transforming passive participants to active stake holders in the development process. The members with no educational, industrial or entrepreneurial background were made self dependent and self reliant by developing, enhancing the decision making capacity, strength and confidence for solving their problems[9].

(f) Micro Credit from the Common Fund

Funds for credit activities are coming through regular savings deposited by all of its members on a weekly or fortnightly basis. Groups meet periodically to discuss their transactions. Limited amount of loan for short duration with a simple and flexible procedure are decided by consensus of members provided for various purposes, defaults are negligible[10]. Innovative Saving Programme "Podupu Lakshmi" launced in Nellore District of Andhra Pradesh based on saving a rupee per day per member the economic prosperity went up and they started climbing the social ladder. The judicious mix of Micro credit and other activities for development and empowerment have made it an effective weapon for holistic and integrated social and economic development of women. Majority of rural SHGs invest the loan for consumption and productive purposes[11]. Study on SHGs reviewed that the beneficiaries had crossed the poverty line with an additional income ranging from 280 to 395 which improved their socio-economic status[12].

---

[8] Rajapriya M., (2008). Social Welfare, Vol. 55, No. 06, Role of Self Help Group women in Value base Emancipation".

[9] Manimekalai N, *et al.* (2003). Grassroot women Entrepreneurship through Micro Credit, Peninsular Economist, Vol. XII. No. 2, pp. 181-185.

[10] Abhaskumar Jha, (2000). Lending to the Poor: Designs for Credit, EPW, Vol. XXXV, No. 8 and 9.

[11] Ledger Wood Joanna, (1995). Sustainable Banking with the poor micro-finance hand book, An institutional and financial perspect *i.e.*, Washington D.C.

[12] Harper, Malcolm, (1992). Profit for the poor cases of micro-finance, oxford and IBH Publishing company private Ltd.

(g) Empowerment through SHGs

SHGs ensures economic independence by income generating activities. Its regular meetings and discussion on many live issues helps rural women in developing communication skills and build confidence to speak at the Grama Sabha and Public meetings. It brings success in their democratic, social and cultural spheres of life. Social development of women by creating equality of status encourage their participation, facilitate decision making and make them self sustaining in the society.

(3) GOVERNMENT INITIATIVES TO PROMOTE SHGs

Government support accelerated SHG movement. Collaborative efforts by government, NGOs and SHGs to promote micro enterprises in the long run generates huge employment opportunity to rural women to reduce poverty in the rural areas[13]. Specific Policies shall be formed to bring occupational diversity by encouraging rural industries and support services. Rural banks made phenomenal progress to increase poor people's access to financial services. The schemes aims at institutional capacity building, promotion of women SHGs, strengthening the capacity of central and state level agencies, income generation, investment of fund, technical support, access to social programmes and use of funds for community asset such as drinking water, sanitation, day care centers, health and child care[14]. Study on rural and tribal women in Maharashtra with 239 families among which mothers of 64 families involved with SHGs have better awareness about child health care, family planning than non participants in the villages level. Following are some of the major initiatives of government towards SHG movement[15].

---

[13] World Bank (2001). World Development Indicators, Washington, D.C., World Bank.

[14] Chelladurai, (2004). Social Welfare Vol. 55, No. 12, "Women Empowerment and Economic Development".

[15] Carr, Marilyn Chen and Renana Jhabvala (1990) Speaking Out Womens Empowerment in South Asia, Vistaar Publications, New Delhi.

(a) Development of Women and Children in Rural Areas (DWCRA)

Groups with maximum membership of 15 are formed by Department of Rural Development. The scheme focus on organisation of women into groups to foster a collective approach to their problems and to enhance their bargaining power by granting a lum sum of Rs. 25000. The members can collectively use it for any income generating activity. Thrift is used as tool for entry and members are encouraged to save their money in a common fund and Training in leadership, attitudinal change, skills for income generation is provided under the scheme.

(b) Mahila Samridhi Yojana (MSY)

It is a unique scheme linking micro-credit with the training to the women members to be formed in to SHGs in the trades such as tailoring, cutting and embroidery, etc. it is implemented by National Minorities Development Finance Corporation through the State Channelising Agencies (SCA) and NGOs. Training is given to a group of 20 women in any suitable craft activity. The group is formed into Self Help Group during the training itself and after the training, micro-credit is provided to the members. The maximum duration of training is for six months with maximum training expenses of Rs. 500/- per month per trainee. During the training a stipend of Rs. 250/- is also paid to the trainees. After the training, need based micro credit subject to a maximum of Rs. 50,000/- is made available to each member of SHG at the interest rate of 5% per annum.

(c) Anganwadi Groups

This group is formulated under the Department of Women Welfare at the habitation level for implementing health, nutrition, and literacy programmes for rural women. Micro finance facility is availed to the members for taking up income generating activities.

(d) Joint Forest Management Groups

Village communities in notified forest areas are formed into Vana Samrakshana Samithis (VSS) to conserve forest wealth, social mobilization and village communities are exhorted to take up alternative income generating activities.

(e) Watershed Management Groups

Farmers in the watershed areas are formed into groups for implementing improved techniques of watershed development with the intervention of a facilitating agency, normally an NGO. On-farm development activities are funded through grant support, these groups are also encouraged to take up microfinance with thrift as an entry point activity.

(f) Rashtriya Mahila Kosh (RMK)

Group formed by NGOs and funded by RMK, a fund set up by the government of India for associating women to undertake income generating activity.

(g) The Council for Advancement of Peoples Action and Rural Technology (CAPART)

It is set up by the Ministry of Rural Development, Government of India to fund Voluntary Organizations and Community Based Organizations engaged in serving rural areas. It occupies a significant space in shaping the development and innovation of NGOs and catalyzing development initiatives to reach the poor.

(h) Swa-Shakti Project (Assisted By IFAD & World Bank)

Rural women's development and empowerment project encompassing states of Bihar, Gujarat, Haryana, Madhya Pradesh, and Uttar Pradesh with a Central Project. Support units in the Department of Women & Child Development of Government of India to facilitate the implementation.

(i) Kudumbashree Project

The project is launched by the Government of Kerala with the support of Government of India and NABARD for wiping out absolute poverty within 10 years. The project implemented through Community Based Organizations for empowerment of women, formation of informal banks for the poor, promotion of micro enterprises and establishment of rural marketing networks and convergent community action.

(j) District Poverty Initiative Project (VELUGU)

In Andhra Pradesh with the aid of World Bank, the project aimed to organize the poorest of the poor in selected districts through convergence of resources, organizational capacity building, linkages and capital support. The project envisages "common interest group" and members are motivated to take up economic activities and community welfare programmes through the common investment fund of Rs. 20,000/-

(k) Swarna Jayanti Shahari Rozgar Yojana (SJSRY)

It is an anti-poverty programme launched by the Government of India for eradicating absolute poverty from urban areas. The community development structure provide the channel for the delivery system of scheme through Urban Self Employment Programme (USEP) and Development of Women and Children in Urban Areas (DWCUA) helps poor women in setting up gainful employment through group activity.

(l) Swarna Jayanti Gram Swarozgar Yojana (SGSY)

It is a modified version of IRDP with the focus on group approach. Cost of group formation and development is met from the scheme fund amounting to Rs. 10,000/- per group over a period of 3-4 years. Grading of group is done once in six months to ascertain their status of performance and corrective capacity building is undertaken. Economic activities is assisted through bank loan cum subsidy.

(m) Bank as a Self Help Promotion Institution

Since the nationalization of the commercial banks there has been a commitment at the highest policy levels, towards improving access to financial services for the poor. Several policy measures like allocation of small loans at subsidized interest rates ranging from 4% to 10% for micro loans, and opening of small rural branches. Linking bank credit to a targeted program of the Government of India. The integrated Rural Development Program (IRDP). Linkage programme of NABARD through its networks and some NGOs act as banking intermediaries, channeling finance through centralizing accounts and financial system at the NGO level.

(n) Swami Vivekananda Youth Movement (1984)

It is a non-political, non-religious, not for profit, registered voluntary organisation engaged in building a new civil society in India through its grassroot to policy level action in Health, Education and Community Development Sectors. Acting as a key promoter in the community towards self reliance and empowerment, it is developing local, innovative and cost-effective solutions to sustain community driven progress. It also rooted to its values of Satya, Ahimsa, Seva and Tyaga which is reflected in its program design and delivery, transactions with its stakeholders, resource utilization, disclosures and openness to public scrutiny. Buying in support from the community, working in health partnership with the government and corporate sectors and sharing its experiences with like-minded organizations are the hallmark. It established its own SHGs and take up microcredit and empowerment programmes.[16]

(o) Marketing Assistance Scheme

It is meant for individual crafts persons, SHGs and other beneficiaries of National Minorities Development Finance Corporation implemented through State Channelizing Agencies and NGOs. With

[16] Swami Vivekananda Youth Movement Annual Report, April 2008 to March, (2009).

a view to support the crafts persons to promote marketing and sale of their products at remunerative prices. The corporation provide grants to SCAs and NGOs to organize state and district level exhibition at selected locations upon the merits of the proposals. In these exhibitions, handloom, handicraft products of minority crafts person are exhibited and sold. Such exhibitions, also serve the purpose of organizing 'buyer seller meet' which is very useful for product development and market promotion for domestic market as well as for exports.

(p) Micro Credit

National Minorities Development Finance Corporation provide financial assistance upto the maximum limit of Rs. 50,000 per beneficiary of Self Help Groups whose family income is below to Rs. 81,000 per annum in rural areas and Rs. 1,03,000 per annum for urban areas to start any income generating activities or any gainful legitimate business activity when undertaken leads to income generation. Under micro financing scheme, groups of individuals belonging to the minorities will include such groups in which predominantly 75% and above members belong to minority community. In exceptional cases this may also include those groups where upto 60% of the members belong to minority community, provided that the other members *i.e.* upto 40% belong to weaker sections including Scheduled Castes/Scheduled Tribes, other Backward Classes and Disabled. Loan is granted for activities like small business or trade comprising starting Tea stall, Dhaba, Meat shop, Fish vending, Pan shop, Vegetable and fruits selling, Vending readymade cloths, carpentry, cycle repairing. Cottage Industry or service activity like Candle making, Papad and Vade making, Wet grinder, Bakery, Processing of dry fish, Shoe shop, Motor winding, Puncture shop, etc. Artisan activities like Block printing, bangle making, jute bag making, weaving, zarizardosi work, kantha work, appliqué work, etc. Agricultural and allied activities like poultry, goat rearing, sheep rearing, duck rearing, piggery, dairy, etc. The

---

[17] Lalitha N. "Women Thrift and Credit Groups-Breaking the Barriers at the Grossroots", Peninsular Economist, Vol. XII, No. 2, pp. 188-191

borrower should preferably be a regular member of a Thrift and Credit Group[17].

(4) IMPACT OF EMPOWERMENT

The empowerment is the process of challenging existing power relations and to challenge patriarchal ideology to transform the structures and institutions that reinforce gender discriminations and to gain access and control over material and informational resources. SHGs are emerging as powerful tool for socio-economic empowerment of the poor in rural areas[18]. After analyzing the problems and prospects of self employed women stated that as women have to play duel role, self-employment is better suited to them and having authority over enterprise she can maintain her own timings and adjustment[19].

SHGs are initially formed on the foundation of the accumulated endowment of bonding social capital already existing in the community. The social capital produced by these as it matures through creation of new tie and linkages strengthens the community capacity. It articulate the community demands as they become aware of their rights which changes the attitude of bureaucratic officials, to be more responsive to the need of the community by building relationship between the state and the society. In this way, eventually becomes an associational framework for collaborative actions that produce public good. It also strengthens the local governance and political democracy by many members being elected in the panchayati raj system in India which is the local democratic governance. In self help groups it is assumed that all poor households need to save and have the inherent capacity to save small amount regularly. Easy access to credit is more important than cheap subsidized credit. Poor are the best judge of their credit needs and good users and re-payers of credit when formed in groups. Credit discipline is imbibed among the members by way of positive impact on income, saving and self

[18] Geetha B., (2007). Social Welfare, Vol. 54, No. 11-12, Self Help Groups, A social Movement.

[19] Khullar Mala, (2009) Emergence of women movement in India, Asian Journal of Womens Studies, Vol. 03, No. 02 pp. 94-129.

confidence. This impact is more when SHGs are linked with NGOs. SHGs provide women opportunity to be together, identify and communicate the problems, exchange experiences, develop forums of solidarity and mutual assistance to build self esteem, planning and to organize against inequality at public levels[20]. Empowerment is the development of skills and abilities of people to enable them to manage themselves. The process of empowerment includes economic independence, knowledge and awareness, self image and autonomy. It provides interventions to alleviate poverty, meet their needs, reduce gender discrimination and improves self-esteem. Economic empowerment improves women's control over material resources and enrich security. The process of empowerment includes education, skill development and increasing awareness about health, nutrition, environment, economic and political conditions to ensure equal participation in the process of bringing social change. Scope for further Investigation can be done in this area to know Progression of SHGs towards right direction for women empowerment, the capacity of formal lending institutions to handle illiterate women, the financial constraints to lend loan to the vast number of SHGs, Sufficiency of loan in the present scenario to start an income generating activity, Demand-supply linkage for all the SHGs in massive scale, the competition issues involved with new micro enterprises started by the SHG members. The micro-credit and SHG movement sometimes perceived as the sole panacea for addressing poverty and women's empowerment is increasingly coming under critical review. The challenge in the micro credit movement is to reach out to the poorest and most vulnerable and marginalized populations like SC/STs, single women and other socially excluded communities. Many of the SHG groups have low levels of credit absorption, low skill base and low asset base, and find it hard to create economic enterprise. At the heart of the problem lies in the need for appropriate institutional mechanisms to address inadequate access to education, lack of investment, poor credit worthiness, poor mobilization, and other structural exclusions in the XII Five year Plan for financial inclusion of gross root.

---

[20] Dadhich, Micro finance a panacea for poverty alleviation a case study of oriental Graeme project in India, Indian Journal of Agricultural Economics, Vol. 56, No. 03.

CONCLUSION

Lalitha Rani N states that the role and integration of women in economic development is always an indicator of economic independence and social status. Usually working women are being respected by the household members and the society. Now a days the women in the SHGs are also respected as they are independent in earning the income and they are contributing to household income, expenditure and savings. The strategy of micro-financing through SHGs can help in a big way in eradicating poverty and empowering women. However, what is needed is a real change in the community attitude to depart from the traditional approach of highly subsidized support to the promotion of self-help. This is a time consuming process but regular follow up and guidance surely, bring substantial improvement. By being a member of SHG there is possibility for better participation, decision making, planning for future by inculcating management skills in financial matters. Women groups have proved that they would indeed bring about a sea change in the mindset of the very conservative and traditional bound illiterate women belonging to rural areas. These groups as a viable alternative to achieve the objectives of rural development and to set community participation with economic power and potentialities proved that with the help of district administration and local officials they could indeed bring in socio-economic development to enhance their self-employment potential. Thus, SHG movement among the rural poor in different parts of the country is emerging as a very reliable and efficient mode for technology transfer. Hence, SHG is agreed to be one of the effective means of empowerment of women to facilitate rural development, building solidarity and socio-economic betterment of the poor. It proved to be successful in addressing the interests of women in a sustained manner.

12

Gender Equity and Inclusive Growth of Women

INTRODUCTION

Indian economy is growing across the world. The country remains shackled with evils like corruption, social barriers, violence against women, deprivation of the minorities. Growth is not uniform across the sectors as many cross-sections of the populae remain outside the process of development. Several social, political and economic factors need to be tackled for sustaining a inclusive growth. Inclusive growth is "a growth process which yields broad-based benefits and ensures equality in opportunity for all". The Inclusive growth implies an equitable allocation of resources with benefits accruing to every section of society hence it is broad-based. It is concerned with the Pro-poor growth and growth with equity. Women are deprived from equity under the social structure. Patriotical bias, Powerlessness and dependency lead women into vulnerable position by making men unjustifiably superior and leaving way for crimes to galore. Violence is always opposed to reason thereby breaches human rights of the people. The legal systems for the protection of women should work with efficacy of criminal law to curb crimes against them. The principle of gender equality is enshrined in the Indian Constitution in its Preamble, Fundamental Rights, Fundamental Duties and Directive Principles by empowering the state to adopt measures against discrimination. Within the framework of a democratic polity, our laws, development policies, plans and programmes have aimed at women's welfare in all spheres. India has also ratified various international conventions and human rights instruments committing to gender equity and justice through inclusive growth strategy.

As per the recent estimates, Population of India in 2016 is 1.31 billion. Women in India constitutes around 48.1% (635 million) of the total population. Indian Government is the key initiator since 1950's to protect women's interest by emphasizing their welfare through gender equity and social justice. The government adopted philosophy of 'Promotion of women's welfare' until 1970, during 1980's towards 'Development of Women' and after 1990's towards 'Empowerment of women' to guide all the major activities towards women's progress. The status given to women in any society reflects the nature of cultural richness and standard of civilization. Swami Vivekananda said, "The Nation which do not respect women can never become great". India is the fastest growing country in the globe with growth rate of 8%. Trade Liberalization and production with advanced technology raises the growth rate of the economy thereby help to face global competition. Gender equality reduce poverty and promote growth by encouraging women's employment. Equal partnership of women in development process ensure the sustainability. But, if Women's are employed in export oriented industries like garments, food processing and handicraft as informal workers for lowest possible wage at poor terms of employment it affects their life. With the emphasis towards Women empowerment to build potential community and ensure human welfare the world started recognizing 1975th year as 'International Year of Women' as per the call of the NGO's, every 8th March as 'International Women's Day', the Decade between 1991-2000 AD as 'SAARC Decade of the Girl child and Year 2001 as the 'Year of Women Empowerment'.

A. NEED FOR WOMEN EMPOWERMENT

Indians learn the essential themes of social and cultural life within the bosom of the family. Women are legal citizens of the country but due to the lack of acceptance from the male dominant society there is a considerable deterioration in their status. Indian women suffered a lot as they were completely devoted inside the family, no share in parental property, lack in medical care, increased infant mortality rates and low priority to education which reduced their growth and deprived rights of equality with men. Women problems and challenges is world-wide phenomena in the developing countries. It is inevitable to create an environment where, women can make independent decisions. Education is the weapon to overcome these inequalities. To bring quick and effective change after independence, Indian Constitution ensured equality, dignity and protection from discrimination. In order to alter the attitude towards segregation of sexes, series of laws were enacted. Now women is encouraged to expose herself to outside business. The economic conditions demand participation of women with men in the production process. Free and Compulsory education, Freedom to hold high offices, Political rights to franchise and contest in elections, Spouses sharing a common social life in cities are the recent trends. These positive situations are vanishing the stereotyped mindset of the society. Hence there is a need for empowering women in health care, nutrition, legal aspects, family welfare, and self-employment in the present scenario. This chapter focus on the study about empowerment by analyzing emerging problems, welfare programmes, role of education and effects of empowerment.

(1) Scope of Women Empowerment

The status of women in the country, particularly those from the disadvantaged sections of the society is unfavourable. A girl child suffers from discrimination even before birth and after birth in the allocation of household resources such as food, education, access to health care and at puberty, sometimes coerced into child marriage. Most women in the rural areas suffer from double burden of carrying out less quantifiable work like cooking, fetching water, sending children to school along with agriculture labour, feeding cattle, milking cow, etc. Women are not just a minority, but the 'marginalised majority' who are sidelined in decision making in the family, and usally cut off from full involvement in the working of the community and getting an equal share in the reward from social institutions. Empowerment of women per se is not only essential for equity, but also constitutes a critical element in our fight for poverty reduction, economic growth and strengthening of civil society. Women and children are always the worst sufferers in a poverty stricken family and need support. Empowering women, especially mothers, is even more important as it is in homes that she nourishes, nurture and moulds the character of her offspring[1]. Women Empowerment has become important issue worldwide. Discussion on political rights are the primary topic of discussion in many formal and informal campaigns globally. It was introduced at the International Women Conference NAIROBI in 1985. Women suffer from the following disadvantages as compared to men hence it is necessary to address issues relating to social and economic deprivations for women[2].

(a) Maternal mortality rate (MMR)

In every minute at least one women dies from causes related to pregnancy, childbirth and abortion. The maternal mortality ratio is the number of women's deaths from causes related to pregnancy and childbirth per 1,00,000 live births. According to Population Reference Bureau (1997), Washington DC, USA the ratio of MMR is 570/100,000. The average MMR in India is 437 per 1,00,000 live births. The rural MMR (448) is 13% higher than urban MMR (397). For trend in Maternal Mortality Ratio (Refer Fig. 4).

(b) Migration

Migration is common because of employment. The women have to perform dual role of earner and home maker. Normally migrant womens are living without basic sanitary facilities. Many women are sexually exploited by the agents of work and prone to sexually transmitted diseases like HIV/AIDS, Many women will be addicted to bad habits like alcoholism, tobacco chewing, etc. Many are not paid equally with the men even though they are working equally. The change in climate also affects the health of the women and the baby in the womb if she is pregnant.

---

[1] Website of Ministry of Minority Affairs.

[2] Anju Bhatia, (2000). Women's Development and NGOs, Rawat Publications, Jaipur, pp. 48-51.

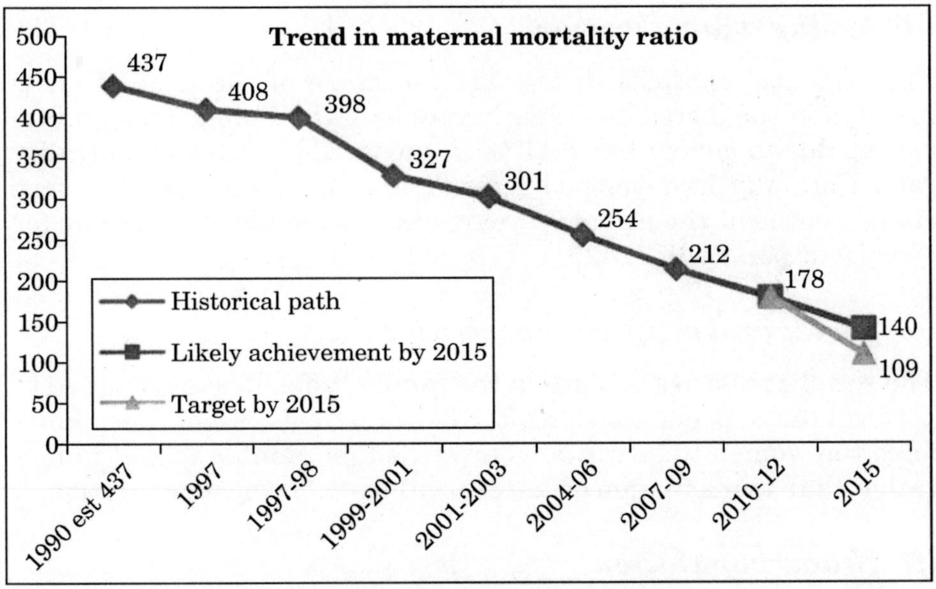

Fig. 4: Trend in Maternal Mortality Ratio

(c) Sexually transmitted diseases

STDs are those diseases which are transmitted by sexual intercourse. The pathogen is present in one partner and the other partner is susceptible to infection with that agent while they are indulging in sexual practices. This allows the pathogen to be transmitted to the other body. Sexually Transmitted Infections include that may not cause clinical disease of the genitals, but are transmitted by sexual interaction. These include Hepatitis B, HIV, HTLV, etc. Women is the victim of sexually transmitted disease due to their vulnerable social and economic conditions. This will increase the risk of infertility and ectopic pregnancy. The risk of transmission from infected men to women is greater than from infected women to men, and many women are powerless to protect themselves. The WHO estimates that the cumulative number of AIDS cases in the world amounted to 2.5 million persons by mid-1993 and that more than 14 million people had been infected by HIV since the pandemic began, a number that is projected to rise to between 30 and 40 million by the end of the decade if effective prevention strategies are not pursued.

(d) Ageing among women

Fundamental changes in the age structure of the population is resulted in the increase of elderly people in the Indian Society. It is caused due to factors like decline in the fertility rate and mortality rate. Normally in developed regions, approximately one for every six persons is at the age of 60 years and this would reach to one for every four persons by 2025.

(e) Social and religious constraints

The socialization takes place in the family.Women is constrained to perform the dependency role after her marriage. Social constraints force the women to be cautious towards the maintenance of family rather than transmission of cultural values to the next generation[3].

(f) Widow population

As per the census department, India's population in 2011 was 121 crore and of this 4.6% or 5.6 crore are widowed with women outnumbering men by a long way. In 2001, only 18.5 lakh or 0.7% of the then population of 102 crore was widowed. Increase in the life expectancy of women resulted in the raise of widowed population. It is a global scenario that women live longer than men. International Population Expert Arokiasamy P. says The age gap between men and women during marriage is the primary cause for widowed population. As life expectancy for women increases, they live as widows for longer period. Among the states Kerala with 6.7% and Tamil Nadu with 6.4%, Undivided Andhra Pradesh with 5.7 and Karnataka with 5.7% ratio. The states with significant elderly population will have more widows.

(g) Crimes against women

It is the direct or indirect physical or mental cruelty to women. Crimes directed specifically against women in which only women are victims. Among the registered cases under crimes against women in India

[3] Neeta Tapan, (2000). Need for Women Empowerment", Rawat Publications, Jaipur and New Delhi, pp. 47-51.

during 2001-14. Crimes like Rape, Kidnapping and Abduction of women and girls, Dowry Deaths, Assault on women with intent to outrage her modesty, Insult to the modesty of women, Cruelty by husband or his relative and cases regarding dowry have increased in 14 years on the other side, Importation of girls from foreign countries, Immoral trafficking and Indecent representation of women considerably decreased. Sati cases are not reported during these period. To understand the total cases registered under crimes against women in India (Refer Table 11).

Table 11: Cases registered under crimes against women in India between 2001-2014

Sl. no	*Crime*	*Year (2001)*	*Year (2014)*	*Variation*	*Remarks*
1	Rape	16075	36975	+20900	Increased
2	Kidnapping and abduction of women and girls	14645	58492	+43847	Increased
3	Dowry deaths	6851	8501	+1650	Increased
4	Assault on women with intent to outrage her modesty	34124	82620	+48496	Increased
5	Insult to the modesty of women	9746	9796	+50	Increased
6	Cruelty by husband or his relatives	49170	123245	+74075	Increased
7	Importation of girls from foreign country	114	13	–101	Decreased
8	Immoral traffic (P) Act	8796	2756	–6040	Decreased
9	Dowry prohibition Act	3222	10146	+6924	Increased
10	Indecent representation of women (P) Act	1052	47	–1005	Decreased
11	Commission of sati (P) Act	0	0	Nil	Normal
	Total crimes against women	143795	341002	+197207	

Source: National Crime Bureau Report

B. GENDER EQUITY AND INCLUSIVE GROWTH IN INDIA

History of women in India has been eventful. Social evils like Child marriages, Sati, Purdah, Jauhar, Devadasi prevailed in the society during the medieval period which diluted the status of women in

India. Women constitute half of total population but projected to be 'weaker sex'. Women, Children, backward castes classes and other minorities often are excluded from the growth story. Inspite of setting women related indicators through gender budgeting, in many cases specific provisions for development of women has failed to bring women on par with man. Poor education, poor health and poor employment continued to prevail except until the recently launched National Rural Employment Guarantee Scheme (NREGS). The women working in the unorganized sector with low wages and poor health condition were severely affected. Indian Government adopted Liberalization, Privatization and Globalization policies after 1990s to accelerate Indian economy towards the global market. Economic trend started changing gradually agricultural orientation to service delivery. The inception of Information Technology into the Indian social and economic units created changes in the phase of productivity aiming to overcome China or Japan in recent future. The initiative to provide food, housing, clothing, education and employment to the large Indian population which is expected to reach nearly 1.5 billion by 2030, is a great challenge. Bringing women into the economic mainstream both as producers and consumers of goods and services must be the basis of any inclusive strategy. The Constitution of India made a deliberate radical departure from the inherited social system, by granting to women equal social and political status. The government began to direct its effort towards mainstreaming of women into the national development process by various legislations to ensure equality, social justice and fraternity[4].

(1) Need for Inclusive Growth in India

Women suffer from many disadvantages as compared to men in terms of literacy rates, labour and autonomy. Social, economic and political empowerment to women through education is the need of the day. Illiteracy has reduced the self-confidence among women from facing challenges in life hence, educating a women is educating a family. Education and Employment is the need of the day for women. There

[4] Parvathy Appaiah, Shankar Rao and Jayanthi P. Shenoy, (2015-16). Human Rights, Gender Equity and Environmental Studies, Jai Bharath Prakashana, Mangalore, Tenth Edition, pp. 37-103.

is a great need for creating awareness on the issues of health, family-life, nutrition, child care, home-management, women's rights, civil responsibilities among the rural women. Social development is only possible through Women Empowerment by eradicating discrimination. The process of women empowerment is conceptualized through personal assertions, building self-esteem and confidence, create ability to protect themselves, encourage full participation in democracy, encourage for education, elimination of gender barriers, ensure employment, land rights, legal aid, freedom and autonomy in the society. Rural empowerment is carried by the interven-tions of 'Self Help Groups'. Though the Government is giving the women empowerment by giving special reservations, the women advancement in India is still not matched to the expectations of inclusive growth.

The eleventh plan which advertised 'inclusive growth' has practically kept women and children out of it to a great extent. Even though the number of voters has been constantly rising, women are socially and politically excluded at the decision making levels. The Integrated Child Development Schemes (ICDS) machinery is still to gear up to meet the challenges of an HIV positive pregnant or lactating mother and her child. Although the country is focusing towards achieving the goal of universal primary education, the poor quality of education has left girls remaining in government institutions to be less competitive because of lack of skills to meet her future needs in life. The social constraints to resist early marriage by a girl and early conception and lack of awareness about sex, sexuality and reproductive health and hygiene has left girls to be the victims of sexually transmitted diseases. Most of the women work in unorganized sectors and fall under the marginal workers or non-workers category and are paid less than the men inspite of having legal provisions for equal pay for equal work. Under the Integrated Rural Development Projects (IRDP) women were not availed with loan facility for the secondary or tertiary sectors but included under primary sectors for availing loan for cows, sheep or goats which used to perish during famine leaving women beneficiaries under a huge debt without any income.

In spite of laws, women even today do not claim the right over the property due to the cultural values that prevail in the society and waive the right against their brothers just to maintain a tie with her family after her marriage without seeking for partition of parental property. According to the report of the High Level Committee on the social, economic and educational status of the Muslim community of India popularly known as the Sachar Report has highlighted the fact that India's largest minority group, the Muslim numbering 13.83 crore approximately have been left out of the development strategies hence, Muslim Women are drastically disadvantageous. Inclusive growth is aimed at poverty reduction, human development, health and employment. The government should seek to the allocation of resources must be focused on weaker sections of the society like women, child, minorities, disabled, etc. The status of Indian women has undergone considerable change but majority of women remain unaware of the personal rights, right to work, right over property, etc. The factors like marriage, extent of literacy, role in the family will affect the quality of life of a women. The empowerment of women in india is higly unbalanced with huge gap that some women who are literate and economically independent will live with better way of life but others will be living under distress conditions. This disparity is also a cause for worry because balanced development is not taking place. However, Indian women still face discrimination in the form of either denial of equal pay or partly payment when compared to men in factories and labour oriented industries. The legal right of a woman pertaining to equal pay at the work place remains unaddressed most of the time because few women are confident enough to complain. Women working in the night shift are more vulnerable to harassment at workplace due to the disregard of people towards the current laws. Indian women are often deprived of promotions and growth opportunities at certain instances.

Typically, the orthodox mindset in the Indian society makes it difficult for a working woman to balance her domestic environment with the professional life. In some families, it may not be acceptable to work after six o'clock. Those families that do accept these working hours may experience considerable anxiety every day about a woman's safety while traveling. So many issues affect a working woman because she is closely protected or watched by her family and the society. According to survey conducted by ASSOCHAM, on 1000 women professionals, around 80 per cent of the households expect their daughters-in-law to prioritize household requirements over the official work. Further, many of them are physically and psychologically abused, by their in-laws and husband but they do not complain or let others know about it, particularly if they have children. Women inclusiveness includes four attributes like providing opportunity, enhancing capability, provide access and ensure security. The Opportunity attribute focuses on generating more and more opportunities to increase their income. The Capability attribute concentrates on providing the means to enhance their capabilities in order to exploit available opportunities. The Access attributes focuses on providing the means to bring opportunities and capabilities together. The Security attribute provides the means to protect themselves against a temporary or permanent loss of livelihood.

(2) Policy Framework for Inclusive Growth of Women

Department of Women and Child Development as a part of the Ministry of Human Resource Development was constituted welfare schemes like Legal Literacy Programme, Awareness Generation Programmes, Prevention of Atrocities against women are evidences of conscious attempts made by the Government to empower women to handle complex situations. The setting of the National Expert Committee on Women Prisoners and The National Commission on Self Employed Women are significant steps in the right direction. It framed National Policy for the Empowerment of Women, 2001 for the advancement, development and empowerment of women.. National Policy on Adult Education was initiated to provide Vocational Education to women after 8th standard belonging to non traditional areas, training educational personnels, their evaluation for better service towards women education, Decentralization of curriculum planning and development. Constitution of Research and Development centres for women studies shall be constituted in the universities and social science research institutions with a purpose to inculcate the research findings into the curriculum was highlighted under the eighth five year plan. The subject Gender Equity is constituted in the undergraduate education to impart gender sensitive education to the young minds. Representative Women Teachers Ratio of 50 per cent was recognized for primary, middle and high school level of education along with promotional avenew in the educational hierarchy. Primary Education Act passed in 1961 in various states through the Constitutional amendment of 1976 some of the subjects of education have been placed under joint responsibility of state and center. The Standard for Conducting Research, Science education, Technical education and higher education will be prescribed by the Centre and run by its financial aid. The equality of women is added in No. 12 in the Twenty Point Programme of Development 1986. National Commission for Women, 1992 a statutory body was created under the National Commission for Women Act, 1990 comprising a chairperson, five members and a member secretary which will investigate into the matters affecting the general interest of women. National Human Rights Commission and State Human Rights Commissions are constituted to protect the human rights of women. The National Plan of Action for the Girl Child (1991-2000) to ensure survival, protection and development of the girl child for a bright future was formulated. Government of India has stepped up for inclusive growth by launching schemes affecting women welfare like Rural Infrastructure(Bharat Nirman), Employment(Mahatma Gandhi National Rural Employment Guarantee Scheme 2005-06), Regional Development (Backward District Development Program), Education (National Literacy Mission and Sarva Shikshan Abhiyan), Rural Health (National Rural Health Mission 2005-06, Janani Suraksha Yojana 2006-07, Total Sanitation Campaign, Mid Day Meal 2008-09, Integrated Child Development Services 2008-09), Agriculture (National Horticulture Mission 2005-06) and Urban Infrastructure (National Urban Renewal Mission), Empowerment (National Rural Livelihood Mission 2010-11) The 73rd Constitutional Amendment Act was passed in 1992 by Parliament which ensure Reservation for Women in Local Self - Government *i.e.* one-third of the total seats for women in all elected offices in local bodies whether in rural areas or urban areas. For Existing Government Interventions (Refer Table 12).

Economic empowerment has been through the formation of thrift and credit based self-help groups (SHGs) formed by women. Increased support for women SHGs in the National Rural Livelihood Mission and in MGNREGA with women having a share of 115.54 (53%) crore person days in 2013-14 have been positive developments. Successful linkages between SHGs and Micro-Finance institutions such as RMK,

Table 12: Existing Government Interventions (Listed by life cycle focus area)

Beneficiaries	***Schemes***
Pregnant & lactating mothers	ICDS, RCH-II, NRHM, JSY, Indira Gandhi Matritva Sahyog Yojana, (IGMSY)- The CMB Scheme
Children 0-3 years	ICDS, RCH-II, NRHM, Rajiv Gandhi National Creche Scheme.
Children 3-6 years	ICDS, RCH-II, NRHM, Rajiv Gandhi National Creche Scheme, Total Sanitation Campaign (TSC), National Rural Drinking Water Programme (NRDWP)
School going children 6-14 years	Mid Day Meals, Sarva Shikshan Abhiyan
Adolescent girls 11-18 years	Rajiv Gandhi Scheme for the Empowerment of Adolescent Girls (RGSEAG), Kishori Shakti Yojana, Total Sanitation Campaign (TSC), National Rural Drinking Water Programme (NRDWP)
Adults	MGNREGS, Skill Development Mission, Women Welfare & Support Programmes, Adult Literacy Programme, TPDS, AAY, Old & Infirm Persons Annapurna, Rashtriya Krishi Vikas Yojana, Food Security Mission, Safe Drinking Water and Sanitation Programmes, National Horticulture Mission, National Iodine Deficiency Disorders Control Programme (NIDDCP), Nutrition Education & Extension, Bharat Nirman, Rashtriya Swasthya Bima Yojana.

Source: Adopted from overcoming the curse of Malnutrition in India: A Leadership Agenda for Action, Coalition for Sustainable Nutrition Security in India, First Edition, September, 2008.

NABARD, SIDBI besides private microfinance institutions have helped in generating additional income, jobs and in creating small enterprises for women. Recently introduced Rajiv Gandhi Scheme for Empowerment of Adolescent Girls (RGSEAG), namely, SABLA which ensures services including health and nutrition to adolescent girls in the age group of 11-14 years school girls and 15-18 years for all girls for nutrition in 200 districts as a pilot. Additionally, a new scheme, the Indira Gandhi Matritva Sahyog Yojana (IGMSY) would provide a better enabling environment for improved health and nutrition to pregnant and lactating mothers and support for providing early and exclusive breastfeeding for the first six months of life on pilot basis in districts initially. NAVDISHA- National Thematic Workshop on Best Practices for Women and Child Development was organised by the Ministry from 20-21 January, 2015 at Panipat reaffirmed that in the Twelfth Plan the Criminal Law (Amendment) Act, 2013, The Sexual Harassment of Women at Workplace (Prevention, Prohibition and Redressal) Act 2013. Ensuring women's social, economic and political empowerment, fulfillment of their rights, promoting their participation and leadership requires comprehensive gender-responsive measures at different levels, including framing legal, policy and institutional frameworks.

(3) Strategies for Inclusive Growth of Women in India

(a) Inclusion through constitutional mandate

The principle of gender equality is enshrined in the Indian Constitution in its Preamble, Fundamental Rights, Fundamental Duties and Directive Principles. The Constitution not only grants equality to women, but also empowers the State to adopt measures of positive discrimination in favour of women. Within the framework of a democratic policies, our laws, development policies, Plans and programmes have aimed at women's advancement in different spheres. India has also ratified various international conventions and human rights instruments committing to secure equal rights of women. Key among them is the ratification of the Convention on Elimination of All Forms of Discrimination against Women (CEDAW) in 1993. The Constitution being the law of the land guaranteed equality to all and equal protection to all by the law of the state, Right against discrimination, state is empowered to make special provisions for the women and children, equal opportunities for all in the public employment, adequate means for livelihood, equal pay for equal work, equal opportunity to promote justice, legal aid for the economically weaker sections, just and humane conditions of work, protection to the educational and economic interest of the weaker section, raising the level of nutrition, promoting harmony and spirit of brotherhood among all the people of the country and positive discrimination favouring women for neutralizing the cumulative socio-economic, educational and political disadvantages in the society.

(b) Inclusion through preventing crimes against women

To uphold the Constitutional mandate, the State has enacted various legislative measures to support services with an intention to ensure equal rights by countering social discrimination, and violence and atrocities against women. The Central government had formulated some Special Laws but all laws are not gender specific, the provisions of law affecting women significantly have been reviewed periodically and amendments carried out to keep pace with the emerging requirements. Normally women are the victims of serious crimes like 'Murder', 'Robbery', 'Cheating' etc, which are spelled as 'Crime against Women'. Indian Penal code (IPC) declared many acts as offences that are punishable with specified punishment under the code. Code specifies offences like Rape, Kidnapping and Abduction for different purposes, Homicide for Dowry, Dowry Deaths, Mental and Physical Torture, Molestation, Sexual Harassment, Importation of girls, etc. The legislators had formulated many acts for protecting offences against women they are The Protection of Women from Domestic Violence Act, 2005, Commission of Sati (Prevention) Act, 1987, Indecent Representation of Women (Prohibition) Act, 1986, The Prohibition of Child Marriage Act, 2006, Prevention of Prostitution Act 1923, UP Naik Girls Protection Act, 1929, The Bombay Devadasi Protection Act, 1934, Prevention of Dedication Act, 1934, Madras Devadasi Act, 1947 and Suppression of Immoral Traffic Act 1956, The Family Courts Act, 1954, The Special Marriage Act, 1954, The Hindu Marriage Act, 1955, The Hindu Succession Act, 1956 with amendment in 2005, Immoral Traffic (Prevention) Act, 1956, Dowry Prohibition Act, 1961, The Medical Termination of Pregnancy Act, 1971, The Criminal Law (Amendment) Act, 1983 these are the efforts to prohibit various crimes against women by imposing punishment.

(c) Inclusion by granting the right for maintenance

Any women has a legal right to claim maintenance from her husband on the ground of desertion or neglect is recognized under section 125 of the Criminal Procedure Code, and under Section 24, of the Hindu Adoption and Maintenance Act, 1956. Even it is extended to her minor children. Further, these laws provide that maintenance can be claimed even prior to divorce, during separation also. Initially, it was believed that a working woman in India is not entitled to claim maintenance, as she is capable of maintaining herself. However, the ambiguity was cleared by a significant decision in Bhagwan *Vs.* Kamla Devi, (1975)2 SCC 386. The Supreme Court held that a working woman can claim maintenance from her estranged husband, if her monthly income is not enough for her maintenance. Further, the Court clarified that the term 'Unable to maintain herself' does not require a woman to be absolute destitute, to entitle maintenance. The right to maintenance is available to the women until she remarries or converts to another religion. Further, there have been instances where the Court has ordered women with substantial earnings, to pay maintenance to her husband.

(d) Inclusion through gender sensitive public finance

Indian Tax Structure is gender biased by nature. We can see the difference in the Personal Income Tax and Gender Differentiated Property Tax. Reduction in Corporate Tax will not benefit women in large numbers as very few are the owners or share holders hence states the 'property lessness' among women. The additional benefit to women can be rendered by increasing the Personal Income Tax exemption limit specially for the female headed households, with aged dependents other than children. Even child care exemptions can be given to the women who are single parent. Tax ememption can be extended to the productive services rendered through Self Help Groups (SHGs) or Women Cooperatives. The System of National Accounts being the internationally accepted standards for measuring economic activity should include care work like cooking, washing, cleaning etc as most of the women engage in this. Even the Indirect tax and Value Added Tax are very regressive by extending upto the consumption level which create impact on the choosing pattern of commodities for daily use by the women. Stimulus packages to support employment and infrastructure projects taken up by government need to be rechecked in terms of utility to women in general. Medical Insurance Policies should be regulated to include single women. The policies for Pension and Post Retirement Benefits need to be reviewed to including the facility for transfer of the policy to the dependent parents or children in case of single headed households. The girl child should not be considered to be a burden and the son syndrome among people have resulted in female infanticide. The Government of India can adopt the old age policy which is adopted in Beijing where under 'care for girl' policy parents of lone females may receive upt to $140 a month for old age pension.

(e) Inclusive growth by strengthening institutional arrangements

National Commission for Women can be strengthened further to achieve womens empowerment. The Ministry of Women and Child Development should work for gender equity through implementation of policies, programmes and schemes through specific women focused schemes and advocacy of the distressed. To make the Ministry to play this role effectively, its women's wing should be strengthened in the XIII Five Year Plan. Consumer Protection Forums shall be constituted to advocate the consumer cases in the block level. Government Hospitals shall be provided with Skilled counselors, Dieticians to safeguard the health and life styles of the poor. Primary Health Centres need to be equipped with advance infrastructure to meet any emergencies. The Appointment of Lady Doctors in all District hospitals shall be strictly monitored. Family Planning and Sex Education shall be rendered to the rural areas through the ANMs. Schools shall be provided with sufficient number of teachers and infrastructure from the Education boards.

(f) Inclusion through skill development programmes

Promotion of skill development which will help the women to overcome the gender stereotypes and facilitate them to grab higher skilled tasks by providing way for higher level employment.Women shall be trained to grab the vocational training based occupations like driving, plumbing, carpentry, painting, tinkering, welding, repairing, etc. Women should be trained to be ASHAs, ANMs, and Project heads for the progress of research and development in the field of agriculture, horticulture, sericulture, fisheries and allied occupations. As the world is driven through technology all the women should be provided with minimum Computer Literacy wherein they could effectively undertake at least the basic banking transactions through utilizing the technological infrastructure. The National Skill

Development Programme (NSDP) has already identified 231 modular courses for women. Promotion of Cottage Industries, Small Scale Industries, Home based products shall be encouraged through proper financial aid and training with the aid of Micro credit. Self Employment Schemes should be linked to the Self Help Groups (SHGs) which are working in the community level. Entrepreneurship development should also be included as an integral part of skill training. To achieve the inclusive growth in India access of women from marginalised and vulnerable communities within these programmes should be ensured. Women's Industrial Training Institutes and Polytechnics should be strengthened to provide advance courses with updated curriculum and training modules.

(g) Inclusion through promoting home based enterprises

Many Non Governmental Organisations and Self Help Groups have initiated women occupations through the Home Base Enterprises which provide basic training to take up occupations like candle making, carpet making, papad production, pickle production, herbal infectants, ready made juice mix, etc. in the rural areas. Women have started exhibiting the home based products in the consumer fairs organized by the local administration. The Government should provide financial aid to those who are willing to start small scale enterprises to effectively reach the consumer market. Subsidies shall be provided to start the home based production units in a small way. MUDRA bank under the Modi Government has initiated a better step in this regard. Linkage of NABARD, Cooperative Societies shall be enriched for the better outcome. Facility shall be offered through organizing consumer fairs and creating awareness by spreading the utilities of home based products through the Akashvani or Doordarshan at the cost of Government will be the best initiative. Common Facility Centres (CFCs) can be started to focus on technological support, skill development, entrepreneurship training, market information, credit facility, infrastructural support.

(h) Inclusion through women friendly trade policy

Trade liberalization has opened up new employment opportunities for women, particularly in export based industries such as textiles, food processing and handicrafts. Most of the women who are economically poor are forced to join garment, fishing, food processing or handicraft occupations for various reasons. In many cases women are employed for lowest wage and compelled to work under poorest terms of employment. The employment is also not regularized in many cases and are not provided with basic amenities for welfare. Many owners do not encourage trade unions in the textiles and matchworks which deprived the right of collective bargaining for their rights. Most of them are employed as informal workers and temporary workers. In order to meet the large scale requirement of finished goods to compete in the global market they started to take more work from the women workers and many are forced to keep sexual relationship with the entrepreneur. For the fear of loosing the employment many are not disclosing the sexual exploitation they face every day. Even though trade liberalization lead the economy towards progress, focus should be given towards giving due share of this growth to women who work for it.

(i) Inclusion of healthy working condition

The work place need to be safe and healthy for the workers. The legislators have formulated many welfare legislations which makes mandatory for the factories, mines, plantations, shops and commercial establishments or motor transport establishments to provide the specified health, welfare and safety provisions at work place. It also prescribes a special set of rules to specify the working hours, rest, weekly half and other benefits for women. Giving birth is the right of the women and the employer should support this cause by granting maternity leave with pay for six weeks prior and after the delivery. It also covers additional leave for women for any illness arising out of the pregnancy. Social security measures like Provident Fund, Employee State Insurance, Gratuity, Workmens Compensation, National and Festival Holidays has to be strictly followed by the organizations. The employment should be free from any type of hazards which will affect the health of the workers. All work for wage hence strict compliance to the Minimum Wages Act, 1948, Payment of Wages Act, 1936 and Equal Remuneration Act should be maintained all the time. The profit earned during the year shall be distributed among the workers according to Payment of

Bonus Act, 1965. Work place shall be free from harassement and should have proper Anti Harassment Committees to investigate the reported cases strictly.

(j) Financial inclusion of women

Women generally need only small loans as they have along with the habit of saving prudent mind in spending economically when compared to men. The Government should support women through granting financial assistance for her studies and personal life. Social Welfare Department can grant Scholarships to the Women either on the merit basis or on the category basis. Stipend and Fellowship can be given at the higher education, vocational training and doctoral studies to encourage womens literacy. Inspite of the progress made by the micro finance movement efforts shall be enhanced towards mainstreaming women into self-employment. Proper directives shall be set under the guidelines of Reserve Bank of India and NABARD to grant loans to women Self Help Groups under priority basis on a very low interest rate. Encouraging small entrepreneurers by granting subsidy to include the excluded women into productivity. The formal credit system should reach the poor and needy women. Hence there is a need for shift from micro finance to livelihood finance. There is a demand for credit and commodity cooperatives, knowledge centres, counseling centres, Vocational Training Institutes, etc. Government Loan Guarantee schemes can be encouraged to facilitate women access to credit. Small Savings Schemes in Banks and Post Offices shall be introduced to increase saving among rural women. Banking facility to remote places can be given through the "Sanchari Banks" in which mobile van equipped with needed infrastructure for banking will be visiting remote areas on a fixed days in the week, timings being fixed after considering the rural life these measures will definitely include women into the mainstream.

(k) Inclusion of women in agriculture

Many places are effected with drought due to scarcity of rain and low price for agricultural commodities has lead the people to depend upon other occupations. In rural India male migration in search of occupation other than agriculture has lead to increase feminisation of agriculture. The agricultural departments should design technical training based on women needs. Encouragement to agriculture through public investment will recognize the gender specific needs of women. Kissan Cards should be issued to all women farmers. Women friendly agricultural technology should be encouraged in farming and farm management. Dry land always depend upon the ground water hence, subsidies for tube well shall be provided. Training shall be given on dry land farming, animal husbandry, plantation, guardening, natural resource management, enterprise development, financial management, and leadership development. Orientations should be organized on pre and post-harvest technologies, storage, preservation, packaging, processing and marketing. Call Centres for farmers to clarify querries about agriculture. Involvement of women can be ensured by linking SHGs to Information Centres in providing information on production, storage, preservation and distribution of agricultural commodities. Development of indigenous livestock varieties and the encouragement of fodder cultivation should be focused on. The Policies should encourage women to take up income generating activities such as poultry, sheep and goats, fish production, seed production of crop varieties, hybrid seed production, etc. Greater attention should be paid to the problem of acute shortage of green fodder and water during summer months, lack of grazing space, and lack of local veterinary health care facilities. Pradhan Mantri Krishi Sinchayee Yojana (PMKSY) is a national mission to improve the farm productivity and ensure better utilization of resources was framed on 1st July, 2015 and Introduced by The Prime Minister, Narendar Modi. Rs. 500 crore is allocated for five years to this scheme, aiming to minimize wastage of water thereby enhance crop per drop by water budgeting in all sectors[5].

(l) Inclusion by granting property rights to women

Women can access to the ownership of land through the Direct Government Transfers, on Purchase or Lease and by way of

[5] Saxena, Monika and Srivastava, B.B.L., (2002). Occupation and Employment Pattern of Women Labour in Agriculture Sector, in Singh, J.L. Pandey, R.K. and Singh, A.K. (*eds.*). Women in Unorganised Sector Problems and Prospects, Sunrise Publications, New Delhi, pg. 31.

Inheritance. Grant of Land Titles to women in Government Transfers shall be encouraged instead of providing joint titles with their husbands by amending state tenancy laws, credit facility to the poor women to purchase land, creating legal awareness on womens inheritance, constitution of supportive schemes can be done in this regard. The empowerment strategies should focus on 'Group Interventions' rather focusing upon individual result. Lease of land for agricultural promotion can be supported through crop insurances to meet the contingencies. Even the joint titles shall be provided with partitiable options so that wives, can get half of the share of land in their single names which will help the divorcee or abandoned wives to lead further life. In the Hindu Succession Act 1956 and The Indian Succession (Amendment) Act, 2002 women's are entitled to an absolute estate like men when they inherit any property[6].

(m)Inclusion by granting facilities for easy and safe transportation

The Central and State Transport policies need to be reviewed to include schemes which provide public transport running between rural and urban routes in sufficient number. Special route buses can be started for easy transportation of working women. The company cab facility for working women for the IT and BPO professionals shall be ensured with proper security systems. Seats shall be reserved in the public transport vehicles for ladies and strict compliance to the rules should be ascertained. Special Discount and Pass facility should be assured to the Women Senior Citizens who possess Senior Citizen Card. Government can start Taxi services only for women in which only women drivers will work which will increase safety and creates employment opportunities of women. The special Trains and Buses may be introduced. Some specific needs such as lowering the heights of entry steps in buses, Regulation of Safety while boarding and getting down from the public transport by prescribing the speed limit within the cities can be taken up. Installation of handrails and First aid facility in the ladies compartments of the train shall be monitored. Each Railway Station

---

[6] Sharma, Ursala, (1980). Women, Work and Property in North West India, Tavistock Publications, Tavistock.

and Bus stands shall be provided with the 'Police Booth' with sufficient number of police constables working 24/7 to safeguard the personal security. All the public transport halting stations shall be kept under the survelience of CCTV Cameras linked to the Police Control Rooms and which has to be consistently monitored. Proper Ladies rest room, waiting rooms and Night shelters with toilet facilities shall be maintained at each stations. Seasonal Train and Bus pass facility can be further enriched by increasing the kilometers and reducing the price to help the poor students. These measures definitely will increase confidence among women and they can work at round the clock to contribute for national growth.

(n) Inclusion through domestic self-reliance

Women are responsible for the procurement of food articles, food production, nutrition and family health. Women groups at villages can be encouraged to start Small production units of solar energy or bio mass sources at village level can be achieved. The panchayat should provide subsidies to start home power generation units for self sustainance at family level. Women can be trained in organic farming of green vegetables, fruits, green leafs, seeds and flowers with high calorie of nutrients for the family members. Small scale Animal Husbandry at home can be encouraged to meet the domestic need. If the panchayat provide the market facility through organizing organic exhibitions once in 15 days that will also yield income generation among the rural women. Women can be encouraged to adopt "Terrace Cultivation" in the urban areas which provide nutritious commodities. Women should be encouraged in community forestry programmes. The support should be given to the projects under the Clean Development Mechanism (CDM) to include reduction of carbon emissions by using fuel-efficient cooking stoves and solar water heaters for domestic purpose and adoption of Compact Fluorescent Light bulbs at home[7].

---

[7] Shramshakti (1988). Report of the National Commission on Self Employed Women and Women in the Informal Sector, New Delhi, June.

(o) Inclusion of scheduled caste (SC) women

Scheduled castes are specified in accordance with Article 341 of Indian Constitution. Social justice to the members of these castes is ensured through the policy of protective discrimination inorder to change the traditional social structure which is based on socio-economic and political inequalities. Economic growth with social justice is the strategy for rural development in India. Article 46 imposes the obligation on the state to promote the socio-economic interests of the scheduled castes and scheduled tribes. Both Central and the State governments have implemented Swarnajayanti Gram Swarojgar Yojana, Indira Awaas Yojana for the upliftment of the families who are living below poverty line[8]. Recently, the government has enacted National Rural Employment Guarantee Act, 2006 to ensure 100 days guaranteed employment to the poor. A Special Component Plan to evaluate the development programmes was taken up in the sixth five year plan. National Scheduled Caste Finance and Development Corporation was constituted in 1989 which provide financial grants for income generating activities at low interest to the below poverty line people. Presently, Almost one-third of them live below poverty line and do not have access to the basic needs and engaged in petty occupations like agriculture labour, construction work, hawking and other low grade jobs. About 16.2 per cent of India's total population constitute people belonging to Scheduled castes wherein 80 per cent live in rural areas. The promotion of their education, health, employment, housing and living conditions is the need of the day. Basic requirement of Women is grant of colonies for Scheduled Cates with facility of healthcare, water supply, road and electricity. They should be encouraged to take up self-employment activities for self-sustainance.

(p) Inclusion of scheduled tribe (ST) women

Electronic media like Doordarshan and All India Radio can generate awareness among the scheduled tribe women about various policies and regulations for their welfare. Knowledge Centres at district level

---

[8] Prasad L.M. "Voluntary Action for Development of SCs and STs: Their Role and Functions, The Indian Journal of Public Administration, Vol. XXXIII, 1, pp. 28-31.

should work in collaboration with E-Sanchalak Yojana at village level in promotion of informations to these people in local languages. Technology and Market support to tribal women for value addition to the Minor Forest Products (MFPs) to enable them to compete even in the Urban market should be preferred through allowing tribal representation in fixing minimum prices to such products. Land Development Facilities and Credit facilities by considering the pattas granted under the land allotment under Forest Regulation Act, 2006. Banking correspondents meeting the tribal women for extension of banking facilities will be a very good measure. Government should provide subsidies and loans at low interest rate for the women income generation activities. Effective implementation of MGNREGA scheme, establishing tribal residential schools, starting tribal research centres and promotion of NGOs which work for the Tribal Community can be strengthened, Scholarship from the Social Welfare Department can be given for promoting literacy among them. Further, registration of tribal migrants by Panchayats under the supervision of nodal officers from tribal region should be encouraged for protection of their rights[9].

(q) Inclusion of single women and widows

Single women are either unmarried, separated or widow's these peoples life is miserable due to the social and economic problems they face in the society. The government should make clear regulations for the pensions, education of their children, housing, health, property right, employment opportunity pertaining to single women. Single women associations at regional level can be encouraged to discuss upon the real problems they face. The age for pension need to be checked along with the quantum when they are left with either children or aged parents. Pension schemes for Widows, Old age and handicap persons can be relooked into the rigid procedure and delay in granting pensions. Widow Rehabilitation and compensation packages can be introduced based upon the intensity of damage. Special job cards offering employment and equal pay under MGNREGA can be taken up. Entrepreneurship and leadership

[9] Darshan Singh, Development of Scheduled Castes in India-A review, Journal of Rural Development, Vol. 28, No. 4, NIRA, Hyderabad, pp. 529-542.

building crash courses can be organized at village level through awareness upon their rights for inclusive growth can be initiated. Provision for legal aid for accertainment of legal remedies can be sought through consumer protection forums for the benefit of Scheduled Tribe Women[10].

(r) Inclusion of elderly women

Special attention need to be given towards the health, nutrition, self dependability and pension provisions. Provision for the Senior Citizenship privileges under the Senior citizenship cards can be extended. Family Counselling, Routine Medical checkup, Access to Day Care Centres and Senior Citizenship Help Line can be encouraged. The Primary Health Centres need to plan for special schemes to monitor the health of elders at village and block levels. Awareness should be generated about various diseases specific to older women like osteoporosis, breast cancer and cervical cancer. Subsidised nutritional food supply and reduction in cost for medical procedure for the elderly women who are living under below poverty line will be a good initiative. Provision for Medical Insurance covering the common diseases like diabetes and Blood Pressure can be introduced at low premium policies. Waiving the income criteria for old age pensions to women above the age of 75 years in rural areas and slums will include them in the mainstream.

(s) Protection and prevention of women from HIV/AIDS

Most of the women in rural areas who are migrant workers, domestic labours and construction employees are infected with HIV. The Government initiative to start VCTC and ART Centres at District Hospitals linked through the Primary Health Centers is working to control HIV infection from the gross root level. For example, Karnataka State Government is aiding projects like Karnataka Health Promotion Trust (KHPT) to constitute rural centers for Rehabilitation and Empowerment of Commercial Sex Workers and Vivekananda Youth Movement in constituting Asha Kirana Hospitals

[10] Barooah, Jeuti, (1993). Single Women in Assamese Hindu Society, Gyan Publishing House, New Delhi, 1993.

to treat the HIV infected persons. As many infected women are deserted by their family and are not included in the various livelihood programmes such people should be identified through the social workers and provided with vocational training to lead independent life for their future life. Awareness Programmes to educate shall be organized in schools and colleges as pre marital relationship is a great contributor to the spread of the infection among youths. General opinion that HIV spreads only through illicit relationship should be irradicated from the society. Commercial Sex Workers need to be educated in the matters of safe sex by compulsory adoption of condoms. NGOs should be aided which are working in detection, prevention and care of the HIV Infected people. The medias shall be used properly to create the awareness about the sexually transmitted diseases. The infected women shall be counseled to ensure emotional, psychological and physical well being. The ICDS guidelines may integrate information on nutritional support to women and children on ARTs. These measures will definitely bring them to the mainstream[11].

(t) Inclusion of women unorganised labours

According to National Commission on self employed workmen (1987) women take up work for wage, piece rate workers, casual labour at extremely low wages and at very uneconomical returns who are suffering from job security and social benefits thereby exploited by way of long working hours, unsatisfactory working conditions and occupational health hazards. These workers have increased many folds during the post independence period. Among which 52 per cent are engaging in agricultural and allied sectors who constitute about 90 per cent of the whole labour force. According to National Commission for Enterprises in Unorganised sector they contribute 50 per cent to the Gross Domestic Product of the country. National Sample Survey Organisation (NSSO) reports that labour market in India has been undergoing drastic changes like inception of informal sector activities, deterioration of quality of employment, weakening of workers organizations and collective bargaining, decline in social

---

[11] Sudhir Varma, (2010). Gender, HIV and Social Work, Rawat Publications Jaipur, pp. 1-7

security hence, these changes shall be treated in accordance with the globalization process. Slow growth, structural inflation and lack of employement and incapability to meet the needs of the growing work force has left option to take proper measures to uplift the condition of these workers. National Rural Employment Guarantee Act, 2005 is a break through for this but suffered from unequal pay and employment only for limited 100 days. If look into the unorganized setors Social Security Act 2008 we can only find some guidelines about social security scheme in the country without specifying the provision properly. Reports of Social Security for Unorganised Workers May 2006, Comprehensive Legislation for Minimum conditions of work and social security for unorganized workers July 2007, Conditions of work and promotion of livelihood in the unorganized sector August 2007, Financing of enterprises in the unorganized sector and creation of a national fund for the unorganized sector (NAFUS) November 2007, Definitional and statistical issues relating to informal economy November 2008, Special programme for marginal and small farmers December 2008, Growth pole programme for unorganized sector enterprise development April 2009, Skill formation and employment assurance in the unorganized sector April 2009, Technology upgradation for enterprises in the unorganized sector April 2009, The challenge of employment in India an informal economy perspective volume I & II April 2009, The global economic crisis and the informal economy in India have highlighted the need for the unorganized sectors. As migration is common among these sector Inter State Migrant Workmen Act, 1979 and registration of migrant workers under the unorganized sector Social Security Act, 2008 along with the issue of Identity cards must be ensured.

(u) Inclusion of women living in the disturbed areas

Indian Northern borders and internally some places are affected with religious or political riots there by women who live in such places will be affected by the continuous army interference, suspended civil rights, restriction over the basic necessities, vulnerability to sexual violence, restrictions upon the personal freedom, violence and atrocities. Hence, special consideration shall be given to their health care during emergencies, schooling, employment, daily livelihood, food and accommodation and free legal aid, etc. The strict rules has to be gender sensitized and Armed Forces Special Powers Act (AFSPA) need to be rescheduled by foreseeing the women problems and living conditions.

(v) Inclusion of women with different abilities

The persons with disabilities (Equal opportunities, protection of rights and full participation) Act 1995 requires for the prevention by the early detection of disability among children through survey. The facility for education by providing learning friendly infrastructure initiated through Sarva Shiksha Abhiyan (SSA) and Integrated Education for Disabled Children (IEDC) schemes. Kasturba Gandhi Bal Vidyalaya (KGBVs) should be designed to include girls with special needs. Training should be provided to the teachers, Anganwadi workers to take care the differently abled children. Providing rehabilitation, vocational training and reservation in public employments must be taken up. Ministry of Women and Child Development run short stay homes, working womens hostel should also make special provisions for the persons with special needs. The schemes like STEP and MGNREGA shall give special preference in this regard. Health cards can be given for subsidized regular medical check ups and absolute subsidy scheme for the construction of toilets in households having differently abled women. Policy makers, participating rural institutions shall be gender sensitized for the better result.

(w) Inclusion of minority women

The Ministry for Minority Affairs constituted minority institution to impart scientific and religious discourse to build leadership among the minority students. The real secular principles and ideologies should be taught at the institutions. The teachers should be trained properly in secularism and diverse cultures and the real theme of religion in various religious epics. Awareness has to be created among the Muslim community about the importance of women education. Religious minorities shall be covered under the National Rural Health Mission (NRHM) and Rashtriya Swasthya Bima Yojana (RSBY) programmes. Sanitation, health and social education shall be departed at religious educational institutions. National Skill Development Mission can give vocational training to minority women to empower them for self employment.

(4) Prescription-Collective Efforts for Inclusive Growth

There is no chance for the welfare of the world, unless the condition of women is improved. It is not possible for a bird to fly on only one wing said Swami Vivekananda. But through centuries society have been trying to fly on only one wing denying women their rightful place. The greatest champions of women have been great men like Gandhiji, Raj Ram Mohan Roy, Ishwarachandra Vidyasagar, Maharshi Karve. Women themselves have to come forward to fight for their rightful place in all walks of life to prevent exploitation against them. India can be a leading economy through inclusive growth. There is a need for more public-private partnerships. The private sector should take more social responsibility and contribute towards making growth more inclusive. Education is extremely important for improving the skills among the people so that everyone can be an equal partner in the country's growth. More and better universities, schools and technical institutes should be created. Inflation, which is running amok today, affects the poor man that should be controlled and finally, rights of women, children, minority communities shall be protected. Empowerment by itself may not place women on an equal footing with men. The greatest need of the hour is change of social attitude towards women. Take the classic case of dowry is still rampant in a virulent even among the highly educated classes. Women's empowerment means a lot, but the ultimate goal of the equalization of man and women would materialize only when her complimentary role is recognized by the society. More inclusive growth must begin with women and children breaking an intergenerational cycle of inequality and deprivations which resulted in poverty, social exclusion, gender discrimination and undernutrition. Engendering National Policies and Plans with special emphasis on the scheduled castes, scheduled tribes, religious minorities, single women, the elderly, women affected by HIV / AIDS, migrant labour, women in disturbed areas, and women with different abilities, among others, remains a challenge in the XII Plan.

CONCLUSION

Presently, the women grabed positions in politics, public administration, army, intelligence, etc. In order to promote gender equity there is a need to change the interaction at home, school, college, university, and workplace by creating an environment that fosters equal treatment. The Ministry of Women and Child Development and Ministry of Human Resource Development, Government of India jointly formulated the general guidelines for "Gender Champions" who are above 16 years and enrolled to educational institutions who are responsible leaders to create enabling environment to treat girls with dignity and respect. All the Vice Chancellors of Universities are instructed to implement this programme in the university and all the affiliated colleges within 31st August, 2015.[12] The process of women empowerment is conceptualized as building self-esteem, confidence, protecting themselves, full participation in democracy, equal opportunity for education, elimination of gender barriers in employment, equal right over property, freedom and autonomy in the family. Women are now seeking equal status with men in all fields of life. They entering all the sectors with utmost confidence and proved to be very good competitors everywhere. Most of them are well educated and working in different capacities like doctors, engineers, CAs, Politicians, Professors, etc. they proved themselves to be good leaders who act more sensibly during crisis. They have exercised 56 per cent of franchise in the elections to bring massive change in the political system. Now we can see that parents have come out of the orthodox mindset and realized the value of providing education to their daughters. Women who were confined only to house keeping, are now accepted as the key players in nation building. India is proud to have the largest number of professionally qualified women in the world. In our country some women have claimed the highest ladder of politics by becoming the president and prime minister of the country. Mrs. Pratibha Singh Patil become the president, Mrs. Vijayalakshmi Pandit was the first women to hold the post in the cabinet. Mrs. Indira Gandhi was the first women Prime Minister of Independent India. Indian women cricket team

---

[12] University Grants Commission, Ministry of Human Resource Development, Government of India, Notification D.O.NO-91-2/2014(GS) dated 3rd August, (2015).

has won Asia Cup in 2004 and 2005. We can list some sports women of the country who brought Laurence to the nation like Sania Mirza in Tennis, Saina Nehwal in Badminton, P.T. Usha in Athletics, Karnam Malleswari in Weight Lifting, etc. Bollywood actress like Aishwarya Rai, Deepika Padukone and Priyanka Chopra has represented Indian cinema in the International Film Festivals. Even though in time, women have fought and won the battle for the right to vote, right to work, equal pay with men, right to own property, right to education but even in the 21st century they do not enjoy complete freedom in the matters of choosing a career, managing finance, choosing life partner, to decide about her life and motherhood as it is influenced by her family members, husband, relatives and society at large.[13] A remarking step was taken by Indian Navy after the Army and Airforce by granting Permanent Commission to seven women officers who were inducted as Short Service Commission officers in the Education and Naval Constructor Cadre in 2008-09. The Navy will also allow woman officers to join as pilots of maritime patrol aircraft like P-8Is, IL-38s and Dorniers from next year onwards. But the force is yet to finalize a policy for allowing women officer on board sea-faring warships. There are currently only about 340 woman officers who have been granted permanent commission in select branches of the Army and IAF, even though they have been allowed to join the three Services since the early-1990s as SSC officers for a maximum tenure of 14-15 years. Overall, women number just 1,436 in the Indian Army, 1,331 in Indian Air Force and 532 in Indian Navy. As reported by Times of India, the Indian Air Force has only now begun to train three woman officers as fighter pilots on an experimental basis. But the Army still has no plans to induct them into the fighting arms of infantry, armoured corps and artillery, which involve direct ground combat with enemy force. With 51 woman officers already serving as "observers" on maritime patrol aircraft, the Navy said "additional avenues" were now also being opened up for them. In 2017, woman officers can choose to join as pilots of maritime reconnaissance planes, as also in the naval armament inspectorate cadre. Thus, eight cadres will now be open for women in the Navy. These are education, law, meteorology, air traffic control, logistics, observers, pilots (maritime reconnaissance aircraft) and

[13] Vaishaliben M. Shah, (2010). Women Empowerment, The Chartered Accountant Student Journal, Vol. SJ1, Issue 1, January, 2010, pp. 11-13.

naval constructor. The Navy is also finalizing the policy for women officers to serve on select (new) warships that have appropriate facilities for them[14].

On 19th June, 2016, three women cadets at the Dundigal Air Force Academy created history by becoming the first commissioned female fighter pilots in the country, living their dreams to secure a combat role in most competitive of Defence branches. Flying officers Avami Chaturvedi, Bhawana Kanth and Mohana Singh were among the 130 flight cadets and 22 women trainees to have been conferred the Presidents Commission at a parade by Defence Minister Manohar Parrikar[15].

Despite some recent positive momentum, the pace of progress in realizing women's safety, protection and empowerment has not been adequate. For example, 16th December, 2012 shocked the whole country with the instance of Delhi Gang Rape. In India rape victims name is not published so the case was called as "*Nirbhaya*", which means fearless, because of her efforts to fight off her rapists and her insistence on making a detailed statement to the police before she died. In which 23 year old female physiotherapy intern, who was brutally beaten, gang raped and tortured in a private bus when she was travelling with her friend. Thirteen days after the assault, she was transferred to a hospital in Singapore for emergency treatment but died from her injuries two days later. The incidence was widely condemned globally. Subsequently, public protests against the government for failing to provide adequate security for women was held at delhi. As an indicator of the scope of the problem of rape prosecution this was the only conviction obtained among the 706 rape cases filed in New Delhi in 2012. However, it appears that the "*Nirbhaya*" case has had an effect on the willingness of rape or molestation victims to report the crime. A recent report released by the National Crime Records Bureau shows that 95 percent of the cases brought to the police were classified as a crime. However, there is a large backlog of cases with fewer than 15 percent of those charged tried in 2012, leaving 85 percent waiting to come to trial. This instance was a grevious crime of madness. These types of many

[14] Rajat Pandit (2016) Times of India Reporter, Article, TNN, Apr. 20,
[15] Deccan Herald, Mangaluru, Sunday, June 19, page 1, Vol. 17, No. 170, 2016.

instances are reflected in the National Crime Records Bureau data, which highlighted that in 2001 total 1,43,795 crimes against women were reported by 2012 it raised to 2,44,270, in 2013 came upto 3,09,546 and in 2014 it was 3,41,002. This shows that inspite of the penal laws and administration of criminal justice in India, crimes against women has increased at the rate of 42.16 per cent within 13 years despite the fact that all crimes against women are not reported. Hence, requires more constructive administration of Criminal Justice and crimes against women shall be punished with more grevious set of punishments which will work as a deterent for future criminal activity.

Bibliography

BOOKS

Anju Bhatia (2000). Women's Development and NGOs, Rawat Publications, Jaipur, pp. 48-51.

Altekar A.S. (1938). The Position of Women in Hindu Civilisation from Prehistoric Times to the Present Day, Culture Publication House, Banaras Hindu University, p. 407.

Barooah and Jeuti (1993). Single Women in Assamese Hindu Society, Gyan Publishing House, New Delhi.

Carol Chapnick Mukhopadhyay and Susan Seymour. Women, Education and Family Structure in India, Westview Press, Boulder, pp. 37-57.

Carr *et al.* (1990). Speaking out Womens Empowerment in South Asia, Vistaar Publications, New Delhi.

Diwan Paras (1997). Law relating to Dowry, Dowry Deaths, Bride Burning, Rape and Related Offence, Universal Law Publication Co, New Delhi.

Debry, Bibek *et al.* (1991). Energizing Rural Development through Panchayats, Academic Foundation, New Delhi.

Feldman D.C and Arnold H.J. (1983). Managing Individual and Group Behaviour in Organisations, Tata Mc Graw Hill, New York.

Gadgil D.R. (1965). Women in the Working Force in India, Asia Publishers, Bombay.

Gore, M.S. (1965). Social Work and Social Work Education, Asia Publishing House, Bombay.

Hokenstad M.C. and Rigby B.D. (1977). Participation in Teaching and Learning An Idea Book for Social Work Educators, International Association of Schools of Social Work, New York.

Hate C.A. (1969). Changing Status of Women in Post Independence India, Allied Publishers Pvt Ltd, Mumbai.

Harper and Malcolm (1992). Profit for the Poor Cases of Micro-Finance, Oxford and IBH Publishing Company Private Ltd.

Hemming Richard (1984). Poverty and Incentives, Oxford University Press.

Indira (1951). Status of Women in Ancient Times, Bombay, pp. 12-13.

Indu Prakash Singh (1991). Indian Women: The Power Trapped, Galaxy Publications, New Delhi, p. 4.

Jai Shree Chandra (1993). Women and Child: A Paradigm for Rural Development, Rawat Publications, Jaipur, pp. 37-45.

Jothmalani, Ram (1985). Dowry and the Law Subversion of Human Right in Gandhi P.K., (*ed.*), Social Action Through Law Partnership for Social Justice, New Delhi.

Kapoor N.D. and Rajni Abbi (2009). General & Commercial Laws, Sultan Chand & Sons Publishers, New Delhi, Seventh Edition, pp. 2.1-2.32.

Krishna Chandra Pradhan (1987). Rural Women Issues and Options, Sonali Publications, New Delhi, pp. 1-4.

Kasibhatta Subrahmanyam (1991). Women and Law, Asia Law House Publication, Hydrabad, 3rd Ed., pp 1-3.

Kakolee Chakraborthy (2000). Women as Devadasi: Origin and Growth of the Devadasi Profession, Deep and Deep Publications Pvt. Ltd, New Delhi, pp. 1-9.

Krishna Gupta (2001). Women, Law and Public Opinion, Rawat Publication, Jaipur, p 69.

Kakolee Chakraborthy (2000). Women as Devadasis, Origin and Growth of the Devadasi Profession, Deep & Deep Publications Pvt. Ltd, New Delhi, pp. 6-7.

Kuber W.N. (1979). Dr. Ambedkar: A Critical Study, Peoples Publishing House, New Delhi.

Lalitha N. (1995). Rural Women Empowerment and Development Banking, Kanishka Publication and Distributors, New Delhi.

Ledger Wood Joanna (1995). Sustainable Banking with the Poor Micro-Finance Hand Book, An Institutional and Financial Perspective, Washington D.C.

Misra S.N. (2013). Indian Penal Code: As Amended by Criminal Law (Amendment) Act, 2013, Central Law Publications, Allahabad, Nineteenth Edition.

Mac Kinnon, Catherine (1979). Sexual Harassment of Working Women, New Haven, Conn: Yale University Press.

Mishra L. (2001). Economy and Labour, Manak Publications Pvt. Ltd, New Delhi.

Neera Desai and Maithreyi Krishnaraj (1987). Women & Society in India, Ajanta Publications, New Delhi, p. 35.

Neera Desai and Maithreyi Krishnaraj. 1987. Women & Society in India, Ajanta Publication, New Delhi, p. 35.

Neeta Tapan (2000). Need for Women Empowerment, Rawat Publications, Jaipur, pp. 47-51, 53-57.

Nelson *et al.* (1997). Women and Politics, Oxford University Press, New Delhi.

Om Prakash Tewari (2002). Womens Rights in India, Sri Sai Law Publications, Faridabad, Haryana, 1st Edition, pp. 36-85.

Paras Diwan (1994). Women and Legal Protection, Deep and Deep Publications, New Delhi.

Parvathy Appaiah *et al.* (2015-16). Human Rights, Gender Equity and Environmental Studies, Jai Bharath Prakashana, Mangalore, Tenth Edition, pp. 37-103.

Park J.E. and Park K. (1983). Text book of Preventive and Social Medicine, Banarsidas Bharot, Jabalpur.

Radha Kumud Mukherjee (1947 & 1951). Ancient Indian Education (Brahmanical and Buddhist) Macmillan & Co. London, 2nd Ed.

Rao R.K. (2005). Women in Education, Kalpaz Publications, New Delhi, pp. 57-69.

Saxena *et al.* (2002). Occupation and Employment Pattern of Women Labour in Agriculture Sector", in Singh, J.L. Pandey, R.K. and Singh, A.K. (*eds.*) Women in Unorganised Sector Problems and Prospects, Sunrise Publications, New Delhi, pg. 31.

Savara, Meera (1982). Changing Trends in Women's Employment, Himalaya Publishing House, New Delhi.

Sonarikar S.S. (1976). Implementation of Labour Enactments, Popular Prakashan, Bombay.

Sharma and Ursala (1980). Women, Work and Property in North West India, Tavistock Publications, Tavistock.

Shukla V.N. (2007). Constitution of India, Eastern Book Company, 10th Ed. pp. 451-57.

Sudhir Varma (2010). Gender, HIV and Social Work, Rawat Publications, Jaipur, pp. 1-7, 48-51.

Tripathi S.C. (2004). Law relating to Women and Children, Central Law Publication, Allahabad, pp. 1-10.

Toohey, S. (1999). Designing Courses for Higher Education, Open University Press, Buckingham.

Vijay Kaushik and Bela Rani Sharma (1998). Encyclopaedia of Human Rights and Women's Development: Indian Women Through Ages, Sarup & Sons Publications, New Delhi, pp. 59-75 & pp. 235-277.

Weick A. (1994). Reconstructing Social Work Education. J. Laird *Ed.*, Revisioning Social Work Education-A social Reconstructionist Approach, New York, The Haworth Press, pp. 11-30.

JOURNALS

Abhaskumar Jha (2000). Lending to the Poor: Designs for Credit, *EPW*, Vol. XXXV, No. 8 & 9.

Butalia, Subhadra (1983). Dowry and Attitudes, *Womens Link Newsletter,* No-18, March.

Chelladurai (2004). Women Empowerment and Economic Development, *Social Welfare*, Vol. 55, No 12, March.

Chiranjeevulu T. (2003). Empowering Women through Self Help Groups-Experiences in Experiment, *Kurukshetra*, March.

Dadhich. Microfinance a Panacea for Poverty Alleviation A Case Study of Oriental Graeme Project in India, *Indian Journal of Agricultural Economics*, Vol. 56, No. 3.

Darshan Singh. Development of Scheduled Castes in India-A review, *Journal of Rural Development*, Vol. 28, No 4, NIRA, Hydrabad, pp. 529-542.

Encyclopedia of Social Sciences, Vol. XV, 1935, p.395.

Gaur K.D. (1995). Abortion and the Law in Countries of Indian Subcontinent, Asian Region, United Kingdom, Ireland and the U.S.A, *Journal of the Indian Law Institute*, Vol. 37, No 3, July-September.

Geetha B. (2007). Self Help Groups: A Social Movement, *Social Welfare*, Vol. 54, No 11-12, Feb-Mar.

Human Capital, February 2009.

Indian Worker Magazine 29 (1993) Vol. XLI.

Jesani, Amar and Iyer, Aditi, Women and Abortion, *EPW*, Vol. XXVIII, No. 48, November 27.

Kucchal S.C. (1975). *The Industrial Economy of India.*

Khullar Mala (2009). Emergence of Women Movement in India, *Asian Journal of Womens Studies*, Vol. 03, No. 02 pp. 94-129.

Lalitha N. Women Thrift and Credit Groups-Breaking the Barriers at the Gross roots, *Peninsular Economist*, Vol. XII, No. 2, pp. 188-191.

Maintenance under Muslim Law Shahbano,to Daniel Latifi (2003). *Criminal Law Journal.*

Mohannarayana K.S. (2010). Mobilisation of Women for Local Governance through Political Empowerment Programmes for SHG'S *Shodha, Biannual Bilingual Research Journal,* July.

Manimekalai N. *et al.* (2003). Grassroot Women Entrepreneurship through Micro Credit, *Peninsular Economist,* Vol. XII. No. 2, pp. 181-185.

Nanavatty and Meher C. Role of Central Social Welfare Board in the Changing Social Context, *The Indian Journal of Public Administration* Vol. XXXIII, 3, pp. 501-511.

Noor Mohammad and others (2004). Rethinking of Women Participation, *Womens Link*, Vol. 10, No. 03, July-September.

Nagasaila, D and Suresh, V. (1992). Can Right to Education be a Fundamental Right? *Economic and Political Weekly*, 27 (45), pp. 2442–2443.

Pradeep M.D. and Aithal P.S. (2015). Learning Through Team Centric Exercise & Key Point Pedagogy-An Effective Learning Model for Slow Learners in Social Work Education Training, *International Journal of Multidisciplinary Research and Development* Vol. 2, Issue 9, ISSN No 2349-4182, September, pp. 265-270.

Prasad L.M. Voluntary Action for Development of SCs and STs: Their Role and Functions, *The Indian Journal of Public Administration*, Vol. XXXIII, 1, pp. 28-31.

Punekar S.D. (1956). The Labour Problems, *Indian Journal of Social Work*, Vol. XVII, No. 3, Dec.

Rao Y.V. and Francis C. Action Oriented Adult Literacy and Education in WCADL, *Journal of Rural Development*, Vol. 12, 6, pp. 651-655.

Rajapriya M. *et al.* (2003). Role of Self Help Group Women in Value Base Emancipation, *Social Welfare*, Vol. 55, No. 06, September.

Rao V.M. Women Self Help Groups profiles from Andhra Pradesh and Karnataka, *Kurukshetra,* Vol. 50, No. 6, pp. 26-32.

Sarkar L. (1987). Women and the Law, *Annual Survey of Indian Law*, Vol. XXIII, Indiana Law Institute, New Delhi.

Sathish P. (2001). Mainstreaming of India, *Micro-Finance, Economic and Political Week* Vol. XL, No. 17, pp. 1732-1738.

Srinivasan S. and Natrajan V.K. Voluntary Health Services in Rural Areas: A Study, *Kurukshetra* Vol. XXXV, 2-3, pp. 15-18.

Veeraraghavan and Vimla (1995). Violence in Families: A Bio Psychological and Naturalistic Perspective, Trends in Social Science Research, *Special Issue on Family Studies*, Vol. 2, No.1, pp. 83-90.

Vaishaliben M. Shah (2010). Women Empowerment, *The Chartered Accountant Student Journal*, Vol. SJ1, Issue 1, January, pp. 11-13.

REPORTS AND GOVERNMENT PUBLICATIONS

Annexure to the "National Perspective Plan for Women 1988-2000 A.D., Report of the Core Group Set Up by the Department of Women and Child Development, Ministry of Human Resource Development, Government of India, 1988.

Annual Report of Swami Vivekananda Youth Movement, April 2008 to March 2009.

Census Survey Report 2011.

Government of India, Pocket Book of Labour Statistics 1984, Labour Bureau.

Government of India, Report of the National Commission on Labour, 2002.

Indian Crime Bureau Report from 2001 to 2014.

Law of Divorce in Islam, ILR 2005, Karnataka Series.

Manual of Integrated Management Information System for NRHM, 2005, Department of Women Welfare, Ministry of Human Resource Development, Government of India, New Delhi.

National Policy on Education (1986). Programme of Action, Ministry of Human Resource Development, New Delhi.

National Health Policy (2002), Government of India, Ministry of Health and Family Welfare.

National Federation and Social Programmes. Social Work Manifesto on HIV/AIDS. January, 2001.

National AIDS Control Organisation, Government of India, Mainstreaming Gender in HIV Programmes. Draft for Review. March 19, 2008.

National Institute of Allergy and Infectious Disease and NIH, USA HIV Infection in Women May, 2006.

National Family Health Survey, NFHS-2, (1998-99). Report of International Institute for Population Sciences, Mumbai.

National Family Health Survey, NFHS-3, (2005-06). Report of International Institute for Population Sciences, Mumbai.

National Family Health Survey, NFHS-4, (2014-15). Report of International Institute for Population Sciences, Mumbai.

National Policy for the Empowerment of Women, 2001.

Population Policy of India, Government of India, Ministry of Health and Family Welfare.

Reports of the Planning Commission of India, New Delhi.

Report of the Committee on the Status of Women in India, New Delhi, Government of India, 1974.

Shramshakti, Report of the National Commission on Self Employed Women and Women in the Informal Sector, New Delhi, June, 1988.

The Manager of Publication, University Education Commission, Government of India, Vol. I, 1948-49, New Delhi.

The National Plan of Action for the Girl Child (1991-2000).

Universal Declaration of Human Rights, 1948. International Covenant on Economic, Social and Cultural Rights, 1966 and International Covenant on Civil and Political Rights, 1966.

University Grants Commission, Ministry of Human Resource Development, Government of India, Notification D.O.NO-91-2/2014(GS) dated 3rd August, 2015.

WHO, Voluntary HIV Counselling and Testing Manual for Training of Trainers 2004.

WHO Handbook of Resolutions and Decisions, Vol. I, 1973, pp. 29,30,31 and Vol. II, 2nd *Ed.*, 1977, pp. 19,20,21,148.

World Bank (2001). World Development Indicators, Washington, D.C., World Bank.

LEGISLATIONS

The Indian Penal Code (IPC), 1860

The Indian Divorce Act, 1869

The Indian Evidence Act, 1872

The Married Women's Property Act, 1874

The Workmen's Compensation Act 1923

The Child Marriage Restraint Act, 1929

The Minimum Wages Act, 1948

State Insurance Act, 1948

The Factories Act, 1948

The Plantation Labour Act, 1951

The Mines Act, 1952

The Employee Provident Fund and Miscellaneous Provisions Act, 1952

The Hindu Marriage Act, 1955

The Hindu Adoptions and Maintenance Act, 1956

The Immoral Traffic Prevention Act, 1956

Hindu Succession Act, 1956

The Karnataka Shops and Commercial Establishments Act, 1961

The Maternity Benefit Act, 1961

The Dowry Prohibition Act, 1961

The Contract Labour (Regulation and Abolition) Act, 1970

The Medical Termination of Pregnancy Act, 1971

The Code of Criminal Procedure (Cr.PC) 1973

The Equal Remuneration Act, 1976

The Indecent Representation of Women (Prohibition) Act, 1986

The Muslim Women (Protection of Rights on Divorce) Act, 1986

The Protection of Women from Domestic Violence Act, 2005.

The Commission of Sati (Prevention) Act, 1987

National Council for Teacher Education Act, 1993

The Pre-Natal Diagnostic Techniques (Regulation and Prevention of Misuse) Act, 1994

Hindu Succession (Amendment) Act, 2005

Protection of Women from Domestic Violence Act, 2005

Right to Education Act, 2009.

The Sexual Harassment of Women at Workplace (Prevention, Prohibition and Redressal) Act, 2013

NEWS PAPER ARTICLES

Deccan Herald, Mangaluru, Volume 19, No. 199, Sunday, April, 10, 2016.

Amit Anand Choudhary, Times of India, 26th April, 2016.

Ammu Abraham, "A Legal Remedy for Harassed Wives", The Hindu, Nov 22, 1992.

The Times of India, "Modi Launches Rs. 8k-cr LPG for poor'Scheme, Monday May 2, 2016.

Rajat Pandit, Times of India Reporter, Article , TNN, Apr 20, 2016, 07.41 PM IST.

CONFERENCE PROCEEDINGS

Gurudath, "Hindu Jurisprudence in Feminist Perspective-A Look" in the Collection of Essays Titled Women Child Law and Society, Vidyavardhaka Law College, Mysore, 2006.

Justice Vishwanath Shetty P, Hon'ble Judge, High Court of Karnataka Bangalore, Inaugural address delivered in the seminar Women-Legal Problems & Perspectives, 25th March, 2004 at Vidyavardhaka Law College, Mysore, Karnataka State, India.

CASES REFERRED

Air India *vs*. Nargesh Mirza [1982] 1 SCR 438

Harvinder Kaur and Saroj Rani's [1984] AIR 1562, 1985 SCR (1) 303

Hussainara Khatoon *vs*. Home Secretary, Bihar (No.1) AIR (1979)SC 1360

Kishen Pattanayak *vs*. State of Orissa AIR (1989) 677

Kharak Singh *vs*. State of U.P. AIR (1963) SC 1295

Kochunni *vs*. State of Madras AIR (1959) SC 75

M.H. Hoskot *vs.* State of Maharashtra AIR (1978)SC 1548

Maneka Gandhi *vs.* Union of India AIR (1978)SC 597

Naurang Singh Chuni Singh *vs.* Smt. Sapla Devi AIR (1968) All 412, 1968 Cri L J 1636

Nandini Satpathi *vs.* P.L.Demi 1978 AIR 1025

Neera Mathur *vs.* LIC 1992 AIR 392

Olga Tellis *vs.* Bombay Municipal Corporation AIR (1986) 180

Satwat Singh Sawhny *vs.* A.P.O. New Delhi, AIR (1967) SC 1836

State of Maharastra *vs.* Madhukar Narayan AIR 1991 SC 207

Sheela Barse *vs.* State of Maharashtra AIR 1983 SC 378

Tahira A *vs.* Ali Hussain Fissalli Chothia AIR (1979) 362

The Sathyarani Chadha and others *vs.* State Delhi Administration AIR, 1986, SC, 205

The Haryana Mahila Santhan and others *vs.* Devi Lal and others Criminal Writ Petition No. 931-936 of 1988

Vishaka *vs.* State of Rajasthan AIR 1997 SC 3011

Women's Resource Centre *vs.* Commissioner of Police AIR (1990) SC 513

WEBSITES

Department of Financial Services, Ministry of Finance, Government of India.

Heaney, T. Issues in Freirean pedagogy. Thresholds in Education / "Freire Issues" Section. 1995, Retrieved on August 7, 2008 from: http://www3.nl.edu/academics/cas/ace/resources/Documents/FreireIssues.cfm.

Ministry of Minority Affairs, Government of India, 2016.

Saakshar Bharath Mission, Department of School Education and Literacy, Ministry of Human Resource Development, Government of India.

Website hosted & maintained by National Informatics Centre, Contents provided by Ministry of Drinking Water and Sanitation, Government of India.

Website of Ministry of Minority Affairs.

Website maintained by National Council for Teacher Education retrieved on 27th April, 2016 at 12.40 p.m.

Subject Index